Reading Thresholds

Reading Thresholds

CAROLYN H. FITZPATRICK
University of Maryland-Baltimore County

MARYBETH B. RUSCICA
St. Vincent's College of St. John's University

D. C. HEATH AND COMPANY
Lexington, Massachusetts   Toronto

Address editorial correspondence to:

D. C. Heath
125 Spring Street
Lexington, MA 02173

Acquisitions Editor: Paul A. Smith
Developmental Editor: Linda M. Bieze
Production Editor: Cormac Joseph Morrissey
Designer: Jan Shapiro
Photo Researcher: Martha L. Shethar
Production Coordinator: Richard Tonachel
Permissions Editor: Margaret Roll

Cover: Sally Cassidy/THE PICTURE CUBE

International Standard Book Number: 0-669-20166-9

Library of Congress Catalog Number: 92-71458

10   9   8   7   6   5   4   3   2   1

Preface

Designed for basic readers, *Reading Thresholds* offers the essential skills students need to succeed in courses now and in careers later. To become active, conscious readers, students must understand the primary elements of paragraphs and essays, and they must be able to use knowledge gained through reading. *Reading Thresholds* enables students to develop their analytical abilities and promotes the transfer of these skills to various reading materials. *Reading Thresholds* provides a foundation of skills for basic readers who enter the course reading at the fourth- to eighth-grade level.

Several features make *Reading Thresholds* accessible to students. First, *Reading Thresholds* motivates students to transfer the skills learned here to academic and "real-life" reading. To assist students in this transition, *Reading Thresholds* contains high-interest paragraph- and essay-length selections from textbooks (covering most disciplines), popular magazines, newspapers, student writing, advertisements, and cartoons. Next, study skills are included within the text. The book begins with information on classroom skills necessary for success in all courses, including reading courses. Later, in Chapter 8, students learn to read textbooks by using the SQ3R model. (However, the second "R" has been changed from "recite" to "record." This change allows students to apply a more practical skill, notetaking, rather than simply repeat information.) Finally, with its developmental arrangement of chapters, *Reading Thresholds* promotes students' confidence in their own reading abilities. This confidence increases students' enthusiasm and makes them more independent readers.

Reading Thresholds, with its developmental structure, guides students through the reading process. Part One introduces students to college survival skills: time management, listening and notetaking, and vocabulary development. Moreover, students are taught to set realistic goals and identify personal learning styles. Addressed at the start of the semester, these survival skills facilitate students' learning and use of classroom time.

Part Two develops students' abilities to analyze reading material. In Part Two, each chapter is also arranged developmentally. Exercises gradually increase in complexity as students work through the chapter. In Chapter Four ("Main Ideas"), for example, students first learn to identify paragraph topics and then main ideas. Students also learn to recognize placements of main ideas and their functions within paragraphs. Individual exercises containing paragraph selections are organized sequentially from lower reading levels to higher ones. As students succeed with the initial readings, they are able to "stretch" to meet the demands of more difficult passages. Later chapters in Part Two build upon the skills students developed in earlier ones. For instance, Chapter Six ("Organizational Patterns") requires that students analyze paragraph structures according to supporting details.

Finally, Part Three motivates students to incorporate all the skills they have developed throughout the textbook. Each of the ten readings includes questions on vocabulary, main ideas, structure, details, and critical reading. To enhance students' use of knowledge gained through reading, discussion questions and writing assignments direct students to apply their knowledge. Although the textbook is arranged sequentially, *Reading*

Thresholds allows complete flexibility in assigning chapters. Because chapters are self-contained, instructors may develop their own sequence of skills based upon their students' needs.

The Instructor's Edition of *Reading Thresholds* includes an Instructor's Guide at the end of the text prepared by Patricia Farabee of the Southern Illinois University, Edwardsville. For each chapter, this Instructor's Guide provides teaching suggestions, reading levels of paragraphs and essays in exercises, and answer keys for exercises.

We wish to thank Paul A. Smith and Linda M. Bieze, our editors at D.C. Heath and Company, for their encouragement and sound guidance. We also appreciate the valuable comments of manuscript reviewers Nancy V. Boozer, Dundalk Community College; Robyn Browder, Tidewater Community College; Charles Hunter, San Jose City College; Patricia Jonason, Johnson County Community College; Kathryn Esther Moore, St. Louis Community College at Meramec; Marguerite Moore, Monterey Peninsula College; Patricia H. Noffsinger, Salt Lake Community College; Daisy Walker, Miami-Dade Community College, North Campus; Suzanne G. Weisar, San Jacinto College South; Phyllis A. Wilkinson, Southern Illinois University at Edwardsville; and Donna Wood, State Technical Institute at Memphis. We gratefully acknowledge the students who allowed their work to be printed here: Amy Demchak, Regina Raffety, and Ray Stolle of the University of Maryland-Baltimore County; and Morgan Dailey, Chris Roesser, and Frank Wharam of Loyola High School, Towson, Maryland.

Carolyn H. Fitzpatrick

Marybeth B. Ruscica

CONTENTS

Chapter 6 Organizational Patterns 147

Chapter 7 Previewing and Skimming 175

Chapter 8 Approaching Textbooks 231

Chapter 9   Critical Reading   265

Chapter 10   Reading Faster   289

Part Three

Reading Applications   311

Appendix   375

PART ONE

Chapter 1

DEVELOPING ACADEMIC SURVIVAL SKILLS

Objectives

1. To determine a personal learning style.
2. To learn to manage time efficiently.
3. To set realistic goals.

Key Concept

Much of your academic success depends on your knowledge of academic survival skills. These basic techniques provide the foundation for your study skills.

Academic survival skills prepare you for academic success. Success in college depends on several factors, including subject knowledge, study skills, energy level, and time management. However, to succeed in college, you must be able to cope with its demands. Academic survival skills help you cope.

These survival skills require preparation. If you wait until midterm time to decide who you are, where you are going, and what you want to accomplish, it will be too late. By that point, you will probably be overwhelmed by tests, projects, assignments, and missed work. To avoid being discouraged and confused later, take a little time at the beginning of the semester to consider your possibilities.

To develop academic survival skills, you must first know yourself. You must determine your learning style, manage your time, and set goals. Once you master these skills, you will be prepared for academic success. You will still study and work but with realistic, achievable goals. You will also learn to study in a way that fits your learning style. Overall, a little planning can make you a more efficient student.

LEARNING STYLE

You may not have ever considered your learning style. This concept refers to the way you learn best. Everyone has a personal learning style, a method that makes it easier for him or her to learn. By knowing your learning style, you can learn more effectively. There are four elements to each person's learning style: environmental, psychological, social, and physical. By examining each part, you can determine the best style for you.

Environmental Aspects

In what environment do you study best? The *learning environment* is the surroundings most beneficial to your learning. If your surroundings make you uncomfortable or distract you, you will not learn effectively. Therefore, you should consider the following significant aspects of your environment.

1. *Sound* plays a major role in our environment. Most people are surrounded by sounds all day—radios, shouting, traffic noise, conversations. Often, you can screen out many unwanted sounds. However, while you are studying, sound can be a major factor in the success or failure of your work.

What sound environment do you enjoy the most when you are studying or concentrating?

_____ Heavy-metal music blaring

_____ Mood music softly playing

_____ Absolute quiet

_____ Normal household background noises—television, radio, conversations

_____ Familiar sounds repeating themselves

Consider your answers. Some students consider absolute quiet unnerving. Others think heavy-metal music is jarring. In either case, that particular sound environment will not help the individual student learn. Use your preferred sound environment to set a mood for learning. Arrange your studying environment according to the sound that best helps you study.

2. *Light* can help you to learn, or it can block learning. Poor light can make study and reading a struggle. Think about your lighting preferences:

_____ One bright ceiling light

_____ Natural light

_____ Track lighting

_____ Several lamps

_____ Fluorescent lights

Each lighting situation creates a different mood. You must decide which one helps you to study. Which one encourages you to concentrate and learn?

3. *Temperature* preferences vary widely. To some people, hot weather means naps. Cold temperatures put others to sleep. If the temperature makes you sleepy or uncomfortable, you cannot learn. Therefore, temperature differences can distract you.

Which temperature makes you alert and ready to work?

_____ Cold 50's
_____ Crisp, cool 60's
_____ Warm 70's
_____ Torrid 80's

Remember that if you are shivering, you cannot learn. Likewise, if the temperature is too hot, you'll probably doze. In either case, the temperature will affect your studying efficiency. Change the thermostat to create a suitable environment. Or open or close windows. As a last resort, go to another room or building to study.

My preferred environment consists of the following:

Sound _____
Light _____
Temperature _____

Given this information, what room or building best suits your environmental preferences? _____

Psychological Aspects

Psychological aspects of your learning style include your method of learning and the personality characteristics you bring to learning. You have probably thought about some of these characteristics: persistence, procrastination, maturity, responsibility, and motivation. You may not, however, have considered others—such as creativity, experimentation, and imagination. Each of these factors influences you to a degree. You must analyze your personality to decide the impact of each factor.

Preparing to Learn. *Maturity, motivation,* and *responsibility* are all linked. These factors affect your approach to learning.

1. *Maturity* means that your actions and thoughts are appropriate for your age. As a college student, you are an adult. Teachers assume that you are a capable, independent person. Therefore, they should not have to explain each assignment in detail. Nor should they have to coach you through each part of a task.

Your instructors are there to teach, and you are there to learn. If you are not as mature as your teacher expects, your learning will suffer. You will not be able to function as effectively as someone who is "ready" for college.

2. *Motivation* means your reason for working at studying and learning. You will be encouraged to learn under several conditions. Sometimes the subject interests you; you already understand the topic, and your instructor teaches, entertains, and inspires simultaneously. Learning under those circumstances is easy. Learning under less than ideal conditions is a mark of a mature, motivated student. If you can motivate yourself to learn when the course is boring, the instructor monotonous, and the subject unfamiliar, then you are prepared to cope with college. You must learn the material and do well in the course because it is required for your degree. This may be an unpleasant truth, but it is also a motivating factor.

3. *Responsibility* suggests an obligation. When you assume a responsibility, you are accountable for the consequences of your action. In a course, you are responsible for your grade. You must perform as a mature, motivated, and responsible student. If you do, then you have the greatest chance to earn a good grade.

Your psychological readiness can vary in learning situations. In some classes, you will be more prepared to learn than in others. Overall, however, you should consider your preparedness as a college student.

My maturity level (is, is not) appropriate for college.
I (am, am not) motivated to do well in college.
I (am, am not) willing to accept responsibility for doing well in college.

Approach to Learning. What is your best psychological approach to learning? How do you learn and work best? How would you describe your attitude toward learning? Consider the following characteristics.

1. *Procrastination.* Do you always wait until the last possible hour before you complete (or start) a task? If you do, then perhaps you work well in a tension-filled atmosphere. You might need the pressure of an immediate deadline to motivate you. If you are a procrastinator, accept this characteristic and use it for your advantage. Know your deadlines, and be sure to leave the

days or hours before deadlines free of other work. You must be able to devote your time solely to the upcoming assignment. You might also try to fool yourself. Schedule false deadlines several days before the real ones. This method will leave you time to review your work.

2. *Persistence*. Does the saying "If at first, you don't succeed, try, try again" apply to you? Do you work at a task until you succeed? If so, then you are persistent and willing to learn from your mistakes. In this case, it is important to allow yourself time to review your errors. Try to determine why you made mistakes. See if you can correct them. Decide whether you can work on a problem alone or whether you should ask your instructor or a tutor for aid. Persistence usually pays off, but it can take extra time.

3. *Patience*. Do you like to work on an assignment immediately, as soon as it is given? Or do you prefer to think about the assignment for a while, consider the task, and decide on the best way to tackle it? Students who want to begin working immediately on a problem are usually experimenters. They will get to work even when they may not know or understand all the aspects of the assignment. These students enjoy starting projects. Even if they do not know how to complete the task, they are willing to experiment. If their methods work, then they complete the assignment ahead of schedule. If their methods fail, then they have to try another approach. If they have allowed ample time, they will probably complete the assignment by the deadline. Also, they may gain knowledge from their experiments. In addition to these experimenters are students who know immediately what to do and begin working confidently on tasks right away.

On the other hand, patient students wait to begin the assignment. These students want to learn all the details of the project. They want to design their approach before they start working. Unlike experimenters, patient students prefer to spend their energy by thinking about the task and then doing it once.

Check the following approaches to learning that seem to describe your method best.

_____ I like to figure things out as I work.

_____ I prefer to get a task right the first time.

_____ I think about how to do something before I actually do it.

_____ I work at a task until I finally can do it well.

_____ I like to design a schedule.

_____ I like to complete an assignment before its due date.

_____ I prefer to wait until I have all the facts and details.

Your answers here have created a psychological profile of your learning style. Use this profile to create your semester schedule of dates and to plan your weekly studying.

Social Aspects

Humans are social beings. As babies develop, they learn how to interact with their parents and siblings. Gradually, their world expands to include other relatives. As children, they learn to develop and maintain friendships. Finally, as adults, people distinguish among strangers, acquaintances, and friends. They respond to each according to the depth of the relationship. However, each person matures in a unique way. Therefore, there are degrees of sociability. Some people feel completely at ease in a crowd. Crowds torment others. Many people enjoy dealing with others on an individual basis. But some adults consider one-on-one encounters frightening.

Think about yourself. In what social situations do you feel most comfortable? These social situations influence your ability to learn. Your learning is affected by your social "comfort level." If you are uneasy in a particular situation, it will be more difficult for you to learn. On the other hand, if you can relax, you can understand material better. Below are some of the various social situations that influence learning. Try to remain flexible about your ability to interact in all situations.

1. *Large groups*. Some people enjoy crowds. They like the variety and excitement. They enjoy mingling and meeting many new people. They prefer to chat about topics rather than to discuss ideas in great detail.

   If you like to be part of a large group, then you should schedule lecture hall classes. Because you can relax in that environment, you can concentrate and learn. You can use this same situation outside of class. For example, you can form study groups of five to eight people. Each individual in the group will bring a different perspective to the material. Thus, a study group can help you learn more, as well as introduce you to new people and their ideas.

2. *Alone*. In contrast is the person who enjoys solitude. This individual feels most comfortable alone. Crowds might overwhelm this person. Sights and sounds might distract him. Of course, anyone who is distracted and uncomfortable will find it difficult to learn.

If you enjoy solitude, then try to arrange independent study courses. If you must participate in large classes, try to arrange to work independently. This independent work will reinforce the large lecture classes and will help you to comprehend the material more completely.

3. *Pairs.* Some people thrive in a one-on-one situation. They enjoy the personal contact and the immediate feedback from partners. For some people, communication is easier in pairs.

   If you function well in this situation, then you might consider working with a tutor. If you become confused in a course, then look for a tutor immediately. The pair approach should help you understand the material. You can explain your concerns, and the tutor can directly answer your questions. As a team, you and your tutor can work through the course material. If you cannot find a tutor for your course, then find a study partner who is taking the same course. You and your partner can help each other learn more.

   Check the social situation that makes you feel most at ease.

   _____ Large group
   _____ Alone
   _____ Pairs

The environmental, psychological, and social aspects of learning are important factors in your ability to learn. However, they are not the only factors that contribute to academic success. To map your personal learning style completely, you must also consider the following physical elements.

Physical Aspects

Many learning theorists have pinpointed two key physical aspects of an individual's learning methods. These two factors—the biological clock and the major sense—affect a person's physical response to learning.

Biological Clock. Each person's energy level increases and decreases according to the time of day. Individuals seem to have an inborn biological clock that dictates energy levels. One person may shine at 8 A.M. Another cannot begin to think until noon. These different performance schedules were once regarded as personality traits and labeled as such ("lazy," "ambitious," "slow-moving").

Today, these schedules are not considered subject to personal choice.

Each person's body seems to be programmed to perform well at a specified time during the day. Some people wake up early, bounce out of bed, and begin their day with a rush of adrenaline. By mid-afternoon, these individuals have lost energy and can perform only routine tasks. Others begin their days slowly, gradually warm up through the morning, and function best in the afternoon. As evening approaches, their energy level drops. Still others, "night-owls," really do not begin to function well until the sun sets. As the sky darkens, they gain energy. Frequently, night people can work long after midnight, an hour about which the morning person has only dreamed.

However, people are flexible. With appropriate preparation, an individual can perform well at any time. For instance, a morning person can deliver a thoughtful speech at an evening banquet. In general, though, everyone has a predetermined performance schedule. It can be modified to meet the demands of a career, family, or school. But it cannot be changed.

Consider your biological clock. At what time of the day or night do you feel the most energetic? If you could choose the hour to begin classes or to study for finals, what time would that be?

Check your peak performance time.

_____ Morning
_____ Afternoon
_____ Evening
_____ Night

Try to schedule your classes and study hours for your peak performance time. This schedule will make learning easier.

Sensory Orientation. Humans are equipped with five senses—sight, hearing, smell, touch, and taste. But each sense is not developed to the same degree in each of us. Some senses are stronger and more defined because they are used more. For instance, early humans probably used their sense of smell to locate game or fire. Modern humans use this sense merely to help determine what is cooking on the stove. Because we no longer rely on this sense for survival, it is not particularly well developed. Likewise, many people do not have a refined sense of touch. They can distinguish hard from soft, coarse from smooth, but they miss fine gradations. In contrast, those who are forced to use only certain senses develop those senses more. For example, many visually-impaired individuals use a refined sense of touch to tell them about the world.

Your senses have a great impact on your learning process. Whether it is sight, hearing, or touch, each person relies on one sense as the first and most important source of information. Of course, each initial impression should be supplemented with information from other senses. However, each individual relies on a major sense, a dominant one, for a first impression.

To determine your dominant sense, answer the following questions.

1. What do you consider your most useful source for information about your courses?

    a. _____ textbook

    b. _____ lecture

    c. _____ laboratory work

2. On what assignment do you prefer to be graded?

    a. _____ research paper

    b. _____ speech

    c. _____ project

3. In which situation are you more comfortable learning?

    a. _____ reading a book or article

    b. _____ sitting in a lecture

    c. _____ participating in an internship

Your choices can help you determine your dominant sense. If you chose *a* for the majority of your answers, then you rely mostly on sight. If you chose *b*, then you prefer hearing. If you chose *c*, then you chose touch; you use your hands a great deal. Based on your dominant sense, you can decide whether you are a visual, auditory, or kinesthetic learner in most situations.

A *visual* learner learns by sight. Sight is the dominant sense. This learner prefers to read a book or watch someone perform a new task. This person may be a television watcher. He likes to *see* something being done. Most people are visual learners.

An *auditory* learner learns by listening. Hearing is the dominant sense. This person prefers to listen to a lecture, discussion, or debate. She is an avid radio listener. Many people are auditory learners.

A *kinesthetic* learner learns by doing. Touch is the dominant sense. This individual prefers to perform a task individually without the assistance of directions or instructions. This person would neither watch a tennis game on television nor listen to a match on the radio. She would be on the court in the park practicing her swing. A minority of people are kinesthetic learners.

Based on these descriptions, classify yourself.

_____ Visual learner

_____ Auditory learner

_____ Kinesthetic learner

Now that you have identified your learning style, you should develop some suitable techniques to reinforce the learning process. The ideas below are suggestions. Not every one will work for every student. Therefore, experiment with each suggestion, one at a time. Determine which are helpful and then try to use them as often as possible. In other words, aim to enhance your strong points and bypass your weak ones. By understanding your learning process and basing your work efforts on that process, you increase your ability to learn.

Visual Learner. A visual learner needs to see in order to work and learn. He can easily learn by reading. He can readily comprehend written directions. Understandably, he needs to keep his sense of sight active while he learns. A visual learner should try these strategies:

1. Definitely read, or at least preview, each textbook chapter before it is discussed in class.

2. While reading a chapter, look at each visual aid. Maps, charts, graphs, tables, and the like are very important to your understanding of the subject.

3. After reading the chapter, highlight key points. Do not underline everything, only the important elements.

4. As the instructor lectures, focus on her. This will help you concentrate.

5. As the instructor lectures, keep your textbook open. When your teacher discusses points from the book, look at the writ ten words.

6. Take lecture notes. Writing notes enhances your memory.

7. When combining the text material and your lecture notes, try to use visual forms—maps, outlines, or diagrams—to summarize important concepts. The more visual you make the ideas, the easier it will be for you to remember them.

8. Do *not* study with the television on. It will distract you.

Auditory Learner. An auditory learner needs to hear in order to work and learn well. To comprehend material, she listens actively. She learns easily from lectures or discussions. Oral directions are easy to follow. Below are some suggestions for you to try if you are an auditory learner. Use the ones that work best as you study.

1. Be an active listener in every lecture classroom. Concentrate on the lecturer.

2. Definitely take written notes as you listen. If possible, tape the lecture so you can replay it at a convenient time.

3. When studying, read your notes aloud. Let your brain hear you say each idea.

4. When you cannot verbalize important material, then at least lip read it to mimic an auditory activity.

5. When possible, use recordings of assigned readings. Simultaneously read and listen to the material. This will increase your memory of it.

6. Do *not* study with the radio playing. The noise, no matter how pleasant, is too great a distraction for you.

Kinesthetic Learner. A kinesthetic learner needs to learn by doing. He needs movement. He must be an active participant in the learning process. Unfortunately, the typical classroom is not designed to help a kinesthetic learner. Therefore, he must simulate a moving environment. Or he must enhance the movements that are acceptable in a traditional classroom. Below are a few suggestions. As you work through this list, you may develop some strategies of your own. If your personal strategies help you learn, then use them repeatedly until they become part of your learning process.

1. Writing is movement. Therefore, take many notes while you read or listen to a lecture.

2. Use a computer. Working with a computer is interactive, and it permits some movement.

3. Definitely try to choose lab courses and internship programs. Their structure enables you to learn by performing tasks.

4. Move around while you study. If movement helps you remember and concentrate, then walk around your room while you review notes or learn new information.

5. Use your fingers to tick off a list of key elements as you review.

6. Do not try to remain still and study for long periods of time. Short, intense study sessions with a defined, limited goal work best for you.

By now, you have analyzed and identified your personal learning style. You have also decided how to use that style to your advantage in an academic situation. As a reminder, complete the list below by filling in the elements of your personal learning style.

My personal learning style consists of the following elements:

Environmental: Sound _____
                Light _____
                Temperature _____
Psychological: *Preparing to learn*
                Maturity level _____
                Motivation level _____
                Responsibility level _____
                Approaching learning
                Procrastination level _____
                Persistence level _____
                Patience level _____
Social: Grouping _____
Physical: Biological clock _____
                Dominant sense _____

TIME MANAGEMENT

Time management is another academic survival skill. Finely tuned study skills, an understanding of your learning style, and realistic goals will not contribute to your success in college if you cannot find the time to implement them. Most students have responsibilities beyond the classroom. They often have work and home responsibilities. In addition, at this point in their lives, many students participate in a variety of social activities. With so many demands, students must manage their time well, or they will be overwhelmed.

Probably, your primary obligation now is to do well academically. Therefore, you should emphasize your course requirements when you schedule your time. Planning for tests, papers, and projects can help you effectively arrange your time and set your priorities. You can plan by developing semester and weekly calendars.

Semester Calendar

On the first day of class, read the course outlines carefully. On a calendar that has large blocks for each day, record each scheduled test or paper. Do the same for each course you are taking. This calendar will become your map for test preparation. It will help you plan your study time effectively.

Your map of the semester's activities will always remind you of the dates of tests and papers. Thus, you can control the amount of time you spend on each course. You will also avoid the frightening prospect of forgetting about a test or project. This method will also enable you to prepare wisely for busy weeks, such as finals week. Finally, if you follow your schedule, you will not need to cram for tests. You will be better prepared to take tests because you have studied the material over a period of weeks instead of the night before. A sample calendar for November is illustrated on the following page.

Sample Calendar for November

Sunday	Monday	Tuesday	Wednesday	Thursday	Friday	Saturday
		1	2 *Psych Test Ch. 1–8*	3	4 *English Essay due*	5
6	7	8 *Spanish Quiz Ch. 6*	9	10	11	12
3	14	15 *Poli. Sci. Test Ch. 1–10*	16	17	18 *English Essay Due*	19
20	21 *History Midterm*	22	23	24 *Spanish Midterm*	25	26
27	28	29 *Psych. Test Ch. 9–14*	30 *English paper due*			

EXERCISE 1   Plan a semester calendar for yourself. Be sure to include all scheduled quizzes, tests, papers, and projects for all of your courses. If any additional assignments are given during the semester, write them in immediately.

Weekly Calendars

After you have prepared your semester calendar, you should create a weekly schedule. Long-term planning can be effective only if it is implemented step by step in the short term. Knowing that a history research paper is due in mid-December will not help you if you do not set weekly goals for yourself with that paper in mind. In this way, you can work through the paper in stages. For example, you might decide to finish the initial bibliography on October 15. Then, you could set the goal of developing note cards by October 30. You should mark each of these goals on your weekly calendar. By doing so, you will not be surprised in early December that a paper is due in two weeks.

In addition to your academic tasks, your weekly calendar should list your work hours, social plans, and other regular obligations or unusual activities. A sample plan for one week in November is illustrated on the following page.

Week of 11/6

Sunday	Monday	Tuesday	Wednesday	Thursday	Friday	Saturday
1-Review Sp. Ch.6	1-Review Sp. vocab.	1-Poli.Sci Study group	1-Review 11/4 Eng. Essay	1-freewrite first draft	1-Synthesize text & lecture notes in Poli Sci, Psych, Hist, Sp.	1-work 10-6
2-Sp. vocab.	2-outline Poli Sci & Psych chaps	2-work 12-8	2-Brain. Storm 11/8 Eng. Essay	2-outline Sp chap	2-first draft Eng. Essay	2-review Sp. vocab.
3-Read Poli Sci. chap.	3-Read & outline Hist. chap.		3-Read Sp. chap.	3-work 6-10		3-Gerri's Party 9
4-Read Psych Chap.	4-work 6-10 p.m.					

By drawing up a weekly schedule, you can avoid cramming too much work into certain days. For instance, using the schedule above, the student could see at a glance that it would be unrealistic to also try to write the first draft of his English paper on Thursday. He simply has enough to do on that day already. The weekly schedule helps you to visualize, actually see, your work load for the succeeding week. Consequently, you can plan ahead and modify your schedule to avoid overloads.

EXERCISE 2   Draw up a weekly plan for next week. Be sure to include your academic assignments, social plans, and work hours.

SETTING GOALS

Most students begin their college careers with high hopes and great expectations. They plan to graduate in record time, receive top honors, work full-time, and maintain their own apartment at the same time. Although their enthusiasm and determination are admirable, these optimistic students are not being realistic. Very few people have the energy, stamina, and ability necessary to perform consistently at the highest level in school, on the job, and at home. Unfortunately, some students recognize that fact of life too late to benefit from their newly found understanding. They fall behind in the rent, receive poor job evaluations, and fail some courses before they are able to recognize that their goals were unrealistic. Nobody could achieve what these students had demanded of themselves.

What can you do to avoid those pitfalls? Your best defense is an objective assessment of yourself.

1. Think about your academic ability.

    Is it easy for you to learn?

    Do you need to review and repeat material in order to remember it?

    Do you like to spend a lot of time on new subjects in order to gain a detailed understand of them?

    Do you find it difficult to learn in a traditional academic setting?

2. Consider your energy level.

    Are you a "Type A" person, filled with boundless energy?

    Are you a "Type B" person, inclined to proceed at a slower pace?

    Do you like frequent rest stops?

    Do you work at a steady pace?

    Do you work in short bursts of high energy?

    Do you tire easily?

    Can you continue to work even when you are tired?

3. Assess your financial situation.

    Do you need to work to pay for tuition, room and board, and books?

    Are you contributing to your family's support?

    Are you working for "pocket money," clothes, entertainment, and so on?

    How many hours a week must you work just to get by financially, to be financially secure, and to be financially well-off?

By taking an objective look at yourself, you can develop realistic goals. If you must work forty hours a week to pay tuition, then it would not be sensible to take eighteen credits each semester. Even those with unlimited energy could not cope with those demands.

Likewise, thorough, methodical students who like to devote a great deal of time to each course should limit themselves to twelve or fifteen credits each semester. On the other hand, if you do not need to work many hours and have a high energy level, then eighteen credits with some labs would be suitable. Based on your self-assessment, be reasonable about your plans for the year. You can decide the number of courses you can carry, the grades you expect to earn, and the number of hours you can work each week. Be sensible and realistic when you set goals for yourself. Expect the best you can give, but do not overschedule your time and energy.

SUMMARY

Your learning style—environmental, psychological, social, and physical—affects how you learn. After determining your learning style, use it to influence and enhance your learning process. Knowing your learning style, you can also set realistic goals and manage time effectively and still consider your personal needs and expectations. With these academic survival skills, you are prepared to succeed in college.

Chapter 2

DEVELOPING LISTENING AND NOTETAKING SKILLS

Objectives

1. To be an effective, active listener.
2. To develop good listening skills as an aid to learning.
3. To develop useful, accurate notes.
4. To organize notes effectively.

Key Concept

Success in the classroom requires good listening skills and effective notetaking techniques. To have good listening skills, you must listen with comprehension. Effective notetaking techniques create notes that can aid your retention and recall of information.

The time students spend in a lecture classroom should be useful. Every student should be able to learn from the lecture. Admittedly, the lecture classroom is an ideal learning environment for an auditory learner. However, every student should use all his or her sensory modes, not just the dominant sense, to aid learning. Therefore, everyone can and should learn from a lecture.

Why, then, do some students fail to benefit from lectures? Why do some students prefer to learn from a textbook, rather than a lecture? Probably, some students do not listen actively to the lecture. They respond with the lowest level of listening, instead of the highest. Consequently, they find it difficult to learn from a lecture.

There are three levels of listening:

1. *Hearing.* Some students are present only physically during a lecture. They passively function on the lowest level of listening, hearing, as they let the waves of sound flow over them. This is an unfortunate situation because a lecture is not a hearing test, and a professor's voice is not just noise.

2. *Parroting.* Sometimes, students regard a lecture hall as a game room. In this situation, the teacher is out to "catch" the student, and the student's strategy to avoid being caught is simple: listen at the middle level, called parroting. When the instructor questions the student, the student repeats verbatim the instructor's words, whether those words are relevant to the question or not. By

parroting, the student avoids the appearance of being inattentive to the lecture. Thus, the teacher has not "caught" him. Of course, the parroting level of hearing and copying sounds does not help a student learn. It merely helps him or her pass that informal oral exam.

3. *Comprehending*. This is the highest level of listening. While functioning at this level, a student is listening, understanding, and *thinking*. This level is the most useful one to students because it helps them learn while they sit in a lecture hall. Thus, lectures become an integral part of the learning process. Of course, listening with comprehension requires thought. Listeners must process the information and knowledge presented. In other words, to listen at the highest level, be an **active listener**.

ACTIVE LISTENING

In order to benefit from a lecture, you must listen with comprehension—that is, you must be an active listener. You must listen for the general structure of the lecture and organize your ideas accordingly. You must think about the material being presented. Such activity requires effort, but you will be rewarded with increased learning. The more you learn from each lecture, the less you will have to learn on your own. The lecture situation can become a learning environment only if you think about the topic being discussed, respond to the lecture, and interact with the instructor.

How can you become an active listener? How can you listen and think at the same time? How can you participate in a learning dialogue in the classroom? You can improve your listening skills in several ways.

Before the Lecture

Even before you enter the classroom, you can prepare yourself so that you will be able to listen and learn. With advance preparation, you can participate actively and control your learning.

1. *Make a decision to learn*. Some courses may seem uninteresting, irrelevant, and boring. However, that gloomy perception has no bearing on your immediate situation. You registered for the course, so you must do all you can to pass it. Therefore, you must pay attention, concentrate, and be willing to learn. A conscious decision to act properly in the classroom indicates your maturity and psychological readiness for the college learning situation.

2. *Read assigned material.* Check the course syllabus for chapters and dates. Then, familiarize yourself with the topic by reading, or at least previewing, the material before each lecture class. This familiarity will help you during the lecture to recognize key points, focus on important ideas, and respond to new concepts. You will gain a limited understanding of the topic and will be able to identify ideas that confuse you. Later, during the lecture, you can immediately question the teacher about the material you find confusing. This is especially important for visual learners.

These pre-class preparations involve you in the learning process. They demonstrate that you know your role as a student: you are the one who must learn. Information and knowledge are not simply absorbed from your environment; instead, learning demands your effort and thought.

During the Lecture

Once you have entered the classroom, you can maintain your concentration and develop your understanding of the topic by applying certain techniques.

1. *Make eye contact.* This contact benefits you, not the teacher, because it enhances your concentration. Instead of staring into space while a disembodied voice drones in the background, you can focus on the lecturer and the topic. This helps you to avoid distraction. It also enables you to recognize clues the instructor might be projecting through body language. This eye-contact technique is helpful for visual learners.

2. *Position yourself for action.* Listening with comprehension requires action. Just as an animal's pose (head cocked, body still, eyes narrowed) lets an observer know when an animal is concentrating on listening, your body language should suggest that you are actively working at listening. Your concentration and emphasis on hearing should be obvious. Sit upright and have your pen ready to take notes. Let your body help your mind perform its job. The correct positioning of your body for listening is especially important to kinesthetic learners.

3. *Uncover the organizational pattern.* Instructors want to make the topic easy to understand and remember. Therefore, they frequently organize their ideas according to a pattern. Some organizational patterns you should know are chronology, importance, definition, comparison/contrast, cause/effect, listing, and problem/solution. (For a detailed explanation of some of these patterns, see Chapter 6.) Try to uncover the lecturer's pattern because organized material is easier to learn than unrelated random facts.

EXERCISE 1   The following are definitions of the organizational patterns that lecturers often use. On the lines provided, name the pattern and give an example of how you have heard the pattern used in class.

1. Explains the meaning of a concept or word.

   Pattern: _____

   Example: _____

2. Shows how two things are alike and/or different.

   Pattern: _____

   Example: _____

3. Explains why something happens and/or the consequences of that occurrence.

   Pattern: _____

   Example: _____

4. Provides a series of events or ideas, usually in numerical order.

   Pattern: _____

   Example: _____

5. Shows the time order, or sequence, in which events occur.

   Pattern: _____

   Example: _____

6. Explains a problem and offers suggestions for resolving it.

   Pattern: _____

   Example: _____

7. Enumerates ideas, usually in order of importance.

   Pattern: _____

   Example: _____

Patterns make the task of understanding and remembering easier by placing ideas in a larger framework. One general concept is always easier to understand and recall than several unconnected ones. Therefore, listen carefully to uncover the instructor's pattern. Use it to organize the material for yourself.

EXERCISE 2

Each of the following is the opening sentence of a lecture. Underline words or phrases that suggest an organizational pattern. Then write the pattern you have uncovered on the line provided.

1. Freud frequently discussed the mind's *ego*, *super-ego*, and *id*. What are they?

   _____

2. The French Revolution did not begin with the fall of the Bastille; its beginnings can instead be traced to the early 1700s.

   _____

3. How do the migratory patterns of whales change?

   _____

4. Most historians recognize five major causes of America's Great Depression.

   _____

5. The majority of people living today belong to one of the five major religions.

   _____

6. Although the health care crisis has been discussed in Congress and reported on by the media, few practical responses have been offered.

   _____

7. Let us trace the inventions that led to the development of the personal computer.

   _____

8. Today, I'd like to discuss the Navajos and the Iroquois, two peoples who were apparently very different from each other.

_____

9. Puberty is frequently discussed but little understood. Let us try to gain an understanding of it today.

_____

10. Although many factors contributed to the Persian Gulf War, some factors were more significant than others. Let us begin our discussion of this topic by examining the most important cause.

_____

4. *Summarize the major points.* Remind yourself of the key elements and reinforce their significance. This strategy will help you to remember and recall the main ideas. It will also enhance your concentration and prevent distraction. Because you can think faster than the instructor can talk, you have an opportunity to daydream. Resist wasting your time; use those few precious moments to reinforce your learning by quickly repeating to yourself or highlighting in your notes the major elements of the lecture so far.

5. *Listen between the lines.* Even though instructors may be presenting only factual information, their tone of voice and body language may suggest their opinions and feelings on the subject or the relative importance of ideas.

   Try to understand the nonverbal clues that instructors may be providing. The hints they give can help you to anticipate the course of the discussion. If the tone seems to suggest that an idea is important, you can assume that more time will be spent discussing it. On the other hand, if body language (perhaps a shoulder shrug or a hand gesture) implies that the idea is insignificant, then you will know that you do not have to emphasize it as you study the general topic.

   In addition, reading the appropriate text chapter prior to class can help you construct a larger framework into which the day's topic fits. As you make connections between each specific lecture and the overall subject, you gain an understanding of the course material, and you remember it more easily.

6. *Take notes.* Writing important elements of the lecture helps to imprint them on your memory and prevents distraction. While you take notes, your attention is focused on the topic. Later, when you

review them, your lecture notes will reinforce the textbook's content or introduce supplementary, but important, material. Notetaking during a lecture serves several purposes:

a. It helps you be active listener, one who is focused on the lecture and comprehending its contents.

b. The notes also help you remember the important points covered by the lecturer.

c. By encouraging you to concentrate and repeat important ideas, notetaking helps you to recall those concepts easily.

At this point, you have already performed certain activities that should make your taking notes fairly easy to do. You have already identified the lecturer's organizational pattern, which you can use to structure your notes. Also, by summarizing the key points of the lecture, you have been condensing the topic into a few major elements. Therefore, you can create your notes by simply writing down those main aspects. The specific format you use for notetaking is your personal choice. Just be sure the notes reflect the highlights of the lecture and don't repeat the whole discussion.

7. *Listen before you write*. Notetaking must be done thoughtfully. Don't begin writing as soon as the instructor begins talking. If you do, you'll certainly write down unimportant items. Wait and listen. When you understand his topic and recognize the organizational pattern, then you can begin to take notes. By focusing your attention and thinking about the topic before writing, you prepare for active, purposeful listening and efficient notetaking.

8. *Listen; then evaluate and question*. At this point, you have spent much time and effort familiarizing yourself with the subject of the lecture. After all, you previewed the topic, organized its thesis and supports, summarized its main elements, and reinforced them by taking notes. Therefore, you should feel confident about your knowledge of the topic, so question yourself on it. If you are unsure of the answers, raise your hand and ask questions. Try to clarify confusing points. Do not wait until later in the vain hope that understanding will suddenly come to you. You have already worked diligently; do not deny yourself the chance to clarify material.

Besides testing your own comprehension of the topic, you can also evaluate and question the lecture itself. Does the instructor offer good reasons to support his point of view? Is it possible to draw other conclusions from the given facts? Based on your background knowledge of the topic and your textbook reading, do you think he has presented all views on the topic? Has he omitted any opposing arguments? Based on your interpretation of his tone and body language, do you think he presented an unbiased view of the subject?

In other words, you should be analyzing the topic. The more you examine the material from different angles, the more you will recall. Active listening demands thinking, which leads to learning.

After the Lecture

The end of class does not mean that your job is done. As an active listener, you have one final task to complete. To reinforce the insights you gained from the lecture, be sure to *review your notes* at your earliest convenience. Complete any half-finished notations; fill in any gaps in the structure; clarify confusing points. If necessary, compare your notes to those of another student in the class. (This is particularly important for those who prefer studying in pairs.) Then, read once again your entire set of notes on that topic. By completing and reviewing your notes, you will reaffirm the importance of the topic and emphasize its primary aspects. This review will ensure that you comprehend and remember what you have heard and learned.

Factors Essential to Active Listening

Before the lecture:

> Make a decision to learn.
>
> Read assigned material.

During the lecture:

> Make eye contact.
>
> Position yourself for action.
>
> Uncover the organizational pattern.
>
> Summarize the major points.
>
> Listen between the lines.
>
> Take notes.
>
> Listen before you write.
>
> Listen; then evaluate and question.

After the lecture:

> Review your notes.

EXERCISE 3   Your instructor will present a lecture to you. Be an active listener by using all the techniques you have just learned. Try to gain as much understanding of the topic as possible.

NOTETAKING

Your teachers have probably encouraged, perhaps even required, you to take notes. However, some students misunderstand the reason for taking notes. They regard taking notes as a dictation exercise, so they try to copy every word the teacher says. Others treat notetaking as proof of their attendance. Occasionally, they will write a word or phrase in their notebook. Neither type of student understands the value of taking notes during a lecture.

You should take notes because the process helps you to learn, to remember, and to recall information.

1. Clear, organized, and relevant notes serve as a record of the lecture. Because of that record, you can understand the topic as you learn it.

2. You can also reinforce your understanding weeks later as you review notes in preparation for a test.

3. Finally, because taking notes demands concentration, notetaking focuses your attention and supports learning.

Therefore, clear, organized, and relevant notes can be useful study and review aids. In order to be able to develop good notes and use them efficiently, you must recognize a few characteristics of notetaking.

Characteristics of Effective Notes

Effective notes are useful tools. First, they can help you learn ideas. They can also help you to remember those ideas for later use. Finally, well-written notes make it easy for you to recall ideas when you need them. In order to do all that, your notes must be clear, organized, and relevant. How do you develop such effective notes?

Clear notes should be brief and in your own words. *Relevant notes* should include the key points of the lecture. Below is a short discussion of those characteristics.

1. *Your notes must be brief.* Notes should not be wordy. They should not provide a transcript of the lecture. Effective notes are composed of the *key words and phrases* from the lecture, not whole sentences. Write the minimum number of words necessary to convey the essential

elements of the discussion. In fact, if you can, try to make your notes even briefer by using *symbols* and *abbreviations*. (A symbol is a mark that replaces a word or concept; an abbreviation is a shortened form of a word.) The following list shows you some examples of the kinds of abbreviations and symbols your notes should contain.

Abbreviations		*Symbols*	
Oklahoma	OK	greater than	>
volume	vol.	and	&
biology	bio	because	b/c
government	gov't	equal	=

As you listen to the lecture or discussion, remember that your chief objective is to listen and learn, not to take notes. Although you must take notes, you should not devote the entire class time to that activity. You should be devoting most of your time and energy to active listening and to participating in the discussion.

EXERCISE 4

For each of the following words, supply a standard abbreviation or symbol, or create one of your own.

1. individual _____
2. therefore _____
3. page _____
4. economics _____
5. *New York Times* _____

6. Korean War _____
7. California _____
8. infinity _____
9. people _____
10. without _____

2. *Your notes should use your own words.* You will find that the lecture is easier to remember and understand if you rephrase and restructure the ideas that were presented. Rewriting the ideas also increases your learning. When you change the teacher's words into your own, you process the information. This processing helps to imprint the material onto your memory. Processing and imprinting are part of the learning process.

EXERCISE 5   Read the following paragraphs, imagining that they are part of a lecture. Take notes on the passage; be sure to use your own words.

> Both coal and oil contain the element sulfur. When these fuels are burned by homes and industries, a gas called sulfur dioxide is produced. Once sulfur dioxide is in the air, it combines with water vapor and falls to the earth as **acid rain**. Winds blowing from west to east carry sulfur dioxide from coal-burning power plants and factories. Many scientists believe that this is why acid rain is common in the northeastern part of the United States and eastern Canada. Acid rain has polluted lakes and ponds and harmed the wildlife living there.
>
> Another form of air pollution is called **smog**. One kind of smog is a combination of smoke, harmful gases, and fog. This type of smog is common in cities with many factories. Another kind of smog is produced when sunlight chemically changes the exhaust gases from cars. Smog can cause burning eyes, coughing, difficult breathing, and even death.
>
> Because many people are sealing their homes to prevent heat loss, **indoor air pollution** is becoming a problem. Gases, particles of soot, and other dangerous substances from stoves, heaters, and cigarette smoke are some of the indoor pollutants.
>
> *(Bierer, Loretta, et al. Life Science.*
> *Lexington, MA: Heath, 1987. p. 339.)*

3. *Your notes should include the key points.* In order to be brief, you must leave out some ideas you hear. Usually, your notes will provide just the framework of the discussion, not its entirety. Therefore, your notes should include the topic, thesis, and supporting details—the essential elements only. Omit all the minor details.

That sounds easy, but how can you distinguish between important and unimportant ideas? Below are a few clues.

Identifying Key Elements

Be aware of the hints your instructor may give you as he or she lectures.

1. <u>The teacher may actually declare that the lecture is important.</u> If she does, believe her. The lecturer is not trying to confuse you; in fact, she is being very honest. Therefore, take notes!

2. <u>The teacher may write concepts on the board.</u> Most of you are aware of this clue, so listen carefully for the squeak of chalk on the board. You can safely assume that if something is written on the board, it is important. Copy it!

3. <u>The teacher may repeat a concept.</u> She may reword an idea to present it in a slightly different form. When she does this, she is emphasizing the concept's importance. Repetition assures comprehension and enhances memory. If you hear an instructor restating a point, note it.

4. <u>The teacher may vary her voice.</u> Few lectures are delivered in a monotone. Teachers know that a single pitch guarantees boredom. Consequently, they try to vary their tone, pitch, and volume as they speak. Their vocal variations provide clues to important ideas. You should familiarize yourself with your teachers' speech patterns and use these auditory clues as notetaking aids.

5. <u>The teacher may use body language.</u> Just as few teachers speak in a monotone, few stand at attention or sit behind their desks the whole time they lecture. Most move around the room as they talk. That movement isn't merely action; it is body language. Observe it and use it to help you decide when to note an important idea.

6. <u>The teacher may refer to the textbook.</u> Often, students overlook their textbook as a source of crucial ideas. (See Chapter 8, for more suggestions on dealing with your textbooks.) If you read the assigned work before class, then you should be aware of the ideas expressed in the text and the different emphasis placed on various concepts. If your teacher stresses the same elements, you can be assured of their importance. Write them down!

If you listen actively to each lecture, you can distinguish essential concerns from nonessential ones. Then, be sure to note the important ones briefly and in your own words. However, for notes to be useful, they must be clear, relevant, and organized.

Organizing Notes

Organized notes have a structure and relate all the parts to the whole. Good notes must be organized so that you can match concepts to their details and examples; this relationship among ideas makes remembering and recalling information easier. There are primarily three ways to organize notes: outlining, mapping, and diagraming. Although some of these methods are more formal than others, all of them condense material and present it visually. If your notes are organized, then you should be able to look at them and easily locate the topic, main idea, and supports. Consequently, well-organized notes help you to review material efficiently and effectively at examination time.

Outlines. You are probably familiar with outlining, a standard organizational technique. A formal outline centers the topic of the lecture at the top of the page, and every noted idea beings a new line. A Roman numeral, written at the left margin, marks each main idea. Secondary ideas are listed and identified by upper-case letters and are indented approximately one inch from the margin. Details are indented another inch and marked by Arabic numbers. Finally, examples, which are identified by lower-case letters, are further indented, almost to the center of the page. The following illustration demonstrates an outline's structure:

TOPIC

I. Main Idea

    A. Secondary Idea

    B. Secondary Idea

        1. Detail
           a. example
           b. example

        2. Detail

        3. Detail

II. Main Idea

    A. Secondary Idea

    B. Secondary Idea

    C. Secondary Idea

Obviously, every outline will differ because it must correspond to a particular lecture's content. Remember, too, that this example illustrates a formal outline; your notetaking outline does not need to be so exact. Instead, the outline you develop during the lecture should simply follow the general guidelines. It should distinguish main ideas, secondary ideas, details, and examples. Moveover, it should visually indicate the relationships of those points to each other.

On the following page is an outline of the lecture your instructor presented earlier. Analyze the outline carefully. Does it fulfill the general requirements? In what ways?

ACADEMIC KNOW-HOW

I. Instructor Assumes:

    A. Student knows what he's doing

        1. courses to take

        2. attends class

        3. does assignments

    B. There to learn

    C. Evidence of learning—must produce

    D. Mature

II. Causes of Failure:

    A. Waits to be warned for trouble

    B. Puts off work

    C. Misses some assignments

        1. No big deal

        2. = 0%

    D. Doesn't understand assignment

    E. Cuts class

        1. attendance important

        2. borderline case

III. Good Student:

    A. Works to capacity

    B. Professional and efficient

    C. Takes many lecture notes

        1. most material there

        2. 3–4 pages per lecture

D. Keeps up with reading (or skims)

E. Reviews notes

IV. Learning = Academic Experience

EXERCISE 6

Read the following passage, "The Energy Crisis," as if it were a lecture you were listening to. Then, outline the passage in the space provided. Remember to be concise and to use abbreviations and symbols.

THE ENERGY CRISIS

Think about things for which you use energy. Energy heats and lights your home, cooks your dinner, and runs your family's car. Imagine how different your life would be without energy. In the past, many people took energy for granted. However, the energy crisis of 1973–1974 changed the attitudes of many people. During that time there were extreme shortages of gasoline. The cost of a gallon of gasoline shot up. Gas stations were only open a few hours each day. People had to wait in long lines just to get a few gallons of gas. This energy crisis made people realize that the country's supplies of fossil fuels were not going to last forever.

I   In 1980, between 90 and 95 percent of the energy used in the United States came from fossil fuels. Fossil fuels—oil, coal, and natural gas—are important sources of energy. However, they are also nonrenewable sources of energy. Today people are using more energy than ever before. As the world's population increases, so will its energy needs. Fossil fuels will probably not be able to meet the energy needs of the future. How will the energy demands of the future be met?

II   Alternate sources of energy are now being explored and developed. Nuclear power now provides the world with more energy than any other energy alternative. Nuclear power plants produce energy by splitting atoms. However, as a result of this process, dangerous waste products are produced. At the present time, scientists have not yet developed a safe way to get rid of these wastes.

III   The sun is another source of energy. Solar energy is a promising energy source because it is a continuous source of energy and it does not have to be renewed. Special collectors and solar panels built on rooftops and hillsides gather the sun's energy. However, these collection devices are expensive and are not always practical. In addition, methods to store solar energy for long periods of time have still not been developed.

IV   Wind, wood, and water are other energy alternatives. However, each one of these energy sources has its drawbacks.

Windmills produce nonpolluting energy but only when the wind blows. Wood is a renewable source of energy, but it is not plentiful in all parts of the country. Burning wood can also add to the problem of air pollution. Energy from moving water is a nonpolluting energy source. However, only areas of the country near the ocean or fast-moving rivers or streams would be able to use this energy resource.

Some life scientists think that living things may provide the key to our energy problems. Does this solution sound impossible? Think about it. All cells produce energy during respiration. Suppose scientists can find ways to capture this energy or to produce it as cells do. Scientists can then apply this knowledge and use it to produce energy on a large scale. Have you ever thought of green plants as nature's solar collectors? Green plants collect and store the sun's energy. By studying this process, scientists may be able to develop better technology for capturing the sun's energy.

(Bierer, Loretta, et al. Life Science. Lexington, MA: Heath, 1987. pp. 344–346.)

Outline

Diagrams. A diagram is a plan or picture that explains a concept. You may be familiar with flowcharts, sentence diagrams, and seating plans; all these are examples of diagrams. Diagrams often use geometric figures—circles, squares, and triangles along with connecting lines or arrows—to illustrate the relationships between an entire passage (or idea) and its parts. Like other organizational formats, diagrams visually represent a concept.

The following diagram is based on the lecture "Orientation" found in the Appendix. How does this diagram compare to the outline of the same lecture?

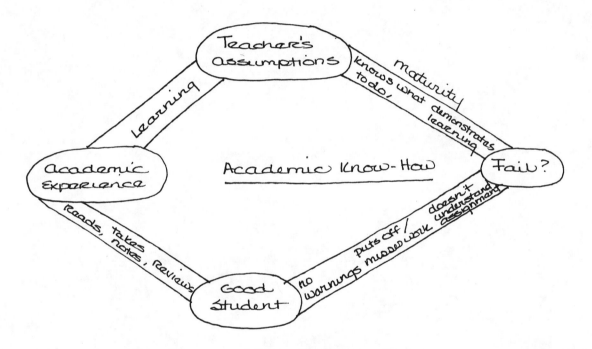

EXERCISE 7

Look again at "The Energy Crisis" passage you outlined in Exercise 6. Diagram the passage in the space provided.

Maps. Outlining and diagraming are effective notetaking strategies if both you and your instructor are organized. If one of you is not, then the outline or diagram will be incomplete. In addition, a spontaneous class discussion, which can arise from students' questions, has no overall structure. That, too, can be difficult to organize into an outline or diagram.

However, there is another notetaking strategy that can help you to structure rambling or disorganized material. Maps let you locate essential elements quickly. Although they are similar to outlines, maps are not as formal or methodical. Thus you have more flexibility as you gather information. In a map, center the topic on the page, as you did with the outline. Then, write and circle each main idea as it is presented. Write each supporting detail on a line connected to the secondary idea it explains. In the same way, "attach" examples to the details they illustrate. The sample map on the following page will help you visualize these features.

TOPIC

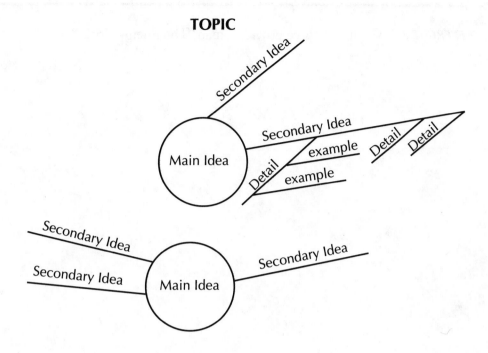

Below is a map of your instructor's lecture. Note how the information is organized and visualized. What differences do you notice between the map and the outline and diagram?

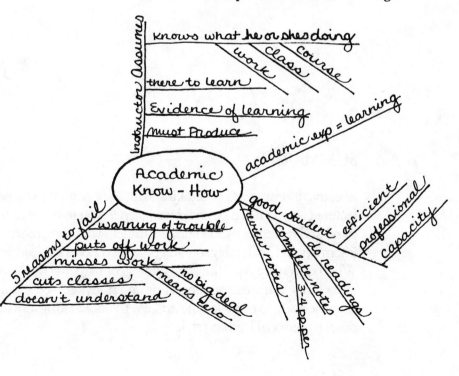

✐

EXERCISE 8   In the space provided, map "The Energy Crisis."

SUMMARY

Effective listening and notetaking skills are essential to success in the lecture classroom. To be an active listener, you must listen to understand and remember. Good notes can help you comprehend and recall information. Clear, relevant, and organized notes are learning aids. Whether you are outlining, diagraming, or mapping the lecture's important points, you are comprehending and studying. You should be sure to listen actively to every lecture and use the notetaking format that best fits your personal learning style.

APPLICATION I

Your instructor will present a lecture to you. Be an active listener by using all the techniques you have just learned. Try to gain as much understanding of the topic as you can. After the lecture, compare your notes with those of your fellow students in small groups. In what ways do the notes differ? What accounts for these differences? Despite individual differences in notetaking style and format, has everyone agreed on the lecture's major points?

APPLICATION II

In another of your lecture classes, use all the listening and notetaking techniques you have learned. After taking and reviewing notes from that class, compare them to notes you took earlier in the year in the same course. Do you see any improvements? Write a paragraph that explains the changes you have made in your listening technique and the results of those changes.

Chapter 3

INCREASING VOCABULARY

Objective

1. To use a dictionary effectively.
2. To use word parts to identify unfamiliar words.
3. To define words from their context.

Key Concept

Your ability to communicate with others depends on your use and knowledge of language. This means that words are important. By expanding your vocabulary, you improve your comprehension and increase your ability to share ideas with others.

Words are powerful. Teachers use words to introduce you to academic knowledge. Newscasters use words to inform you of the day's events. Advertisers use carefully selected words to encourage you to purchase their products. Even politicians use specific words to persuade you to vote for them. A well-developed vocabulary lets you participate in such social interactions. Words empower you. Consider these situations in which your word knowledge proves helpful to you.

1. As a reader, you can focus on an author's message instead of stumbling over unfamiliar words.

2. As a student, you can gain access to the concepts presented in lectures, books, and journal articles.

3. As a consumer, you can judge the merits of products and contracts for yourself.

4. As an individual, you can communicate more effectively and accurately with others.

To increase your vocabulary, you must focus on three strategies:

1. Using a dictionary efficiently.
2. Using words parts to define unfamiliar words.
3. Determining meanings of words from their context.

DICTIONARY USAGE

Dictionaries come in many types, each with a specific purpose.

1. **Standard college dictionaries**—such as *Webster's Collegiate Dictionary*, the *American Heritage Dictionary*, or the *Oxford American Dictionary*—provide basic information on a word's definition and use. It would be helpful to you to have this type of dictionary in your personal library.

2. **Unabridged dictionaries** contain all the words in the English language. They give complete information on a word's origins (its etymology), its definitions, and changes in its use over centuries.

3. **Specialized dictionaries** for nearly every academic discipline define the words used within that field.

You can find unabridged and specialized dictionaries in the reference section of your school library.

Before using any dictionary, examine the first few pages carefully. These pages will give you information about the dictionary's organization and the abbreviations it uses, a pronunciation guide, and a list of its tables, charts, or graphs. As the sample table of contents from *Webster's Third New International Dictionary* on the following page shows, dictionaries provide more than just word definitions. Examine this table of contents carefully. What information other than definitions does this dictionary contain?

_____

_____

_____

_____

_____

_____

CONTENTS

A Dictionary of the English Language

Tables

(at or near *italicized* word)

Full-Page Illustrations

3a

(Gove, Philip Babcock, Editor in Chief. Webster's Third New International Dictionary. Springfield, MA: G. & C. Merriam Co., Publishers, 1976. p. 3a.)

Definitions

Although a dictionary may contain a great deal of other information, its most important function is to provide the definitions of words. How are words defined? How do dictionaries develop definitions?

Words are defined by their usage. This means that words can change their meanings over the course of centuries or even decades. Consider, for instance, the term *broadcast*. In the early part of this century, when most people lived in farming communities, the term meant "to scatter seeds for planting." Even today, this definition remains part of the specialized language for agriculture. However, most people would define the word *broadcast* as "the electronic transmission of a radio or television program." Therefore, the definition changed when a new invention became part of the popular culture. Compare the two definitions of *broadcast* reprinted here from two dictionaries, one published in 1961, the other in 1980. Consider how the usage, and thus the definition, changed.

1. **broadcast**—verb. 1. To scatter or sow broadcast. 2. *Radio & Television.* To send out broadcast from a radio or television transmitting station.

(*Bethel, John. General Editor. Webster's New Collegiate Dictionary. Springfield, MA: G. & C. Merriam Co., Publishers, 1961. p. 106.*)

2. **broadcast**—verb. 1. send out by radio or television. 2. to speak or appear in a radio or television program. 3. to make generally known. 4. to sow (seed) by scattering.

(*Ehrlich, Eugene, et al. Oxford American Dictionary. New York: Oxford University Press, 1980. p. 77.*)

In entry 1, the original meaning of the word, "to scatter," appears first as the most common definition. A second definition, specific to one industry, is also supplied. However, within twenty years, the use of the word has changed significantly. The second dictionary entry begins with "to send out by radio or television" as the most common definition; the next two definitions are also based on this usage. It is the fourth definition, "to sow (seed) by scattering," which is the least common and was once the original meaning.

As you can see, words change their meanings over time. Therefore, you need to use a current dictionary. Can you think of other words whose meanings have changed over time? (You might consider a word such as *hardware*, which has a new meaning, specific to the computer industry.)

Additional Information

In addition to definitions, each entry for a word offers a great deal of information. Analyze the following entry carefully:

> **record** (rek´-ord) n. 1. information preserved in a permanent form, especially in writing. 2. a document etc. bearing this. 3. a disk bearing recorded sound. 4. facts known about a person's past, *has a good record of service; have a record or a police record*, to have past criminal convictions that are on record. 5. the best performance or most remarkable event etc. of its kind that is known; *hold the record*, to be the one who achieved this. **record** adj. best or highest or most extreme hitherto recorded, *a record crop*. **record** (ri-cord´) v. 1. to set down in writing or other permanent form. 2. to preserve (sound) on a disk or magnetic tape for later reproduction. 3. to register on a measuring instrument. *for the record*, so that facts may be recorded. *off the record*, stated unofficially or not for publication. *on record*, preserved in written records. *record changer*, that part of a record player that moves the records into playing position or removes them after playing. *record player*, an apparatus for reproducing sound from disks on which it is recorded.
>
> *(Ehrlich, Eugene, et al. Oxford American Dictionary. New York: Oxford University Press, 1980. p. 562.)*

In this entry, the word and its pronunciation are listed first. Next the part of speech is named:

1. For *record*, the first use of the word is as a noun, a thing. The five definitions that follow are arranged in descending order of importance and use. In other words, the first definition listed is the one most frequently used. Notice, too, that within definition 4, a specific example of the word used in that sense is given. Often, dictionary editors will provide usage examples to clarify the definition.

2. The second entry of *record*, as an adjective to modify a noun, also includes an example.

3. The third entry for the word is as a verb, to show action. Its verb has a different pronunciation. After the three definitions of *record* as a verb, the editors have listed specific set phrases in which the word *record* appears.

Meaning and Context

The sample dictionary entry for *record* presents the basic information you need in order to understand a word: its pronunciation, its part(s) of speech, its meanings in order of importance, and examples of special uses. All of this information is important, for you may find that the first definition is not the one that "fits" the passage you are reading.

Consider the following sentences:

Before she reached the finish line, the sprinter has *run* as fast as possible.

The nylon jacket has a *run* in it.

The gambler had a *run* of good luck.

Is the word *run* used the same way in each sentence? Is the meaning the same in each sentence? If you tried to use the same definition for *run* in each sentence above, then your sentences would not make sense. In the first sentence, *run* is a verb and means "to move quickly." In the second sentence, *run* is a noun and means "a flaw in fabric." In the third sentence, *run* is a noun that means "a streak." So you can see that the appropriate meaning depends on the context in which a word is used. Therefore, check each meaning carefully to determine the correct one for your sentence. Make sure the chosen meaning "fits."

EXERCISE 1

Use a dictionary to determine the meanings of the italicized words in the sentences that follow. Make sure that you identify the part of speech and meaning that best fit the sentence.

1. Before the fall of the Berlin Wall, many Eastern European countries were *satellites* of the Soviet Union.

   Part of Speech: _____

   Meaning: _____

2. Jackson *begrudgingly* agreed to follow the new rules.

   Part of Speech: _____

   Meaning: _____

3. With the last *game* in the set, Chris Evert won the tennis match.

   Part of Speech: _____

   Meaning: _____

4. The food critic's *prejudices* are well know to his readers; this critic prefers Southern cooking and avoids innovations.

   Part of Speech: _____

   Meaning: _____

5. The judge's *high* ideals have made him the most respected man on the Supreme Court.

   Part of Speech: _____

   Meaning: _____

6. The workers *rallied* against the new administrative reforms.

   Part of Speech: _____

   Meaning: _____

7. The *rag* printed the most vicious story about the company.

   Part of Speech: _____

   Meaning: _____

8. The salary *floor* begins at $3.35 an hour.

   Part of Speech: _____

   Meaning: _____

9. By the end of their training exercises, the soldiers were *seasoned* veterans.

   Part of Speech: _____

   Meaning: _____

10. The large man *stormed* into the restaurant.

    Part of Speech: _____

    Meaning: _____

EXERCISE 2   Define the words listed below. Use two or three different dictionaries to assist you in determining the major meaning of each word. Note any specialized use of the word. Also, write a sentence for each primary definition of the word.

1. discriminate

_____

_____

2. port

_____

_____

3. interface

_____

_____

4. liberal

_____

_____

5. slash

_____

_____

WORD PARTS

Languages develop over hundreds of years. You have already studied how the meaning of words can change with time. Now, look at how the words themselves can change, too.

Words are made up of parts: prefixes, roots, and suffixes. A *prefix* is a syllable added to the beginning of a word. A *root* is the base form of a word, its foundation. A *suffix* is a syllable added to the end of a word. Every word has a root; *not* every word has a prefix or suffix added to it. However, by adding prefixes and/or suffixes to a word, you can change the meaning of the word.

Example:

root:	*cycle*
root + suffix:	cycle + ing = *cycling*
prefix + root + suffix:	bi + cycle + ing = *bicycling*

When you changed the form of the word by adding a prefix and a suffix to it, you also changed its part of speech and its meaning. How could that happen? The changes in the word's part of speech and its definition occurred because *word parts have meanings.*

Many English words and word parts come from other languages: German, French, Spanish, Latin, Greek, and others. Although a prefix or suffix is only part of an English word, in its original language that part had meaning by itself. Therefore, if you know the meanings of word parts from other languages, it may be possible for you to figure out definitions for unfamiliar words. To learn new word parts, you can examine a word's origins (or etymology) in a dictionary. Look carefully at the following entry:

biography (bi og´ ra fi) [Gr. *biographia,* fr. *bios* life + *graphein* to write]

(Webster's New Collegiate Dictionary. *Springfield, MA: G. & C. Merriam Co., 1961. p. 86.*)

In this entry, the origins of the word *biography* are given. The word comes from a Greek word *biographia,* composed of two parts; *bios* (meaning "life") and *graphein* (meaning "to write"). Knowing these Greek word parts can help you later identify other words in which they appear. By keeping a list of roots, prefixes, and suffixes as you discover them, you increase your ability to identify unfamiliar words.

EXERCISE 3

Use a dictionary to locate the origins of the following words and write them in the space provided. Report your findings to your classmates. Also, use each word in a sentence.

1. chauvinistic

   Origin: _____

   Sentence: _____

   _____

2. sociology

   Origin: _____

   Sentence: _____

   _____

3. liberate

   Origin: _____

   Sentence: _____

   _____

4. photosynthesis

   Origin: _____

   Sentence: _____

   _____

5. tripod

   Origin: _____

   Sentence: _____

   _____

The lists of prefixes, roots, and suffixes on the following pages will help you begin your study of word parts. Please note that the lists for prefixes and suffixes are arranged by meaning, because many prefixes and some suffixes have the same meaning.

Prefixes

Meaning	Prefix	Origin	Example
after	post	Latin	postdate
before	ante	Latin	anteroom
	pre	Latin	preconceived
evil, bad	mal	Latin	malformed
from	ab	Latin	abnormal
not	a	Latin	amoral
	anti	Greek	antitrust
	de	Middle English	defrost
	dis	Latin	discomfort
	il/im/in	Latin	illogical, impermanent, inability
	non	Latin	nonsense
	un	Old English	uncoordinated
numbers			
one	mono	Greek	monarchy
	uni	Latin	unicorn
two	bi	Latin	bicycle
three	tri	Latin	triangle
four	quad	Latin	quadrupled
five	quint	Latin	quintuplet
	pent	Middle English	pentathlon
six	ses, sex	Latin	sextet
seven	sept	Latin	septennial
eight	octa	Latin	octagon
nine	non	Latin	nonagenarian
ten	dec	Latin	decade
with	com/con	Latin	congregation
	syn/sym	Greek	sympathetic

Roots

Root	Origin	Meaning	Example
aqua	Latin	water	aquarium
bio	Greek	life	biology
chronos	Greek	time	chronology
demos	Greek	people	demography
hydr	Greek	water	hydrogen
institu	Latin	place in	institution
optic	Greek	vision	optician
physis	Greek	nature	physical

Root	Origin	Meaning	Example
psych	Greek	mind	psychology
pyro	Greek	fire	pyrotechnics
soma	Greek	body	psychosomatic
sophos	Greek	wise	sophomore
theos	Greek	God, religion	theological
vita	Latin	life	vitamin
zoo	Greek	animal	zoology

Suffixes

Meaning	Suffixes	Origin	Example
capable of	able/ible	French	intelligible
characterized by	al	Latin	original
	ish	Old English	peevish
	ory	Latin	conciliatory
one who performs	ent/ant	Latin	president
	er	Old English	lawyer
	ist	Greek	physicist
	or	Latin	counselor
state	ence/ance	Latin	perseverance
	ity	Latin	activity
	ment	Latin	amazement

EXERCISE 4

In the words that follow, you will find many of the prefixes, roots, and suffixes listed in the tables above. However, each word has a new word part. For each word, use a dictionary to define all the word parts. Record the type and the meaning of the new word parts. Then, write two other words that use the new word part. The first one has been done for you.

	New Word Part	Type	Meaning	New Examples
aquatic	ic	suffix	related to	psychic, aerobic
predicament				
theocracy				
institutional				
sympathetic				

	New Word Part	*Type*	*Meaning*	*New Examples*
disapprove				
thespian				
congenial				
malevolent				
chronometer				
antebellum				

EXERCISE 5   Use the prefixes, roots, and suffixes below to form words to complete the following sentences. The first one is done for you.

Prefixes	Roots	Suffixes
auto (self)	ambulate (walk)	ate (in the state of)
mis (hate)	bio (life)	ology (study of)
uni (one)	gyn (woman)	ium (place)
circum (around)	phone (wound)	y (characterized by)
tele (far)	anthro (mankind)	ist (one who)
	cycle (wheel)	
	philos (love)	
	sophos (wise)	
	aqua (water)	
	graph (write)	
	psyche (mind)	

1. An instrument that allows you to send written messages over great distances is a *telegraph*.

2. A story of one's own life is an _____.

3. The study of mankind is _____.

4. The study of the mind is _____.

5. A place where marine animals are kept is an _____.

6. A person who studies mankind is an _____.

7. A one-wheeled vehicle is a _____.

8.   Handwriting analysis, the study of handwriting, is also called

_____.

9.   A person who rides a bicycle is called a _____.

10.   When a star signs his name for a fan, he is giving his

_____.

EXERCISE 6

Use the lists of prefixes, roots, and suffixes provided in this chapter, along with a dictionary, to create a list of 10 words and their definitions. With this list, create a quiz that matches words and their definitions. In groups of four, exchange quizzes and take them. What new words have you learned? How did knowledge of word parts enable you to define the new words?

WORDS IN CONTEXT

It can be frustrating to encounter new words as you are listening to a lecture or reading a textbook passage. Sometimes you must interrupt your reading to check a dictionary for the word's meaning. At other times, you might have to listen to a discussion of a term you don't understand. If this situation occurs too often as you are reading or listening, then you will begin to focus on the new words rather than on the content you need to learn. Consequently, you will not be able to read or listen carefully, and your learning will suffer. You will not control your learning situation, because the unknown words will affect your analysis. There is a solution, however. You can gain control of the learning situation by using the context of a passage or lecture to make an educated guess about the word's meaning.

What is *context*? A word's context is the passage or sentence in which it appears. It is the ideas surrounding a word. Sometimes authors will deliberately use the context to offer clues to an unfamiliar word's meaning. They may alert readers to a word's definition by using certain punctuation marks. At other times, both writers and lecturers will use examples, definitions, descriptions, summaries, and synonyms or antonyms to help you define words. Although these context clues will not give you the exact meaning of a word, they will provide enough information for you to understand the word in that specific context. If you understand at least a general sense of the word, you can continue reading and learning or listening and learning. Later, you can check the word's definition in a dictionary.

Punctuation

Certain marks of punctuation—dashes, colons, commas, or parentheses—help a writer to define terms for an audience. Usually, the definition of a new term will be enclosed or set off by these marks. Analyze the following sentences, and try to define the italicized words.

> The actor's *egotism*, his focus on himself, made him a poor candidate for the panel discussion.
>
> Like many American writers, the author was an *autodidact*: he had taught himself by reading others' novels.
>
> To learn new word parts, you can examine a word's origins (or *etymology*) in a dictionary.
>
> *Alliteration* (repetition of similar sounds) plays a major role in poems.
>
> The patient suffered from *agoraphobia*—the fear of open spaces.

Define the following words:

egotism _____

autodidact _____

etymology _____

alliteration _____

agoraphobia _____

What punctuation clues in each sentence alerted you to the definitions?

Example or Explanation

Often, a writer or lecturer will signal in one of two ways that an example or explanation is being provided. Transitional expressions (such as *for instance* or *for example*) or the abbreviations *i.e.* (meaning "that is") or *e.g.* (meaning "for example") will precede the example or explanation. Consider the following examples; try to define the italicized words by analyzing the example or explanation.

> Although the salesman was well dressed, charming, and articulate, he was a *charlatan*; that is, he falsely declared himself an expert on the subject.
>
> Mabel impressed her teachers because she was a *polyglot*—e.g., she could speak French, Italian, Russian, and Cantonese fluently.

Left in the refrigerator for over three months, the eggs were *putrescent*—i.e., they smelled rotten.

Hank's *insouciance* towards his education made him a poor student; for instance, he never read the assigned materials, completed his homework, or attended class.

Define the following words:

charlatan _____

polyglot _____

putrescent _____

insouciance _____

In the following cartoon, how do the examples help you define the term *oxymoron?*

(MacNelly, Jeff. "Shoe," Baltimore Evening Sun, *15 Jan. 1991.*)

Definition

If a term is vital to your understanding of material, an author or lecturer may simply provide a definition. Consider the following examples:

Embryology is the study of the development of an animal before birth.

A *neurosis* is the psychological term for a mental disorder that may produce depression or abnormal behavior.

A *quark* is the smallest part of matter.

A novel that traces the development of a character from innocence to experience is a *bildungsroman*.

Define the following words:

embryology _____

neurosis _____

quark _____

bildungsroman _____

Description

Often, a writer will define a concept by describing its characteristics. Analyze the following examples:

His *arrogance* is unbearable; he constantly asserts his superiority over everyone else.

The university president stated her opinions about the new grant *unequivocally*; she presented her views definitely and forcefully.

The Egyptian *hieroglyphics* intrigued us; these stick figures and characters symbolized many aspects of Egyptian culture.

His interest in *herpetology* repels most people; in his home, he has over fifty varieties of snakes and other reptiles.

Define the following words:

arrogance _____

unequivocally _____

hieroglyphics _____

herpetology _____

Summary

Writers will sometimes provide summaries of words to define them. Frequently, an author will first gave familiar information and then state the new term. To follow are some examples. Use the summaries to identify the meaning of the italicized words.

My aunt talks constantly about anything and rambles on for hours; her *garrulous* nature drives the family crazy.

The traitor, once a trusted military aide, sold classified material to the enemy; this *quisling* was convicted for his betrayal of the country.

Jackson has given most of his money and time to assist the homeless; this *humanitarian* was rewarded by the town council.

Psychics claim to see the future and know all by gazing into a crystal ball; most of us do not possess such *omniscience*.

Define the following words:

garrulous _____

quisling _____

humanitarian _____

omniscience _____

Synonyms and Antonyms

Synonyms are words that have the same meaning; antonyms are words that have opposite meanings. Both can be used to help define unfamiliar words. Analyze the italicized word in each sentence below in light of the antonyms and synonyms provided.

The couple's wealth was evident in their lovely, expensive home, its formal garden and swimming pool, and the Mercedes in the driveway; the neighbors envied the couple's *affluence*.

The jury did not *exonerate* the defendant; instead, the jury returned a guilty verdict.

Terry's good manners were appreciated by others; her *gentility* made her a popular guest.

His intellectual knowledge was not *innate*; he had developed it through his education.

Define the following words:

affluence _____

exonerate _____

gentility _____

innate _____

This last technique for determining meaning in context may be difficult to use sometimes. If you do not know anything about a word's meaning, you may be unsure of whether the author is providing a synonym or antonym. In that case, try to use another context clue. For example, perhaps you could not determine that *wealth* and *affluence* are synonyms in the first sentence. However, additional clues are provided: expensive home, formal garden, swimming pool, and Mercedes. Those details describe a life-style that only the rich can afford. Therefore, you can decide that *affluence* means "wealth."

EXERCISE 7

Using context clues, define each of the italicized words in the sentences that follow. Check your answers in a dictionary.

1. Even though the art critic was an *agnostic*, she appreciated medieval religious paintings and themes.

   _____

2. During the Crusades, the knight's *peregrinations* led him from Western Europe to the Middle East, a journey of several thousand miles.

   _____

3. My computer *port*—i.e., the slot for attachments—was filled with peanut butter.

   _____

4. The child's bright eyes, alert expression, and charming smile were captured in a great photograph; the child certainly has many *photogenic* characteristics.

   _____

5. Because the employee constantly circulated rumors about the company and told everyone of the company's confidential plans, he was fired; his *indiscretion* had cost him a job.

   _____

6. The computer company's profits increased drastically; obviously, the owners had found a *lucrative* business.

   _____

7. The manager stood upright, raised his fists, and glared menacingly at the shaking clerk; the manager's *pugnacious* nature did little to make him an effective administrator.

_____

8. The poet's *panegyric*—a poem praising a person—pleased the audience.

_____

9. A figure with four sides is a *quadrangle*.

_____

10. During the Second World War, Japanese-Americans were placed in *internment* camps; in these isolated areas, they were forced to live in barracks until the end of the war.

_____

_____

EXERCISE 8

Read each paragraph carefully and use context clues to define the italicized words. Record your definitions in the space provided below each paragraph.

1. Weather changes from day to day. But the kind of weather that your area has from year to year is the same. Some areas have hot, dry summers and cool, wet winters. In other areas, it is hot and rainy all year long. The temperature and moisture conditions that an area has over a long period of time is called its *climate*. Climate helps to determine the kinds of plants and animals that can live in an area. A group of *ecosystems* with similar kinds of climates and similar plant and animal communities is called a *biome*.

(Bierer, Loretta, et al. Life Science. Lexington, MA: Heath, 1987. p. 186.)

climate: _____

ecosystems: _____

biome: _____

2. *Depressants*, or "downers," are drugs that slow down the central nervous system. These drugs decrease the heart and breathing rates and make a person feel sleepy. There are different kinds of depressants. *Narcotics*, such as heroin and codeine, are strong habit-forming depressants that are made

from the drug opium. Doctors prescribe narcotics to relieve pain and tension and relax the muscles. Other depressants are called *barbiturates*. Barbiturates, which are often used in sleeping pills, are powerful drugs. If taken in large amounts or in combination with other depressants, they can slow down the body functions so much that death results.

(*Bierer, Loretta, et al. Life Science. Lexington, MA: Heath, 1987. p. 503.*)

depressants: _____

narcotics: _____

barbiturates: _____

3. . . . [T]he family is a biological unit that includes three fundamental relationships: *marriage* (two or more individuals sharing a socially recognized mating relationship), *parenthood* (parent-child relationships), and *siblingship* (child-child relationships). Although rooted in biology, these three basic familial relationships are also socially defined. The form of the marriage, as well as the rights and responsibilities of the marriage partners, varies considerably from society to society. And in all societies, the parent-child and sibling relationships are variously defined and continually refined according to the relative age and the sex of those concerned. . . . But all families are built upon a central core which consists of a father-husband, a mother-wife, and their children-siblings. We refer to this central core as the *nuclear family*.

(*Mendoza, Manuel, and Vince Napoli. Systems of Society. Lexington, MA: Heath, 1990. p. 222. 5th ed.*)

marriage: _____

parenthood: _____

siblingship: _____

nuclear family: _____

4. Listen. What do you hear? Is a clock ticking? Can you hear traffic? Is someone talking? All the sounds you hear involve *sound waves*. A sound wave is a compressional wave produced by a back-and-forth motion. For example, when a bell rings, the sides of the bell move back and forth rapidly, making sound waves. The rapid back-and-forth motion is called a *vibration*. As the bell vibrates, it pushes together, or *compresses*, the air around it, making a compressional wave.

(*Nolan, Louise. Physical Science. Lexington, MA: Heath, 1987. p. 394.*)

sound waves: _____

vibration: _____

compresses: _____

5. The printed lines of a play do not indicate the many
   nuances of expression—the continual shifting of pace, the
   changes in emotional tension, the accenting of one word
   rather than another, the pauses, inflections, movements,
   and gestures—that create a living character. It is here that
   actor and director make their personal contribution, as a
   result of which one performer's *interpretation* of a role
   differs markedly from another's. The *notation* of music is
   even more limited in this regard than language. The
   composer is able to set down the pitches and their values in
   time; he indicates whether a passage should go fast or slow,
   soft or loud; and he may add other details that serve as
   clues to the character of the piece. But the life of the
   music, its mood and feeling, cannot be written down in
   symbols.

   *(Machlis, Joseph. The Enjoyment of Music. Shorter ed. rev. New York:
   Norton, 1963. p. 67.)*

nuances: _____

interpretation: _____

notation: _____

symbols: _____

SUMMARY

As you increase your vocabulary, you will become a more conscious
reader, for you will be able to focus on the content of a passage, not
the words used. By using a dictionary, recognizing word parts, and
defining words by their context, you will gain power as a reader, as a
student, as a consumer, and as an individual.

Read the following paragraphs carefully and note the italicized words. Use your knowledge of word parts and words in context to determine their meanings. Then, answer the questions at the end of each selection.

1. The original art of the Germanic peoples was *abstract*, decorative, and geometric, and ignored the world or *organic* nature. It was confined to the decoration of small, *portable* objects—weapons or items of personal *adornment* such as bracelets, pendants, and belt buckles. Most characteristic, perhaps, and produced in considerable numbers by almost all tribes, was the *fibula*, a decorative pin usually used to fasten garments. The fibulae were made of bronze, silver, or gold and were profusely decorated, often with inlaid precious and semiprecious stones.

   (De la Croix, Horst, and Richard G. Ransey, Gardner's Art Through the Ages. 5th ed. New York: Harcourt, Brace & World, 1970. p. 281.)

   a. Define the following words: *abstract, organic, portable, adornment,* and *fibula.* What clues in the passage alerted you to the meanings of these words? How did your knowledge of word parts help?

   b. What does the prefix *semi* mean in the word *semiprecious?*

2. A *novel* can be defined as a prose narrative that is longer than a short story. Some novels are very long, some barely longer than a long short story. But all novels are more complex, more *ambitious* undertakings than stories. Often a novel introduces many more characters than a short story, and many novels give a much more detailed picture of the society in which the characters move. A novel also enables the writer to make a more powerful statement about the world or the universe than does a short story. While a short story generally reveals a writer's *artistry*—the mastery of form and detail—a novel reveals, in addition, the size of the writer's vision and ability to deal with complex situations.

   (Hodgins, Francis, and Kenneth Silverman. Adventures in American Literature. Heritage ed. New York: Harcourt Brace Jovanovich, 1980. p. 447.

   a. Define the following words: *novel, ambitious,* and *artistry.* What clues in the passage alerted you to the meanings of these words? How did your knowledge of word parts help?

   b. Why are novels contrasted with short stories? How does this contrast help to characterize novels?

3. Its very name tells us that a *microcomputer* is a small computer. . . . [S]everal types of computers are classified as microcomputers. Most people think of a microcomputer as being small enough to fit on a desktop. In addition, although some powerful models can serve several users *simultaneously*, most microcomputers are used by only one person at a time. For this reason, microcomputers are also often called *personal computers*.

(Colantonio, Ernest. Microcomputers & Applications. Lexington, MA: Heath, 1989. p. 12.)

a. Define the following words: *microcomputer, simultaneously,* and *personal computers.* What clues in the passage helped you to determine the meanings of these words? How did your knowledge of word parts help?

b. What does the prefix *micro* mean? How do you know? Name at least three other words that begin with this prefix.

4. Air, like food, is *essential* to life. Human activities affect the quality of the air in many ways. Exhaust from cars and smoke from factories contain gases. These gases are dangerous to breathe in large quantities. Furthermore, when such gases combine with water in the atmosphere, they form acids, which fall to the earth as *acid rain.* Acid rain can *pollute* lake water, poison fish, and damage trees.

(Gritzner, Charles. World Geography. Lexington, MA: Heath, 1989. p. 98.)

a. Define the following words: *essential, acid rain,* and *pollute.* What context clues helped you define the words?

b. What causes acid rain?

5. The *muckrakers* were people with the progressive spirit. They were reporters who wrote stories on public problems for popular magazines. Theodore Roosevelt, who did not like them, gave them their name. He meant to suggest that they were people who spent time digging in dirt when they could have been doing more *glorious* things. That was not really fair. Muckrakers generally did very careful research before writing their articles. They were, in fact, the nation's first *investigative* reporters.

(Maier, Pauline. The American People. Lexington, MA: Heath, 1986. p. 524

a. Define the following words: *muckrakers, glorious,* and *investigative.* What context clues or word parts helped you define the words?

b. What is the origin of the term *muckrakers?*

6. The concern girls have over achieving the figure of a fashion model has an *extreme* form in the problem of *anorexia nervosa.* Anorexia nervosa is an eating disorder which occurs largely among young adolescent girls, although it is also found among some young women, and, in some cases, among boys. It is characterized by self-induced starvation, *bizarre* attitudes toward food, and distorted body image. Although they are often *emaciated,* anorexic girls believe they are fat and become *preoccupied* with dieting. So distorted are their perceptions of their own bodies that they do not see themselves as emaciated, but, rather, as fat.

(*Zigler, Edward, and Matia Finn-Stevenson.* Children. *Lexington, MA: Heath, 1987. p. 594.*)

a. Define the following words: *extreme, anorexia nervosa, bizarre, emaciated,* and *preoccupied.* What context clues helped you define the words?

b. What prefixes are found in *disorder* and *preoccupied?* How do these prefixes help you define the words?

7. All of us at some time allow ourselves the luxury of daydreaming. A common *tendency* in these dreams is to picture ourselves as able to afford all the things we *associate* with wealth. A look through a mail-order catalogue or a visit to a large department store *whets* our appetite for a never-ending list of products. However, nothing can bring us back to reality sooner than reaching into our pockets and finding how little we have to work with. The problem we are faced with is that our *resources,* here identified as money, are limited. The only way we can resolve our problem is to make choices. After looking at our resources, we must examine our list of wants and identify the things we need immediately, those we can *postpone,* and those we cannot afford. As individuals, we face the central problem involved in economics—deciding just how to *allocate* our limited resources to provide ourselves with the greatest satisfaction of our wants.

(*Gordon, Sanford, and George Dawson.* Introductory Economics. *6th ed. Lexington, MA: Heath,. 1987. p. 9.*)

a. Define the following words: *tendency, associate, whets, resources, postpone,* and *allocate.* What context clues helped you define these words? How did your knowledge of word parts help?

b. How does the paragraph define *resources*? What other resources might economists consider important?

8. Historically the best-known *advocate* of relationships between body types and personality was William Sheldon. Sheldon classified physiques into three *somatypes* and suggested that each body type was associated with a set of personality characteristics. *Endomorphs* are large torsoed, short, and fat, and were said to be outgoing, *jovial*, *gregarious*, and sociable. *Mesomorphs* are muscular and were said to be *callous*, noisy, assertive, and vigorous. *Ectomorphs* are tall and lean, and were said to be restrained, inhibited, neurotic, and shy.

(Ingersoll, Gary. Adolescents in School and Society. *Lexington, MA: Heath, 1982. p. 36.*)

a. Define the following words: *advocate, somatypes, endomorphs, jovial, gregarious, mesomorphs, callous,* and *ectomorphs*. What context clues helped you to define the words? How did your knowledge of word parts help?

b. What is the root of *gregarious*? What other words are formed from this root? List at least three.

9. *Bribery* is offering something of value to a person to influence his or her judgment or conduct. Such actions are considered illegal, or at least *unethical*, in the United States, though they may be part of the normal way of doing business in some foreign companies. Yet the distinction between bribery and gift giving is often blurred. For instance, a salesperson has the chance to get a big order from a large firm. The firm's buyer hints that he needs a new motor for his boat. The cost of the boat motor is hidden in the selling company's accounts. Is it bribery or a gift?

In 1975, it was disclosed that, in order to sell the TriStar jet to Japanese airlines, Lockheed paid out about $12 million, most of it in bribes. A $1.7 million secret payment was made to Japan's prime minister. He was tried and convicted, but later reelected to Japan's *Diet*, or parliament. Boeing concealed $7.3 million in "commissions" to sell thirty-five airplanes to Spain, Honduras, Lebanon, and the Dominican Republic.

(Meggins, Leon, et al. Business. *Lexington, MA: Heath, 1985. p. 50.*)

a. Define the following words: *bribery, unethical,* and *Diet*. What context clues helped you define the words?

b. What prefixes are found in *illegal* and *unethical*? How does understanding these prefixes help you define the words?

10. If there is a specifically *turbulent* part of adolescence, it is probably associated with adolescents' needs to establish *psychological* independence from their parents. Their dependent relationship of childhood must be altered as they near the independent status needed in adulthood. During this shift parents and adolescents are often at odds with one another. Parents still see the need to exert control over their children, whom they regard as dependent and *immature*. Adolescents feel treated "like a child" and prefer to think of themselves as adults, worthy of adult trust and adult responsibilities. Some joke that adolescence is a period of storm and stress—for the parents.

(Ingersoll, Gary. Adolescents in School and Society. *Lexington, MA: Heath, 1982. p. 145.)*

a. Define the following words: *turbulent, psychological,* and *immature*. What context clues alerted you to the words' meanings?

b. What differences are implied in calling a person aged 13–19 an *adolescent*, a *juvenile*, a *teenager*, or a *young adult*? What do these differences in a word's suggested meaning tell you about language?

APPLICATION II

This chapter has provided ways for you to increase your vocabulary. Now, you must continue to expand it. Begin your own vocabulary study by creating a vocabulary notebook. For each word you record, list its meaning, its word parts (and their meanings), and its part of speech. In addition, write a sentence of your own to demonstrate the word's meaning in context. To practice your new words, use them in writing and in conversations with others. Also, create vocabulary cards for words you must know for academic courses. On one side of a 3" by 5" index card, write the word; on the back side, write the word's definition. Carry these cards with you and practice their meanings whenever you have a few extra minutes. Finally, select at least ten words from your notebook. Submit this list of words and sentences to your instructor.

PART TWO

Chapter 4

MAIN IDEAS

Objectives
1. To identify paragraph topics.
2. To identify main ideas in paragraphs.
3. To identify controlling ideas in topic sentences.
4. To understand the functions of stated topic sentences and their placements and to develop unstated topic sentences in paragraphs.

Key Concept

Paragraphs usually discuss only one subject, a *topic*. Writers will often signal their main idea about this subject in one sentence, a *main idea* or *topic sentence*. Within this topic sentence is a *controlling idea*. The controlling idea states the writer's opinion or limitation about the topic. This controlling idea predicts and controls the development of the paragraph.

A writer usually develops only one subject, a *topic*, in a paragraph. The writer's statement about that subject is a *main idea* or *topic sentence*. This topic sentence expresses an author's view on a topic, predicts the development of that topic, and controls the discussion within the paragraph. When you recognize a paragraph's topic sentence, you find the key to the paragraph. You will be able to anticipate the development of the topic. Conscious readers identify these elements.

TOPICS

Your first clue to a writer's purpose, the reason for writing, is the paragraph topic. Think of a topic as the title of the paragraph. This title will give you a basic idea of the paragraph's content. Titles of newspaper articles prove this point. Each newspaper piece uses a headline to tell readers its topic. After reading the headline, readers can decide whether or not to read the article.

When you read the newspaper, you look for articles that interest you. You locate these articles by looking at the headlines. Examine the following headlines. Each one tells you the topic of the article.

Headline	Topic
New York Giants Victorious in Super Bowl	The winners of the Super Bowl
Budget Cuts Cause Factory Layoffs	Impact of budget cuts on industry
New Federal Taxes pass Congress	Enactment of new taxes by Congress

Each newspaper headline presents the topic of the article.

EXERCISE 1

Read each of the newspaper headlines below. Write the topic for each headlined article in the space provided.

1. Prices Rise, Stock Market Falls 100 Points

    Topic: _____

2. Space Shuttle Atlantis on New Mission

    Topic: _____

3. New Medicine Halts Flu Virus

    Topic: _____

4. Tornados Rip Through Midwest

    Topic: _____

5. International Conference Calls for Limits on Pollution

    Topic: _____

General and Specific Topics

Depending on their context, topics can be general (broad) or specific (narrow). A general topic covers a number of elements. For example, the topic *whales* can be general if the writer then lists different types of whales and their characteristics. A specific topic, on the other hand, identifies one element in a group. The topic *whales* can be specific if the writer is describing marine animals. Whales would be only one of the many types of ocean animals.

The chart on the following page, with the most general topic at the top, represents this concept of *general* and *specific*.

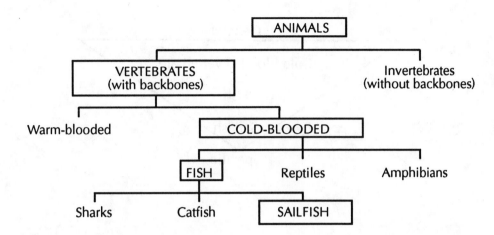

As you follow the boxed terms, *animals* is the most general and *sailfish* is the most specific. The items in the middle of the chart can be either general or specific, depending on their context. For example, the term *cold-blooded vertebrates* is relatively specific when you compare it to the broad term *animals*:

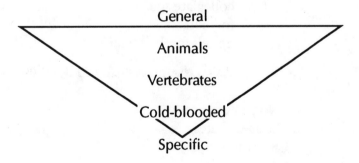

However, the same term is general when it is compared to the term *sailfish*, a particular type of cold-blooded vertebrate:

General

Cold-blooded vertebrate

Fish

Sailfish

Specific

To identify a topic accurately you must recognize ideas as either general or specific.

EXERCISE 2

Read the following lists of topics carefully. Decide whether the list is becoming more specific or more general. Complete the list by writing either a more specific detail or a more general term in the blank at the bottom.

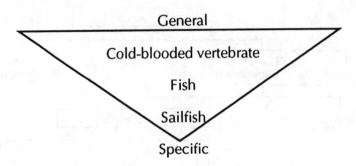

Example: sports (general term)
collegiate sports
football
State's football team

~~State's star running back~~ (specific term)

1. North America
   United States
   Southwest
   Arizona

   _____

2. *I Love Lucy*
   Comedy Shows
   Television Shows

   _____

3. Real Estate
   Developments
   Commercial Developments
   Shopping Malls

   _____

4. Corvettes
   Sports Cars
   Automobiles

   _____

5. The *Mona Lisa*
   Leonardo da Vinci
   Italian Painters
   Renaissance Painters

   _____

Paragraph Topics

Paragraphs, unlike newspaper articles, usually do not have titles that tell readers the topic. To identify a paragraph topic, you need to examine the specific details (examples or descriptions) in the paragraph. These details provide an overall impression of the paragraph and its topic. In the paragraph below, underline the specific details. Then identify the topic.

> Rainfall varies widely from region to region in Africa. Some areas near the equator receive heavy, tropical rains, but parts of the Sahara are among the driest in the world. In most of Africa, rainfall is seasonal. Much rain falls during the wet season, but during the dry season, months may pass without a drop of rain.
>
> (Gritzner, Charles. World Geography. *Lexington, MA: Heath, 1989. p. 425.*)

The following details give you a clue about the topic:

1. In some areas, there are tropical rains.

2. The Sahara has some of the driest parts of the world.

3. Rainfall occurs during certain seasons.

These details will help you determine the paragraph's topic.

Below are some possible topics for the paragraph. Think of each topic as a title. Which one is the best?

1. The topic *seasonal rainfall in Africa* is too specific. Although seasonal rainfall is mentioned in the paragraph, it is only one example of the levels of rainfall in Africa. As a topic, it gives incomplete information about the paragraph.

2. The topic *weather in Africa* is too general. The paragraph does not cover all aspects of African weather.

3. The topic *various rainfalls in Africa* is appropriate. The paragraph discusses the types of rainfall throughout the entire continent.

    Choose a topic for a paragraph that covers *all* of the details listed.

EXERCISE 3   Underline the specific details in the following paragraphs. From these details, identify a paragraph topic that names the main idea in the paragraph.

1.   Bats, like other creatures, must fit their lifestyles to the changing seasons. When cold weather comes, the insects vanish from the air. Some bats resolve this food problem by migrating southward. Others stay in their caves and go into hibernation. Body temperatures fall to near the temperature of the cave. The rate of heartbeat and metabolism slows. They must hang to their places in the cave, waiting for the return of spring. Then some biological "clock" awakens them again when the insects are hatching and there is food to be picked from the air.

    (Laycock, George. "Life in Caves," in Through the Starshine. *Ed. Donna Alvermann et al. Lexington, MA: Heath, 1989, p. 468.)*

Topic: _____

2.   Of all the Andean countries, Peru has had the most economic success. Today Peru exports cotton and sugarcane grown on the coast and coffee grown in the highlands. Minerals—including copper, iron, lead, zinc, and silver—make up more than half of Peru's exports. Among the newest sources of income are oil and timber production in the Amazon lowlands

east of the Andes. In addition, Peru has plants that process agricultural products and refine metals and oil. It is also trying to draw tourists to its lofty mountains, sandy deserts, tropical forest, and ancient Inca ruins.

(Gritzner, Charles. World Geography. Lexington, MA: Heath, 1989, p. 275.)

Topic: _____

3.   All mollusks have certain characteristics in common. The soft body of a mollusk is covered by a fold of tissue called the mantle. The mantle of most mollusks makes a hard shell. The shell protects the mollusk's soft body. All mollusks also have a head and a muscular foot that is used for movement. Although many mollusks are sea animals, some mollusks live in freshwater and others live on land.

(Bierer, Loretta, et al. Life Science. Lexington, MA: Heath, 1987. p. 204.)

Topic: _____

4.   Most beach sand is made of many different minerals. The greatest amount is quartz, however, because quartz is very hard and weathers slowly. Beaches in tropical areas are sometimes made up of grains of shells or coral. Waves grind the shells and coral into grains and then deposit the grains on the shore. These beaches are usually white and softer than the hard, quartz-sand beaches. Along the east coast of Florida, you can see the beaches change from quartz sand to shell sand as you drive south. Some beaches in Hawaii are black. Black beaches are formed from grains of volcanic rock. You even have a choice in Hawaii, as some islands have a white beach on one side and a black beach on the other.

(Tillery, Bill. Earth Science. Lexington, MA: Heath, 1987. p. 215.)

Topic: _____

5.   You are living in an age when science fiction seems to come true. Since 1958 more than 50 space vehicles have flown near to or landed on the moon. Twelve American astronauts in the Apollo program landed on the moon. What discoveries did they make? They found the moon's outer layer had been completely shattered by space objects striking its surface. Many of the elements found on the moon are the same as those found on Earth but in different proportions. Rock samples from the moon have been dated to be 3.9 billion years old. The astronauts also found that the moon's basins, lunar seas, are covered with volcanic rocks and that there are moonquakes.

(Tillery, Bill. Earth Science. Lexington, MA: Heath, 1987. p. 61.)

Topic: _____

TOPIC SENTENCES

Many paragraphs have one sentence that states the author's main idea about the topic. This main idea, also called a *topic sentence*, acts as a transition between a paragraph's topic and its details. A topic sentence is more specific than a topic because the topic sentence records a writer's main idea about the topic. At the same time, a topic sentence is more general than the details (the examples or descriptions) in the paragraph.

General   Topic
              TOPIC SENTENCE
Specific   Details

A topic sentence has two functions:

1. It unifies the paragraph by stating one main idea; and

2. It organizes the details presented in the paragraph.

Read the following paragraph carefully. Identify the topic and the details given.

The only tropical ecosystem in the continental United States, the [Florida] Keys shelter an astounding number of animal and plant species. Sea turtles, crocodiles, manatees and roseate spoonbills thrive in their nourishing waters. The Key deer, an endangered subspecies now reduced to a few hundred survivors, is found nowhere else. Miles and miles of coral reef support more than 300 kinds of fish. Key Largo alone has more native species of trees and shrubs than any state in the continental United States.

(Sawhill, John. "Last Great Places." Nature Conservancy. (May/June 1991): 6.)

Topic: _____

Details: _____

_____

_____

_____

_____

The topic of this paragraph is *animals and plants in the Florida Keys.* In the paragraph, the author provides examples of the animals and plants found there: the sea turtles, crocodiles, manatees, and spoonbills, the Key deer, the coral reef, and Key Largo's plant life.

The sentence that links the topic and the details in the paragraph is the first one: "The only tropical ecosystem in the continental United States, the [Florida] Keys shelter an astounding number of animal and plant species." This sentence acts as a bridge between the topic and the paragraph's details.

EXERCISE 4   Read each of the following three comic strips carefully to determine a topic and the details. Next, create a title for the strip; your title should name the topic. Finally, construct a topic sentence that gives the main idea of the comic.

(*Schulz, Charles. "Peanuts." Baltimore* Sunday Sun, *28 October 1990.*)

Title: _____

Topic Sentence: _____

_____

The Stanley Family

Barbara & Jim Dale

(Dale, Barbara and Jim. "The Stanley Family." Baltimore *Sunday Sun*, 28 October 1990.)

Title: _____

Topic Sentence: _____

_____

(Howard, Greg. "Sally Forth." Baltimore *Sunday Sun*, 28 October 1990.)

Title: _____

Topic Sentence: _____

_____

EXERCISE 5	Each of the following set of sentences forms a paragraph. However, the sentences have been scrambled and are not in their correct order. Read each set carefully to determine a topic. Next, select the one sentence that unifies and organizes the other sentences; this sentence will be the topic sentence. Circle its letter.

1. a. Liquid water moves across the land in streams and rivers.

    b. It also moves through the atmosphere as invisible vapor.

    c. Water is always on the move.

    d. There is more water vapor moving through the atmosphere than there is water in all the rivers on land.

    e. Water moves through the atmosphere as tiny droplets called clouds.

    f. The study of water on and within the earth, and in the atmosphere, is called hydrology.

    (Tillery, Bill. Earth Science. Lexington, MA: Heath, 1987. p. 126)

2. a. It is common for teenagers to have three or more jobs before they graduate from high school.

    b. It is unlikely that their wages will be much less than five dollars an hour.

    c. Today's society furnishes its youngsters with innumerable job opportunities.

    d. If they become inconvenienced by or uninterested with their work, they can easily find employment elsewhere.

    e. At the age of sixteen, males and females alike can be anything from a lifeguard to a data processor.

3. a. People are helping to conserve water by using water saving devices on faucets and in showers.

    b. Sewage treatment plants reduce the amount of harmful chemicals and bacteria in waste water.

    c. Laws have been passed to limit the dumping of sewage and chemical wastes into waterways.

    d. Clean water is a basic need of all living things.

e. Many industries that cause thermal pollution are now cooling the water before returning it to rivers and streams.

(Bierer, Loretta, et al., Life Science. Lexington, MA: Heath, 1987. p. 343.)

4. a. If you develop a critical eye, you'll always be able to see new things to try in writing.

b. Learning to write is not an easy process, but it can be a very satisfying one.

c. In short, be patient, and give it time.

d. Don't expect to master the craft immediately.

e. When you are working on accomplishing something, you may lose sight of other parts of your writing.

f. Learning to write takes time and practice; and many, many professional writers say that they feel like learners at the trade of writing all of their lives.

(Tchudi, Susan and Stephen. "Why Do People Write?" in Through the Starshine. Lexington, MA: Heath, 1989. p. 88.)

5. a. There is nothing of the woeful history of Acadie in these cheerful melodies.

b. Originally for at-home listening, it soon became an accompaniment for dancing.

c. The vocals, usually in French, are nasal and shrill enough to be heard over the dancing feet; to an outsider they are an acquired taste.

d. Music is the single most distinctive element in today's Cajun cultural revival.

e. But the music itself—fiddle, triangle, accordion, guitar, and the more modern drums—is irresistibly infectious.

(Smith, Griffin. Jr. "The Cajuns: Still Loving Life." National Geographic. Vol. 178, no. 4 (October, 1990): 55.)

CONTROLLING IDEAS

Within the topic sentence is a *controlling idea*, the writer's opinion or limitation about the topic. This controlling idea predicts the discussion, or development, of the topic in the paragraph. From the topic sentence, you can guess the type of details, the development of ideas, needed to prove the controlling idea.

Look at the following topic sentence. The questions following it will help you locate the controlling idea.

Americans over the age of 17 should be required to vote in national elections.

What is the entire sentence about? _____

What is the author's comment, or opinion, about this subject?

_____

If you said that the topic of the sentence is *Americans over the age of 17*, you are right. The author's comment about this topic is that these Americans "should be required to vote in national elections." This comment is the controlling idea. You can now predict that the rest of the paragraph will provide the writer's reasons for favoring compulsory voting.

In addition to presenting an opinion about a topic, a controlling idea can also limit a topic. Answer the questions that accompany the following topic sentence.

Country music offers its listeners vivid performances, memorable lyrics, and stunning instrumental numbers.

What is the entire sentence about? _____

To what major issues does the author limit the discussion?

_____

In this sentence about the topic *country music*, the author addresses only three issues: "vivid performances, memorable lyrics, and stunning instrumental numbers." The rest of the paragraph should provide examples of these controlling ideas.

Sometimes, the controlling idea can limit the topic by simply stating a list. Look at the following topic sentence.

To complete your federal tax return, you must follow five steps.

What is the topic sentence about? _____

What limits does the author place on the subject?

_____

With this topic sentence, you can predict that the discussion will cover the five steps needed to complete a tax return.

EXERCISE 6

You have already learned to identify a topic sentence by determining the topic and details of a paragraph. Now, use this skill to provide topic sentences (below) for each of the advertisements on the following pages. First, create a title—topic—for the advertisement. Next, examine the details given in the advertisement carefully. Finally, write a topic sentence (below) that presents either an opinion or a limitation about the product or service.

U.S. Army advertisement

Title: _____

Topic Sentence: _____

_____

CUNA Mutual Insurance Group advertisement

Title: _____

Topic Sentence: _____

_____

Lane advertisement

Title: _____

Topic Sentence: _____

_____

U.S. Army advertisement in Newsweek 8 October 1990.

CUNA *Mutual Insurance Group advertisement printed in* Southern Living, *Vol. 25, no. 10 (October, 1990).*

When's the last time you were this comfortable?

<u>Introducing a chaise rocker recliner designed with head-to-toe support.</u>

If it sounds too good to be true, have a seat. We've filled the space between the seat and the ottoman with cushioned support, making for a noticeably more comfortable recliner experience.

And like all our recliners our new chaise comes in a variety of colors and styles, and is backed by a limited lifetime warranty.

For a free brochure highlighting the advantages of our new recliner, and a list of dealers near you, write Action Industries, Inc., Dept. E100, Box 1627, Tupelo, MS 38802. Or call 1-800-447-4700.

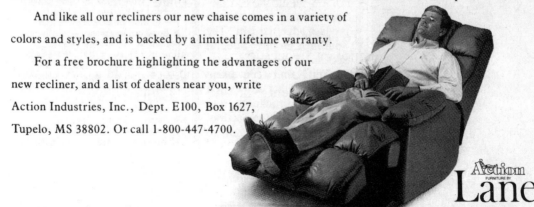

Action
FURNITURE BY
Lane®
make yourself comfortable

Lane advertisement printed in Southern Living, *Vol. 25, no. 10. (October, 1990).*

EXERCISE 7

In each of the topic sentences below, circle the controlling idea. If the controlling idea presents an opinion, write 0 on the line to the left. If the controlling idea states a limitation, write L on the line to the left.

_0_ 1. Owning a pet can be time-consuming, expensive, and rewarding.

_L_ 2. All college students should be required to learn a foreign language.

_L_ 3. Congress failed to approve the new budget bill for several reasons.

_L_ 4. The movie _Mountains of the Moon_ portrays Sir Richard Burton, the Victorian adventurer, as a complex, brilliant, and stubborn explorer.

_L_ 5. Building a fire requires four easy steps.

_0_ 6. Drug-enforcement laws must be made more strict.

_L_ 7. Psychologists have three general classifications of personalities: introverts, ambiverts, and extroverts.

_0_ 8. All homeowners should be required to recycle plastics, paper, and aluminum or tin.

_0_ 9. Additional federal funds must be made available for space and oceanic exploration.

_L_ 10. A weekly exercise program provides several benefits.

To predict the discussion of a paragraph easily, turn the topic sentence into a question. The answer to this question is the support the writer will offer to explain the topic sentence. Analyze the following topic sentence, and turn it into a question.

> Within the past decade, medical advances have provided four major benefits.

If you asked, "What are the four major benefits of medical advances?" then you have predicted the development of the paragraph. You can assume that the author will list each medical advance and explain it in the body of the paragraph.

EXERCISE 8   For each topic sentence, create a question from the controlling idea. Next, using your question as a guide, explain how the author might develop the paragraph.

1. Journalists face multiple ethical problems with each story they write.

    Question: _____

    Development: _____

2. Foreign travel provides many benefits for Americans.

    Question: _____

    Development: _____

3. Local festivals give towns a means of raising money, entertaining others, and advertising the town's qualities.

    Question: _____

    Development: _____

4. Hospitals should be required to care for poor patients.

    Question: _____

    Development: _____

5. America's foreign policy has changed drastically in the past decade.

    Question: _____

    Development: _____

6. College students should be required to take courses in community service.

    Question: _____

    Development: _____

7. The play *Tru* offers insights into author Truman Capote's life.

    Question: _____

    Development: _____

8. Popular culture, in the form of movies, television programs, advertising, and music, gives us a glimpse into Americans' values.

    Question: _____

    Development: _____

9. The exhibition of French Impressionists' paintings is exciting and informative.

    Question: _____

    Development: _____

10. Wilderness areas must be protected from developers.

    Question: _____

    Development: _____

FUNCTIONS OF TOPIC SENTENCES

You already know that a topic sentence serves as a bridge between a paragraph's topic and its details. Therefore, to locate a topic sentence, ask questions about the topic and details in a paragraph. The following three questions will help you locate stated topic sentences:

1. What is the entire paragraph about? (The answer will be the *topic*.)

2. What information about this topic does the author provide? (The answer will be the *significant details*.)

3. What do the details tell you about the topic? What conclusion can you draw after reading the paragraph? (The answer will be the *controlling idea* in a topic sentence.)

To test these questions, read the paragraph below carefully and answer the questions.

> The Ganges River . . . forms a broad and fertile plain. This plain extends southeastward from the northern mountains. It has both good soil and ample rainfall. The most densely populated part of India is found in the Ganges lowland. The area is also one of South Asia's most productive farming regions, supplying much of India's wheat and rice. The southeastern part of the Ganges Plain is a large floodplain. There, the

Ganges and Brahmaputra rivers meet. The delta area, criss-crossed by ribbons of river water, is one of the world's most fertile areas. It also is one of the wettest. North of the delta, the town of Cherrapunji, in India, receives about 450 inches (1,143 centimeters) of rain each year. And in one 12-month period, 1,042 inches (2,646 centimeters) of rain fell. This is almost 87 feet!

(Gritzner, Charles. World Geography. *Lexington, MA: Heath, 1989. p. 379.*)

1. What is the entire paragraph about?

   Answer: *The Ganges River* (Topic)

2. What information about this topic does the author provide?

   Answer: a. Plain extends southeast from mountains.
   b. Plain has good soil and plenty of rain.
   c. The Ganges lowland is very productive farming region.
   d. The southeastern part is a floodplain.
   e. This delta area is very fertile and wet. (Significant details)

3. What do the details tell you about the topic? What conclusion can you draw after reading the paragraph?

   Answer: *The Ganges River creates a large and productive area.* (Controlling idea)

   Your answer to this question provides a paraphrase of the stated topic sentence. In other words, your sentence contains the main idea of the paragraph, but it uses your own words, not the author's, to state it. To locate the stated topic sentence, you must now ask one more question.

4. Is there a sentence in the paragraph that contains the same main idea as yours? (The answer will be the *stated topic sentence*.)

   Answer: *"The Ganges River . . . forms a broad and fertile plain."* This sentence, the first one in the paragraph, gives you a similar main idea. Although this sentence may not resemble yours in word choice, it presents the same information. Thus, this sentence is the paragraph's stated topic sentence.

EXERCISE 9   For each paragraph, use the procedure you just learned to locate the stated topic sentence.

1.   Natural resources fall into two types, renewable and nonrenewable. *Renewable resources* add a new supply each growing season or will become available again sometime soon in the future. Wood, food, and wool are examples of such resources. A *nonrenewable resource* is one that is not available again from the earth once it is taken and used. Examples of nonrenewable resources are metallic substances such as copper, iron, and aluminum. Nonmetallic substances such as oil, coal, clays, and chemical fertilizers are also nonrenewable resources. . . .

(Tillery, Bill, Earth Science. Lexington, MA: Heath, 1987. p. 434.)

a. What is the entire paragraph about? (Topic)

_____

b. What information about this topic does the author provide? (Significant details)

_____

_____

c. What do the details tell you about the topic? (Controlling idea)

_____

_____

d. Is there a sentence in the paragraph that contains the same topic and controlling idea as yours? (Stated topic sentence)

_____

_____

2.   Almost half of the Revolutionary generation was female. Fine ladies, servant girls, black slave women, middle-class matrons, and American Indian women all contributed to the development of American life. They may be invisible in history books but they were present everywhere that men were. They were on farms and plantations, in the cities and in the forests. They ran businesses, served with the armies, and participated in political decision-making. The sex stereotypes and legal restrictions that so severely hampered women's ac-

tivities in the nineteenth century were relatively weak in the eighteenth. Consequently, women participated in the social, economic, political, and military activities of the day in ways that would be thought highly improper if not impossible for women a generation later.

(De Pauw, Linda Grant, "Founding Mothers," in Roads Go Ever On. *Ed. Donna Alvermann et al. Lexington, MA: Heath, 1989. p. 479.)*

a. What is the topic?

_____

b. What significant details does the author provide?

_____

_____

c. What is the controlling idea?

_____

_____

d. What is the stated topic sentence?

_____

_____

3.   People have studied the planets and outer space for thousands of years. However, actual space exploration began only about 30 years ago. Many fascinating discoveries have been made in this short time. Dramatic pictures of the surface of Mercury, Venus, Mars, Jupiter, and Saturn have been received from space probes. Space probes have landed on Venus and Mars, sending pictures and information back to Earth. Astronauts have visited the moon. There they conducted experiments and collected soil and rock samples from the moon's surface. Space-shuttle crews have placed satellites in orbit and conducted experiments to provide data about living and working conditions in space. Scientists are using this information to plan future space exploration.

(Tillery, Bill. Earth Science. Lexington, MA: Heath, 1989. p. 81.)

a. What is the topic?

_____

b. What significant details does the author provide?

_____

_____

c. What is the controlling idea?

_____

_____

d. What is the stated topic sentence?

_____

_____

4.   People who live and work together share many habits, ideas, skills, traditions, and values. All these habitual ways of thinking and acting make up the society's culture. Culture is the way of life that a group of people develops and passes on to its children. Every group of human beings—from the most ancient to the most modern, from the smallest to the largest—has a culture. A group's language, tools and skills, beliefs and traditions, ways of organizing itself, and much more are all part of its culture. Culture has been described as a "blueprint for living." From birth to death, most of human life is spent learning, following, and passing on this blueprint.

(*Jantzen, Steven, et al.* World History. *Lexington, MA: Heath, 1988. p. 15.*)

a. What is the topic?

_____

_____

b. What significant details does the author provide?

_____

_____

c. What is the controlling idea?

_____

_____

d. What is the stated topic sentence?

_____

_____

5.   A traditional Japanese gardener designs his site to be in harmony with its surroundings. If nearby hills, distant mountains, or notable buildings can be seen from the property, he is likely to include them in a vista, using a venerable technique the Japanese call *shakkei*, or borrowed scenery. If water is plentiful, he might create a cascade, stream or pond. As he arranges rocks, digs waterways, raises hills, or places trees, he will remember the gardens of his predecessors, which will help him shape the site at hand.

(Coats, Bruce. "In a Japanese Garden." National Geographic 176 (November, 1989): 644.)

a. What is the topic?

_____

_____

b. What significant details does the author provide?

_____

_____

c. What is the controlling idea?

_____

_____

d. What is the stated topic sentence?

_____

_____

You might have noticed that stated topic sentences are frequently first in a paragraph. However, a topic sentence can be placed at any point within a paragraph. A topic sentence's placement is determined by its purpose within the paragraph. Thus, you must learn to identify other placements of topic sentences and their purposes in paragraphs.

Placement: First Sentence

As the first sentence in a paragraph, the topic sentence *introduces* the details that explain the controlling idea. This type of paragraph can be represented by an inverted triangle:

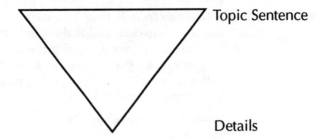

Topic Sentence

Details

In this paragraph, the topic sentence opens with a general statement about the topic. Because of their specific information, the details form the bottom of the triangle. With this topic sentence placement, an author makes sure that readers will immediately know the purpose of the paragraph.

To practice this strategy, locate the topic sentence in the following paragraph. Write the topic sentence on the line provided and circle its controlling idea. Finally, in the space provided, diagram the paragraph.

> The Industrial Revolution was made possible because of four great inventions. In 1765, James Hargreaves built a mechanical spinning wheel for making cotton thread, called the spinning jenny. In 1768, Richard Arkwright invented a spinning machine called the water frame. It made a much stronger thread. Then, between 1774 and 1779, Samuel Crompton invented the spinning mule. It combined features of both the spinning jenny and the water frame. Both Arkwright's and Crompton's machines required more power than horses or water could produce. In 1785, James Watt invented a steam engine that was powerful enough to drive the new machines.
>
> (*Maier, Pauline*. The American People. *Lexington, MA: Heath, 1986, p. 285.*)

Topic Sentence: _____

_____

Diagram:

Placement: Last Sentence

As the last sentence in a paragraph, the topic sentence *summarizes* the paragraph's details. In other words, this placement reverses the traditional order of topic sentence first followed by details. Because this placement begins with specific details and ends with a general topic sentence, it is diagramed as an upright triangle:

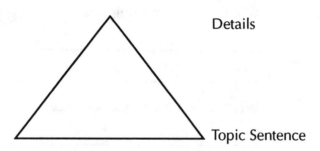

Writers choose this placement for one of two reasons. First, an author may wish to create suspense or mystery. Consider, for instance, the structure of a joke. If a comedian were to tell the punch line before telling the joke, then nobody would laugh. Consider, also, a movie that identifies a criminal before the audience learns of the crime. In each case, learning the punch line or solving the mystery becomes less important and the rest of the paragraph fails to interest the audience. Second, when addressing a controversial topic, a writer may first provide evidence to convince the reader of a specific opinion. Then, the writer will state the topic sentence. For example, to demonstrate the need for space exploration, a scientist might first discuss the benefits of knowledge gained from past exploration. By presenting convincing information, the writer leads the reader to the conclusion stated in the topic sentence.

To practice this strategy, use the general procedure for locating a topic sentence. Read the following paragraph and answer the questions.

> The living things in the meadow depend on one another. The animals eat green plants or other animals that eat green plants. When the animals die, their remains decay, enrich the soil, and help plants grow. The plants and animals of the meadow interact with each other. They also interact with many nonliving things in their environment, such as light, water, and temperature. The study of how living things interact with each other and with their nonliving environment is called ecology.

(*Bierer, Loretta, et al.* Life Science. *Lexington, MA: Heath, 1987. p. 152.*)

1. What is the topic?

   _____

2. What significant details does the author provide?

   _____

   _____

3. What is the controlling idea?

   _____

   _____

4. What is the stated topic sentence?

   _____

   _____

5. Diagram the paragraph here.

Placement: First and Last Sentences

In this type of paragraph, the topic sentence appears twice: at the beginning and the end of the paragraph. This placement combines the functions of the two preceding placements. An author *introduces* an opinion or limitation in the first sentence, develops supporting details about the main idea, and then *summarizes* the main idea in the final sentence. This repetition of the topic sentence—although not always in exactly the same words—ensures that readers will follow the discussion. This type of paragraph is diagramed in an unusual way:

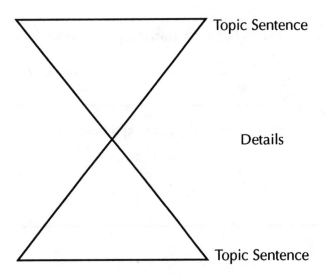

To practice this strategy, locate the topic sentence in the following paragraph, and then diagram the paragraph.

The development of language is essential to the formation of culture, because without language there could be no mature culture. Language does more than just facilitate communication. It allows us to think about the past and future as well as the present. Once our ancestors began to construct symbols, they could communicate about an object without its being present. In this manner, one person's past experiences could be communicated to another. Through symbol systems people could store such communicated experiences in their memories; this stored knowledge is the essence of culture. Language, then, facilitates the accumulation and storage of a social heritage, and the transmission of that social heritage from one generation to another.

(*Mendoza, Manuel G. and Vince Napoli. Systems of Society. 5th ed. Lexington, MA: Heath, 1990. p. 41.*)

1. What is the topic?

   _____

2. What significant details does the author present?

   _____

   _____

3. What is the controlling idea?

   _____

   _____

4. What is the stated topic sentence (or sentences)?

_____

_____

5. Diagram the paragraph here.

Placement: Middle of the Paragraph

Finally, a topic sentence may be located in the middle of a paragraph. In the middle, the topic sentence serves as a *transition* between the details given at the beginning and at the end of the paragraph. When a topic sentence has two parts, two controlling ideas, a writer will place it in the middle. To diagram this type of paragraph, draw a diamond:

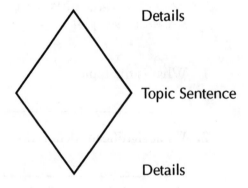

Details

Topic Sentence

Details

To practice this placement strategy, read the paragraph on the following page carefully, and answer the questions following it.

The development of electronic instruments and music has brought together many skills that were once isolated. In the past usually a composer wrote music, a performer played it, and an engineer recorded it. But these distinctions are starting to disappear. To begin with, the task of performing on today's electronic keyboards is not a simple one. Previously, the keyboard player used one instrument, usually a piano. Today's keyboard player, however, might be called on to use an electric piano, a combo organ, and a string synthesizer, all during the same performance.

(Kettlekamp, Larry. "Performing and Recording Electronic Music," in Through the Starshine. *Ed. Donna Alvermann et al. Lexington, MA: Heath, 1989. p. 139.)*

1. What is the topic?

   _____

2. What significant details does the author provide?

   _____

   _____

3. What is the controlling idea?

   _____

   _____

4. What is the stated topic sentence?

   _____

   _____

5. Diagram the paragraph here.

Unstated Main Ideas

Paragraphs are easier to understand if they contain a stated topic sentence. However, some paragraphs do not have stated main ideas. A writer might choose to omit a topic sentence for a number of reasons. For example, the writer might wish to surprise readers. Or the writer may want to force readers to draw their own logical conclusions. When a topic sentence is not stated, for whatever reason, you must develop one by inferring it from the information given in the paragraph. Analyze the following paragraph:

> When words can be changed so easily [on a computer], writers are freer to experiment with ideas. For some, this may lead to a brainstorming or free-writing approach to composing text. The flow of ideas is simply entered into the computer as it occurs. After the ideas are on paper, they can be reorganized, expanded, or deleted. Many people feel that this freedom expands their creativity, and this is the main advantage of word processing for them. Others simply find that the main benefit is the removal of the drudgery of revising and correcting their work.
>
> (*Kershner, Helena* G. Introduction to Computer Literacy. *Lexington, MA: Heath, 1990. p. 250.*)

In this paragraph, no one sentence gives you the topic and the controlling idea. Therefore, you must develop them yourself using the procedure for locating topic sentences.

1. What is the paragraph about? (Topic)

   Answer: *advantages of word processing on a computer*

2. What information about the topic are you given? (Significant details)

   Answer: *Some writers feel free to experiment with ideas; others enjoy the increased creativity; for some, revising and editing are easier.*

3. What do the details suggest about the topic? What conclusion can you draw? (Controlling idea)

   Answer: *there are three major advantages to writing on a computer*

4. Make your conclusion a complete sentence. (Unstated main idea)

   Answer: *Writers identify three major advantages of using a computer for composing.*

To practice this strategy, read the following paragraph carefully, and develop a topic sentence.

More than any other form of life, humans are able to shape the environments they inhabit. They can also harm the environment. Such harm may be caused either knowingly or unknowingly. A person who takes wood from a forest for fuel may not know that this action, if done by thousands of people, will change the whole environment. People who dispose of rubbish in a river may see little immediate damage. But, if many other people also use the river as a dumping place, the river will one day become too polluted to support fish life. Even a small change, multiplied thousands of times, can damage an entire ecosystem.

(Gritzner, Charles. World Geography. Lexington, MA: Heath, 1989. p. 96.)

1. What is the topic?

   _____

2. What significant details does the author provide?

   _____

   _____

3. What is the controlling idea? What conclusion can you draw?

   _____

4. Make your conclusion a complete sentence.

   _____

   _____

By developing a topic sentence, you will unify the paragraph and organize the details presented. This procedure will help you remember the information in the paragraph. Because this type of paragraph has no stated topic sentence, there is no diagram to represent it.

Summary of Placement Strategies

The table on the following page summarizes the placement strategies for stated topic sentences and the purpose of each placement.

Placement	Purpose
Beginning	Introduces supporting details
End	Summarizes supporting details
Beginning and end	Introduces and summarizes supporting details
Middle	Provides transition from details that support one controlling idea to details that support another controlling idea

EXERCISE 10

For each of the following paragraphs, use the technique you have learned in this chapter to locate the topic sentence or to discover an unstated one. Diagram each paragraph.

1.   Lincoln Ellsworth was a made-to-order American hero. Like his contemporary Charles A. Lindbergh, he was brave and independent, tough and resourceful, and modest to a fault. Like his other contemporary, and sometime rival, Richard E. Byrd, he was an aerial explorer who performed spectacular feats in the Arctic and Antarctic. In 1926 he took part in the first flight across the North Pole and the Arctic ice cap, from Norway to Alaska; in 1935 he made the first coast-to-coast flight across Antarctica. He claimed more than 400,000 squares miles of Antarctica, much of it now known as Ellsworth Land, for the United States. Twice he vanished for weeks into the polar outback while millions tracked the ensuing search in headlines, and twice he emerged blinking and smiling shyly in the spotlight. Ellsworth always got through.

(Jackson, Donald Dade. "The Quiet Heroism of Lincoln Ellsworth." Smithsonian 21 (October 1990): 171.)

a. What is the topic?

_____

b. What significant details does the author provide?

_____

_____

c. What is the controlling idea?

_____

_____

d. What is the topic sentence?

_____

_____

e. Diagram the paragraph here.

2.   Just about everyone writes. However, some people become *writers*, those who enjoy writing for its own sake, who write for fun or profit. Many people become writers by chance. They never intended to become writers or thought of themselves as writers, but suddenly they became involved in a job in which they needed to write. Many of these people felt they had no particular skills or abilities in writing until they were in a situation in which they had to write. They learned to write by writing, by getting responses from people around them, and through reading. Somewhere in the process, they became writers.

(Tchudi, Susan and Stephen. "Why Do People Write?" in Through the Starshine. *Ed. Donna Alvermann et al. Lexington, MA: Heath, 1989. p. 85.)*

a. What is the topic?

_____

b. What significant details do the authors provide?

_____

_____

c. What is the controlling idea?

_____

_____

   d. What is the topic sentence?

   _____

   _____

   e. Diagram the paragraph here.

3.   Rabies is caused by a virus. Usually an animal becomes
   infected when it is bitten by a rabid animal, one that is in the
   last stages of this usually fatal disease. Once the rabies virus
   enters the body, it multiplies and spreads, reaching the brain
   and other parts of the nervous system. The process may take
   days, weeks, or even months. In the final stages of infection,
   an animal may seem sleepy and shy, or it may be restless and
   aggressive. In either case, the victim has the rabies virus in its
   saliva, and the victim usually becomes paralyzed, stops breathing, and dies.

   (Pringle, Laurence. "Vampire Bats," in Through the Starshine. *Ed. Donna
   Alvermann et al. Lexington, MA: Heath, 1989. p. 250.)*

   a. What is the topic?

   _____

   b. What significant details does the author provide?

   _____

   _____

   c. What is the controlling idea?

   _____

   _____

   d. What is the topic sentence?

   _____

   _____

e. Diagram the paragraph here.

4.   As the [Civil W]ar called up more and more men in both the Union and Confederacy, women found themselves facing new responsibilities. In the South, planters' wives and daughters learned how to manage their plantations. Women on smaller farms plowed the ground and grew their food. In the North, farmers' wives sometimes had new farm machinery that allowed them to do as much work as many men using hand tools. In both the Union and Confederacy, women also took paying jobs as government workers or in industry. On both sides, a few women served as spies. Many more were nurses. At first, however, women were not welcome in military hospitals. Clara Barton, who later founded the American Red Cross, and Dorothea Dix worked to change that situation. The large number of wounded soldiers also made women's help necessary. The North set up a training program for nurses under Dr. Elizabeth Blackwell, the first American woman to graduate from medical school. The Confederacy officially welcomed women as nurses in September 1862.

(Maier, Pauline. The American People: A History. *Lexington, MA: Heath, 1986. pp. 409–410.)*

a. What is the topic?

_____

b. What significant details does the author provide?

_____

_____

c. What is the controlling idea?

_____

_____

d. What is the topic sentence?

_____

_____

e. Diagram the paragraph here.

5.   As the civil rights movement continued, four black college students in Greensboro, North Carolina, began a sit-in at a segregated lunch counter. On February 1, 1960, they took seats and sat and waited all day for service. The waitress would not serve them. Still, the students refused to leave. The next day, more blacks came and sat at the counter. The sit-in spread to other lunch counters. Six months after the movement began, Greensboro's white leaders gave in. At last, blacks could be served at any lunch counter in the city.

(Maier, Pauline. The American People: A History. Lexington, MA: Heath, 1986. p. 679.)

a. What is the topic?

_____

b. What significant details does the author provide?

_____

_____

c. What is the controlling idea?

_____

_____

d. What is the topic sentence?

_____

_____

e. Diagram the paragraph here.

SUMMARY

Conscious readers use reading strategies to identify a paragraph's topic, its main idea, and topic sentence. By locating a stated main idea, you will know the author's view on the topic, be able to predict the discussion of the topic, and identify the author's purpose in writing the paragraph. With this information, you control the reading process.

In each of the following paragraphs, identify the topic and the controlling idea, and write them on the lines provided. Underline the topic sentence. If there is no stated topic sentence, use the reading procedure to develop one and write it on the line below. Finally, diagram the paragraph.

1. Biological needs are universal; they include such things as food, clothing, and shelter. However, the type of food and the way it is prepared, as well as the utensils used to eat it, vary according to cultural preference. Rice, for example, can be eaten with a fork or with chopsticks. It can be served with shrimp or black beans. Clothing needs are determined in part by weather conditions, but that does not explain why one society uses polyester knit suits, another uses clothing made of cotton, and a third uses animal skins. Cultural preferences are responsible for these differences. Culture also accounts for the fact that in some societies women's bodies are completely covered while in others with a similar climate they may wear grass skirts and have their bosoms exposed. People living in similar climates might live in wooden huts or in high-rise apartment buildings.

    (Mendoza, Manuel G. and Vince Napoli. Systems of Society. *Lexington, MA: Heath, 1990. p. 313.)*

Topic: _____

Controlling Idea: _____

Unstated Topic Sentence: _____

_____

Diagram:

2. As the area of a habitat such as a rain forest is decreased, the number of species of plants and animals it can support also declines. The relation between these two qualities of the natural environment, area and diversity, is consistent. A reduction of the habitat to one-tenth its original area means an eventual loss of about half its species. In other words, if a forest of 10,000 square miles and a hundred resident bird species is cut back to 1,000 square miles, it will eventually lose about 50 of the bird species.

(Wilson, Edward O. "Rain Forest Canopy: The High Frontier." National Geographic (December 1991): p. 104.)

Topic: _____

Controlling Idea: _____

_____

Unstated Topic Sentence: _____

_____

Diagram:

3. In the 1920's, entertainment became an industry. The first radio station in the United States to broadcast presidential election results was KDKA in Pittsburgh. The first of those broadcasts was in 1920. At that time almost no one owned a radio. But by 1929, 12 million families had radio sets. Local stations and two national stations, the National Broadcast Company (NBC) and the Columbia Broadcast Company (CBS), competed for listeners. Often millions of people listened to the same broadcast. As a result, the radio helped tie Americans together. The movies also helped link Americans because people living in different sections of the country saw the same films. The movies were not as new as radio. Silent films had been around since the early 1900's. Never before, however, were film stars as adored as they were in the 1920's. Americans rushed to see movies featuring their favorite actors

and actresses. Stars such as Mary Pickford, Greta Garbo, Rudolph Valentino, and Charlie Chaplin were known to almost everyone. Then, with *The Jazz Singer*, a movie of 1927, the "talkies" were born. By the 1930's millions of Americans were going to the movies every week.

(Maier, Pauline. The American People: A History. Lexington, MA: Heath, 1986, p. 579.)

Topic: _____

Controlling Idea: _____

Unstated Topic Sentence: _____

_____

Diagram:

4. To coordinate their activities, fishes communicate in many and sometimes unusual ways. Some rely on sight and distinctive body-color patterns. Most have special sense organs on their skins that can "hear" the movement of their cohorts through the water around them. Others talk to one another in private languages of clicks, grunts and growls. And still others communicate with electric pulses that they generate in highly specialized muscles.

(Levine, Joseph. "For These Fish, School Never Lets Out." Smithsonian 21 (July 1990): 88–90.)

Topic: _____

Controlling Idea: _____

Unstated Topic Sentence: _____

_____

Diagram:

5.   If anyone was ever, as the cliché goes, "ahead of his time" it was Richard Burton [the 19th-century British explorer]. In an age when many of his countrymen looked down on anyone whose skin was another color, and the armies of Victoria were slaughtering spear-carrying Africans by the thousands, this pioneer anthropologist mastered 25 languages and 15 dialects (not to mention his linguistic studies of monkey jabber), and filled 43 volumes with erudite observations about native customs and natural phenomena encountered on his travels. His rage to learn—especially anything that was taboo—had a no-holds-barred, 20th-century ring but even today it seems virtually obsessive. At a time when his fellow explorers would delicately refer to trousers and drawers as "unmentionables," Richard Burton risked scandal and even prison with his endless meditations on sexual habits that he had observed in the farthest corners of the world.

    (*Kernan, Michael, "Sir Richard Burton, Scholarly Swashbuckler." Smithsonian 20 (February 1990): 127.*)

Topic: _____

Controlling Idea: _____

Unstated Topic Sentence: _____

_____

Diagram:

6.   The fact that the jury system, decreasing in use everywhere else in the world, has enjoyed such popularity in the United States is probably due, in part, to our country's early experience of using the jury to wrest power from an oppressive government. The deep respect in this country for the jury system is founded on the belief that jury trials can prevent the government from getting too powerful and also prevent, or at least hinder, the enforcement of unfair laws. Since jurors, unlike judges, do not have to explain their verdicts or give reasons for acquitting (freeing) someone, they play the role of the conscience of the community. Juries have proven themselves over time to be an effective and humane system for resolving disputes.

(Kolanda, Jo and Judge Patricia Curley. Trial by Jury. *New York: Franklin Watts/A First Book, 1988. p. 26.)*

Topic: _____

Controlling Idea: _____

Unstated Topic Sentence: _____

_____

Diagram:

7.   The Second World War is often described as a "total war." Although it began as a relatively restricted conflict between the Anglo-French allies and Germany over the political future of Poland in early September 1939, it gradually spread, drawing in country after country. In April 1940, Denmark and Norway were invaded by the Germans; a month later it was the turn of Belgium, the Netherlands, Luxembourg and France. Italy joined in on Germany's side in June and, after attacking British forces in Egypt and East Africa, took part in the invasion of Yugoslavia and Greece. In July 1941, Russia became involved as Axis forces—including units from Rumania and Hungary—poured across her borders in Operation Barbarossa. Five months later, Japan (at war with China since 1937) attacked American, British and Dutch possessions in the Far East to produce a truly global war. By 1945, campaigns had been fought in areas as far apart as the Atlantic and the Pacific and in climates as diverse as those of North Africa and Southeast Asia.

(Pimlott, John. "Introduction," in The Second World War. *Ed. Charles Messenger. New York: Franklin Watts, 1987. p. 4.)*

Topic: _____

Controlling Idea: _____

Unstated Topic Sentence: _____

_____

Diagram:

8.   Throughout their history, Europeans have looked outward to the rest of the world. The Portuguese explored the west coast of Africa and around the Cape of Good Hope across to India in the 15th century. A Genoese sea captain called Christopher Columbus tried to sail to India by going west across the Atlantic Ocean. In 1493 the words "the New World" were first used to describe his discovery of the islands of the Caribbean. These islands are known to this day as the West Indies because Columbus thought (mistakenly) that by sailing as far west as possible, he had arrived in India!

(Roberts, Elizabeth, Europe 1992: The United States of Europe? New York: Watts/ Gloucester Press, 1990. p. 8.)

Topic: _____

Controlling Idea: _____

Unstated Topic Sentence: _____

_____

Diagram:

9.   The economy of Europe, although devastated by World War II, is now one of the strongest in the world. Europe has been industrialized for two centuries. In the past 25 years Europeans have doubled their income, having twice as many goods and services at their disposal as they had in 1965. This compares with an increase of only 60 percent in the United States and an increase of 40 percent in Japan. However, U.S. income is higher than European income.

(Roberts, Elizabeth. Europe 1992: The United States of Europe? New York: Watts/ Gloucester Press, 1990. p. 30.)

Topic: _____

Controlling Idea: _____

Unstated Topic Sentence: _____

_____

Diagram:

10.   Think Palm Beach [Florida] and you think money. That narrow strip of sand and coral that is Palm Beach has long been the playground of the idle rich. They drive more Rolls Royces per capita than Londoners. Through countless balls and benefits they raise more charity dollars per capita than any other city in the world. But there is another Palm Beach, a much bigger and more varied one. This is Palm Beach County, home of Palm Beach and also North, West, and South Palm Beach; Lantana; Hypoluxo Island; Boca Raton; Lake Worth; Delray; and more. These towns are rich and poor, stately and tacky, home to fabulous hotels and modest trailer parks and as culturally diverse as any part of Florida north of Miami.

(Older, Jules, "Palm Beach, for Richer or Poorer." Baltimore Sunday Sun (2 December 1990): 51.)

Topic: _____

Controlling Idea: _____

Unstated Topic Sentence: _____

_____

Diagram:

APPLICATION II

Select a section of two or three pages from one of your textbooks. Identify the topic sentences for each paragraph in this section. In a paragraph, explain the relationships of these topic sentences to the overall main idea of the section.

APPLICATION III

Write a paragraph on one of your favorite movies or television programs. In the paragraph, explain your reasons for liking this program. Place your topic sentence in the position that best suits your purpose. Then, underline your topic sentence, and submit the paragraph to your instructor.

Chapter 5

SUPPORTING DETAILS

Objectives
1. To understand the functions of details.
2. To locate primary support statements in a paragraph.
3. To identify secondary support statements in a paragraph.

Key Concept
To support a main idea, a writer provides details. Details offer various levels of examples to support main ideas. *Primary support statements* directly develop the topic sentence. *Secondary support statements* provide specific examples, descriptions, or explanations of primary support statements.

When a friend tells you that a particular movie is good or interesting, you probably ask for more information. What makes the movie good or interesting? Who are the stars? What is the plot? The answers to these questions give you details about the movie and support your friend's favorable comment. For example, your friend can prove her statement by giving examples of some of the special effects used in the movie, by naming the major actors, and by retelling the story. These details help you understand the original comment about the movie.

You ask the same type of questions in class. When your chemistry teacher explains that a lab experiment has seven steps, you probably ask, "What are those seven steps?" In both cases, you question the speaker about details that support main ideas. By asking these questions, you enter into a conversation with the speaker. When you read, you should question the writer as you would a friend or teacher. This questioning makes you a conscious reader, one who talks with a writer.

Writers, too, use this method. Writers know that readers need explanations to understand ideas. To answer readers' questions, writers develop their ideas by giving details. Primary support statements directly develop the topic sentence. Secondary support statements offer specific examples, descriptions, and explanations about the primary support statements. These statements help you to understand the development of ideas.

TYPES OF DETAILS

Writers develop their main ideas by using different kinds of details. They may provide statistics, historical evidence, a list of procedures, comparisons or contrasts, causes or effects, examples, definitions, descriptions, narrations (stories), or reasons. Each type of detail can support the main idea. Look at the following examples of these types of details:

Statistics: Nearly 30 percent of America's wetlands have been destroyed by commercial development.

Historical Evidence: In April 1861 Confederates fired on Fort Sumter to begin the American Civil War.

List: To bake a cake, you must have the right ingredients, follow the recipe's directions, and bake the cake for the required time at the specified temperature.

Comparisons/Contrasts: Two aerobic sports, jogging and swimming, offer participants similar benefits: a good workout for the heart, development of several muscle groups, and flexibility in exercise.

Causes/Effects: Because they practice reading strategies, conscious readers learn and remember more.

Examples: Car manufacturers are interested in passenger safety; for example, nearly 80 percent of all new cars have driver-side air bags.

Definitions: A *polyglot* is a person who speaks several languages.

Descriptions: The homeless man was dressed in torn jeans, a ragged plaid shirt, a dirty baseball cap, and patched sneakers.

Narrations: After studying all day, Jamil went to dinner and a movie with friends; then, he returned home to study some more.

Reasons: Prices rise because the supply is low and the demand is high.

These details have similar features. Each is specific and concrete. Many present factual evidence or descriptions. For these reasons, details are more specific than a topic or topic sentence.

The table on the following page shows the level of information for a paragraph's topic, topic sentence, and details.

Paragraph Element	Level of Information
Topic	Very general, a short phrase that identifies the broad subject of discussion
Topic sentence	More specific; identifies the writer's opinion or states a limitation in the controlling idea
Details	Most specific; provides examples of the controlling idea

Your clue for identifying a paragraph's details lies in the topic sentence. Look at the following topic sentences carefully. Locate the controlling idea. What types of details might the author use to support each topic sentence?

1. Changing a tire requires four steps. _____

2. A liberal arts education provides a solid foundation for undergraduates. _____

3. Women have made great strides in equality in the past twenty years. _____

4. Two new computers differ in their prices, functions, and storage abilities. _____

5. The abandoned building on First Street needs major repairs.

_____

Your answers might look like these:

1. A list of the four steps.

2. The reasons a liberal arts education provides a solid foundation.

3. Examples and statistics of the changes in women's status.

4. Contrasts of prices, functions, and storage abilities. (You should also expect to see examples of these three features.)

5. Description of the building.

By asking how a paragraph will be supported, you can predict the details an author might use. Thus, your task of locating details becomes easier. In Chapter 4, "Main Ideas," you used the same technique to determine a writer's purpose. You turned the controlling idea into a question. This question helped you understand the writer's purpose. This purpose indicates the type of support a writer might use. Your use of this technique to find details makes you a conscious reader. As you read, you carry on a conversation with the author.

EXERCISE 1   For each of the following topic sentences, underline the controlling idea. Next, turn the controlling idea into a question. Then, from this question, guess the type of details a writer might use to support the topic sentence.

1. Every college student <u>should be computer literate</u>.

   Question: _____

   Type of Details: _____

2. Homeless people <u>face many obstacles</u> in their return to employment.

   Question: _____

   Type of Details: _____

3. In the past few years, <u>rap music has captured the imagination</u> of many listeners.

   Question: _____

   Type of Details: _____

4. Taos, New Mexico, <u>offers vacationers ski areas</u>, Native American culture, a thriving arts community, and the legacy of D. H. Lawrence, the famous British writer.

   Question: _____

   Type of Details: _____

5. Learning a foreign language <u>offers insights</u> into a country's culture.

   Question: _____

   Type of Details: _____

6. The beginnings of the American Revolution <u>can be traced from the French and Indian Wars to the Battles of Concord and Lexington.</u>

   Question: _____

   Type of Details: _____

7. The benefits of <u>living on campus outweigh the disadvantages.</u>

   Question: _____

   Type of Details: _____

8. Although the Persian Gulf War has been likened to the Vietnam conflict, <u>there are many differences.</u>

   Question: _____

   Type of Details: _____

9. Television programs <u>fall into one of five categories.</u>

   Question: _____

   Type of Details: _____

10. The past two decades have brought <u>many changes in the way Americans view the family.</u>

    Question: _____

    Type of Details: _____

PRIMARY SUPPORT STATEMENTS

Details offer various levels of support. Primary support statements directly develop a topic sentence. You can recognize these statements because they immediately answer the questions you construct from the topic sentence's controlling idea.

Examine the following topic sentence. What type of support might this paragraph contain?

Americans should have four-week vacations each year.

The controlling idea in this sentence is "should have four-week vacations each year." The primary support statements should provide reasons for the writer's opinion.

Now, consider the following statements. Do these sentences give reasons for the writers's opinion?

1. Americans can complete household tasks and relax.

2. Workers would have several breaks around the holidays.

3. Studies indicate that workers are more satisfied and productive when they have four-week vacations.

4. This vacation period would increase the travel industry and have a positive impact on the economy.

Each statement above *does* provide a reason to support the controlling idea. Of course, each statement needs more explanation to convince an audience.

1. What typical activities do Americans complete during vacations?

2. Why do workers need breaks around the holidays?

3. What are the results of studies on job satisfaction and productivity?

4. How would this vacation affect the economy?

The four reasons do not provide all the additional information you may want. But they do give a clear idea of the support in the paragraph and provide a basic outline of it. These four statements are *primary support statements.*

Read the paragraph below. Its topic sentence is in bold type and its primary support statements are italicized for you.

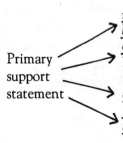

Primary support statement

> In China, the family was central to society. **Everyone's role in the family was fixed from birth to death.** *The elderly had privileges and power; the young had practically none. The oldest man was in charge of all the family's goods and possessions.* He also had final approval of the marriages that the women of the family arranged for his children and grandchildren. *The oldest woman—usually the grandmother—had authority over all the younger women. Children were expected to obey their parents and grandparents without question.* The most important virtue in Chinese society was respect for one's parents.
>
> (Jantzen, Steven, et al. World History. Lexington, MA: Heath, 1988. p. 78.)

Each primary support provides examples of family roles "fixed from birth to death." The first one identifies the general principle that the oldest have power. The second, third, and fourth list the specific family members and their roles in a Chinese family. Therefore, each primary support statement directly develops the controlling idea in the topic sentence.

The following diagram shows the relationship among the paragraph's elements:

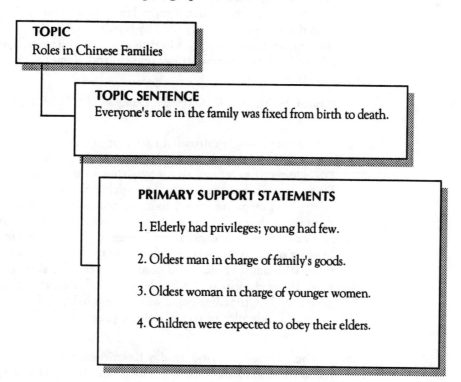

TOPIC
Roles in Chinese Families

TOPIC SENTENCE
Everyone's role in the family was fixed from birth to death.

PRIMARY SUPPORT STATEMENTS

1. Elderly had privileges; young had few.

2. Oldest man in charge of family's goods.

3. Oldest woman in charge of younger women.

4. Children were expected to obey their elders.

Notice that the paragraph elements—topic, topic sentence, and primary support statements—move from most general to specific. Notice, too, that the primary support statements form a basic outline of the paragraph. Therefore, primary support statements have two functions: (1) they develop the topic sentence, and (2) they provide an outline of the paragraph.

EXERCISE 2

In the following paragraphs, underline the topic sentence, circle the controlling idea, and number the primary support statements.

1.   The civilization of Greece and Rome gave birth to many of the most prized ideals of the modern world. In government, the Greeks developed the ideas of democracy and individual worth. Greek science encouraged the use of human reason. Greek art and architecture established standards of beauty based on balance, scale, and proportion. As they founded cities around the Mediterranean Sea, the Greeks spread their ideas far beyond their homeland. The Romans were not such original thinkers as the Greeks, but they were fearsome con-

querors and skilled empire builders. They took up Greek culture and extended it to new lands as their empire spread. Their own great contribution was law—a single law that united many peoples and gave new meaning to the idea of citizenship. During the period of Roman rule, a new religion, Christianity, arose. Beginning in the land of Palestine, Christianity spread throughout Roman lands. Christianity too united many peoples, this time by bonds of faith. Even after the Roman empire fell, the heritage of Greco-Roman culture lived on. Its achievements became central elements in Western civilization.

(*Jantzen, Steven, et al.* World History. *Lexington, MA: Heath, 1988. p. 92.*)

2.   It is increasingly difficult to grow up in America. If a teenager is not glued to the television set, he or she is spending large amounts of money at a movie theater or sporting event. Drugs and alcohol are nearly inescapable at many social gatherings, and teens are forced to make decisions about those substances that will have an impact on the rest of their lives. It is crucial to be accepted and appreciated. The need for belonging often overpowers judgment and values. Teenagers are faced with adult choices and consequences. The ability to make those choices is clouded by a lack of education and experience. The time has come when there is little division between the splendor of youth and the pressure of maturity.

3.   The interior of a modern-day Renaissance Festival is set up like a little European town, with literally scores of shops, amusements, and food vendors. The shops and amusements alone offer an abundance of activities. Hoards of merchants sell any souvenir imaginable. Blacksmiths sell swords and armor, woodworkers their handicrafts, glassblowers trinkets, and clothiers apparel (Renaissance style, of course). Dozens of other providers of goods are also eager to trade their merchandise for cash; so are those who provide services, which include anything from tarot or runestone readings to the refreshments and meals whose delicious aromas waft up and down the causeways. Proprietors of amusements, games, and other tests of skill offer distraction in exchange for a bit of your money, as well. Archery, Frankish axe throwing, darts, and a Jacob's ladder, among other things, are ready to entertain and challenge; sometimes, prizes can be won. It is possible to spend hours at all these shops and amusements; more than likely, each shop or game will demand at least two visits, even if the second one is just to browse or spectate.

4.   Two kinds of logic are used [in motorcycle maintenance], inductive and deductive. Inductive inferences start with observations of the machine and arrive at general conclusions. For example, if the cycle goes over a bump and the engine misfires, and then goes over another bump and the engine misfires, and the goes over another bump and the engine misfires, and then goes over a long smooth stretch of road and

there is no misfiring, and then goes over a fourth bump and the engine misfires again, one can logically conclude that the misfiring is caused by the bumps. This is induction: reasoning from particular experiences to general truths. Deductive inferences do the reverse. They start with general knowledge and predict a specific observation. For example, if from reading the hierarchy of facts about the machine, the mechanic knows the horn of the cycle is powered exclusively by electricity from the battery, then he can logically infer that if the battery is dead the horn will not work. That is deduction.

(*Pirsig, Robert.* Zen and the Art of Motorcycle Maintenance. *New York: Bantam Books, 1974. pp. 99.*)

5. Animals form social groups for many reasons. One reason is safety in large numbers. For example, a herd of antelopes is less likely to be attacked by a lion than a lone antelope. In some social groups, large numbers of animals help to keep each other warm. Penguins in Antarctica crowd together to break the icy winds and to lessen the effects of the cold. Migrating animals often form social groups. Animals travel-ing in large groups are less likely to get lost.

(*Bierer, Loretta, et al.* Life Science. *Lexington, MA: Heath, 1987. p. 324.*)

EXERCISE 3

To understand the relationship of primary support statements to the controlling idea, read the following sets of topic sentences and primary support statements. Underline the controlling idea of the topic sentence. Next, circle the letter of the one primary support statement in each set that does *not* develop the topic sentence.

1. Each student should be required to be computer literate.

   a. Since computers are used frequently in educational settings, students have a greater access to information.

   b. Using a computer for word processing can save time and make revisions easier.

   c. Students should know how to use automatic teller machines.

   d. Computers are present in all career fields, so students should be familiar with the functions and uses of computers.

2. The roles of women have changed greatly within the last fifteen years.

   a. Women now head major corporations.

   b. Professions that were once restricted now employ women.

   c. Working mothers account for 75 percent of all women in the workplace.

   d. Women athletes now have more opportunities for competition.

3. Hobbies offer challenges, enjoyment, and sometimes financial gain for people.

   a. Many hobbies encourage the development of new skills.

   b. Hobbies can become so encompassing that people concentrate on them alone.

   c. Hobbyists enjoy using and appreciating their handicrafts.

   d. Some hobbies can be turned into small businesses.

4. Traveling offers many rewards for vacationers.

   a. One can experience a new culture or region, even in the same country.

   b. Traveling provides a good way to explore national parks.

   c. Through traveling, vacationers meet new people.

   d. Traveling can be expensive.

5. Saturday morning cartoons have changed over the past twenty years.

   a. In the 1970s, cartoons based their humor on slapstick routines.

   b. Cartoons today often promote advertisers, not entertainment.

   c. Today's cartoons focus on action-packed adventures.

   d. Today, it is more difficult to tell the heroes from the villains.

Secondary Support Statements

Secondary support statements directly illustrate the primary support statements by offering examples, statistics, descriptions, narrations, comparisons or contrasts, or definitions. Consider the following paragraph:

> Americans should have four-week vacations each year. Americans can complete household tasks and relax. Workers would have several breaks around the holidays. Studies indicate that workers are more satisfied and productive when they have four-week vacations. This vacation period would increase the travel industry and have a positive impact on the economy.

With only a topic sentence and four primary support statements, this paragraph does not completely develop its topic. Each primary support statement needs more explanation, more specific examples and details, to convince readers. Secondary support statements can supply this information.

Read the paragraph below. How does the addition of the italicized secondary support statements increase your understanding of the topic?

> Americans should have four-week vacations each year. Americans can complete household tasks and relax. *Too often, many Americans choose to paint the house, complete some remodeling, or build decks during their vacations. They return to the office exhausted. The vacation did not accomplish its major goals: relaxation and rejuvenation.* Workers would have several breaks around the holidays. *With four weeks to choose from, workers can plan their vacations to fit their needs. They can enjoy quiet holidays, without cramming work and holiday preparations into a brief, tiring week.* Studies indicate that workers are more satisfied and productive when they have four-week vacations. *In most European countries, workers enjoy this longer vacation. Office managers have long noted that workers return to the office or plant eager to resume their duties. Moreover, productivity increases when workers are given a chance to relax completely.* This vacation period would increase the travel industry and have a positive impact on the economy. *With longer vacations, people would take the time to explore other areas of the country. The travel industry would see an increase in tours. In addition, the entire economy—from automobile manufacturers, hotels and restaurants, to camping equipment industries—would benefit as more vacationers need additional services and goods.* For all these reasons, Americans should have an extended vacation period.

Each primary support, which offers a reason, now has some explanation following it. This explanation, given in the secondary support statements, provides more information than the original paragraph did. The new paragraph is, therefore, more convincing and more interesting to read.

Your recognition of secondary support statements aids your understanding of this paragraph. The paragraph now has four levels of ideas and examples, each more specific than the last. The chart below demonstrates these levels:

Paragraph Element	*Level*
Topic	General; a short phrase about the subject of the paragraph
Topic sentence	More specific statement of the writer's main idea about the topic; identifies the writer's opinion or states limitations in the controlling idea
Primary support statements	Provide specific supports of topic sentence
Secondary support statements	Provide specific examples of primary supports

From this chart, you can see that the topic is the most general of these elements. Secondary support statements are the most specific. With knowledge of these levels, you can diagram, map, or outline paragraphs effectively to see the development of ideas.

Study the partial outline on the following page, based on the sample paragraph about four-week vacations.

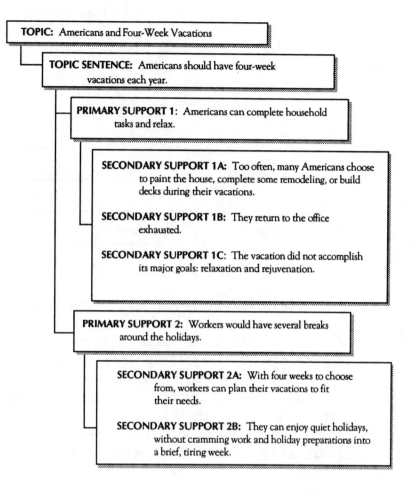

TOPIC: Americans and Four-Week Vacations

TOPIC SENTENCE: Americans should have four-week vacations each year.

PRIMARY SUPPORT 1: Americans can complete household tasks and relax.

SECONDARY SUPPORT 1A: Too often, many Americans choose to paint the house, complete some remodeling, or build decks during their vacations.

SECONDARY SUPPORT 1B: They return to the office exhausted.

SECONDARY SUPPORT 1C: The vacation did not accomplish its major goals: relaxation and rejuvenation.

PRIMARY SUPPORT 2: Workers would have several breaks around the holidays.

SECONDARY SUPPORT 2A: With four weeks to choose from, workers can plan their vacations to fit their needs.

SECONDARY SUPPORT 2B: They can enjoy quiet holidays, without cramming work and holiday preparations into a brief, tiring week.

Below, complete the diagram of the paragraph with the third and fourth primary supports and their secondary supports.

Primary Support

3. _____

Secondary Support

3a. _____

_____

3b. _____

_____

3c. _____

_____

Primary Support

4. _____

Secondary Support

4a. _____

_____

4b. _____

_____

4c. _____

_____

As you can see, identification of paragraph elements allows you to diagram the paragraph effectively. In addition, this diagram shows you the relationships among the ideas in a paragraph.

Occasionally, a paragraph many contain two other types of sentences: an introductory sentence and a concluding sentence. An introductory sentence will provide a general comment before the topic sentence. A concluding sentence will summarize the paragraph and end it. Simply identify these opening and closing sentences to complete your understanding of the paragraph.

EXERCISE 4

Read each of the following paragraphs carefully. Identify the topic sentence, primary supports, and secondary supports. Diagram each paragraph in the space provided. If you find introductory or concluding sentences, simply label them.

1.   Birds' feathers are actually forms of scales like the scales on reptiles. Each kind of feather serves a different purpose. Soft down feathers grow close to the skin. Air is trapped between the spaces of these down feathers. The bird's body gives off heat that warms the air in these spaces. If you've ever worn a down jacket or slept under a down comforter, you know how warm and light down is. Over the down feathers is a second kind of feather that rounds out a bird's streamlined body. A third kind of feather, the large flight feathers, grow in the wings and tail. The flight feathers give birds the lift and balance needed for flying.

(Bierer, Loretta, et al. Life Science. Lexington, MA: Heath, 1987. p. 290.)

Diagram:

2. Once the Second World War began, more women than ever went to work outside the home. Some 57 percent of adult women were wage earners. Of the six million women who took jobs during the war, almost half worked in manufacturing. They filled positions traditionally saved for men. Women worked, for example, as welders or as steelmakers. "Rosie the Riveter" was a popular song about a female worker. Even more striking, most of the new female workers were older than 35 years, and about 75 percent of them were married. Some even had children.

(Maier, Pauline. The American People. *Lexington, MA: Heath, 1986. p. 629.)*

Diagram:

3. . . . [I]rrational stereotyping begins early in life. The child, watching a TV Western, learns to spot the Good Guys and the Bad Guys. Some years ago, a social psychologist showed very clearly how powerful these stereotypes of childhood vision are. He secretly asked the most popular youngsters in an elementary school to make errors in their morning gym class. Afterwards, he asked the class if anyone had noticed any mistakes during gym period. Oh, yes, said the children. But it was the *unpopular* members of the class—the "bad guys"—they remembered as being out of step.

(Heilbroner, Robert. *"Don't Let Stereotypes Warp Your Judgments."* Reader's Digest. 80 (Jan. 1962): 67. Condensed from Think, *published by International Business Machines Corp., 590 Madison Avenue, New York, N.Y. Copyright 1961 by Robert L. Heilbroner.*)

Diagram:

4.   In earlier periods, art, music, and most theater had been largely the concern of the upper classes. By 1900, however, artists, writers, and musicians were appealing to a much larger audience. For the first time, we can speak of *mass culture.* There were at least three causes for the rise of mass culture around the turn of the century. First, the spread of public education broadened literacy in both Europe and North America. The millions of new readers created an enormous market for newspapers, magazines, and books that were written in simple, colorful language. Second, improvements in communication made it possible to meet this broad demand for information and entertainment. The new, high-speed presses and linotype machines could turn out thousands of pages in a few hours. The phonograph brought music directly into people's homes. The third cause was a gradual reduction in working hours. By 1900, most industrial countries had limited the working day to ten hours. Most people worked Monday through Friday and half a day on Saturday. Thus, men and women of the lower and middle classes had more leisure time than ever before. They could take part in activities that their grandparents never had time to enjoy.

(Jantzen, Steven, et al. World History. *Lexington, MA: Heath, 1988. p. 570.*)

Diagram:

5.   Lichens are not moss, but many of their common names—oakmoss, Iceland moss, reindeer moss—reflect the early days when they were classified with mosses. They tend to share mosses' habitats, growing on trees and rocks and in such places as the damp soil of road cuts. But they also grow in places where mosses cannot. They grow in almost every natural habitat imaginable, from deserts to tropical rain forests—even on the backs of certain beetles in New Guinea, and inside rocks (along with algae) in the otherwise barren dry valleys of Antarctica.

(Sharnoff, Sylvia Duran. "Lichens give food, drugs, perfume—and poison." Smithsonian 15 (April 1984):137.)

Diagram:

✏

Each of the following set of sentences forms a unified paragraph. Identify the correct order of sentences, and label the topic sentence (TS), the primary supports (PS), the secondary supports (SS), and the concluding sentence (CS).

PARAGRAPH A

_____ 1. This majestic forest was also bountiful, for at the entrance stood a great chestnut tree, and scattered throughout the rest of the forest were cherry trees, crab apple trees, and big, thick raspberry and blackberry bushes, but only the great chestnut tree had a good season each year.

_____ 2. At one point the trees formed a tunnel by joining limbs and branches over my favorite path.

_____ 3. During my adolescent years, the forest overflowed with beauty.

_____ 4. It was like walking under a sea that had every shade of green ever imagined, and when the wind blew, it was like listening to the waves of an ocean.

_____ 5. As well as these fruits, there were pine cones, as big as a little kid's head, scattered all over the ground where they had fallen.

_____ 6. Not too far into the forest was a clear, blue, small stream that only minnows could survive in.

_____ 7. The sound of birds singing, quick glimpses of deer, squirrels meandering about, and sometimes people passing by riding horses always kept me company.

_____ 8. The trees, which towered miles over my head, were filled with leaves of all different kinds.

_____ 9. These clearings were like oceans of long sea-green grass and dandelions.

_____ 10. Farther into the woods were a couple of cleared out spaces that were relatively close together and a little larger than football fields.

PARAGRAPH B

_____ 1. For those students who plan to go into business, computer programming represents their first valuable experience in interdisciplinary studies.

_____ 2. If policy decisions were based on students' current attitudes, then computer-related education would overwhelm colleges.

_____ 3. Computer literacy emphasizes the integration of knowledge.

_SS_ 4. For example, in writing a program dealing with guaranteed annual wages, the student must have at least a minimal acquaintance with the principles of economics, finance, government, and labor relations.

_____ 5. Teachers use computers, for instance, as teaching aids that range in sophistication from drill devices to tutoring systems that can diagnose student errors and provide corrective instruction.

_____ 6. Educators constantly search for methods of synthesizing knowledge.

_____ 7. The good news remains that schools are testing some great ideas that might serve as models for computer education in the future.

_____ 8. A good curriculum incorporates its own best criticism.

_____ 9. Students use computers to create models of phenomena that range from the human metabolism to wars and revolutions.

_TS_ 10. Computer education serves as a means of achieving this goal.

PARAGRAPH C

_____ 1. The whole festival is constantly filled with the sounds of musicians or the ruckus of some other event.

_____ 2. Most of these events successfully incorporate a great deal of audience interaction, which is otherwise very difficult to do in a large-scale performance or is neglected altogether.

_IS_   **3.** Three events are special enough to require their own areas.

_____   **4.** The final result is that all the shows at the Renaissance Festival are unique and memorable.

_____   **5.** These are the human chess match (where people are used as giant chess pieces on an oversized playing board), the jousting matches, and the event at the "mud pit," where two grimy protagonists attempt to rally supporters to cheer them on as they do battle to determine the king of the pit.

_____   **6.** At the Renaissance Festival are half a dozen stages and other specialized areas where planned events take place.

_____   **7.** Throughout the entire day, different performances rotate from stage to stage and begin at intervals of every two hours.

_____   **8.** These performances are usually short plays that commonly either mock some Shakespearean piece, such as the hilarious *Macbeth in Twenty Minutes or Less*, or deal with some other Renaissance theme in some humorous way.

_____   **9.** Other shows feature magicians or other tricksters who keep the audience laughing—the festival's main goal.

PARAGRAPH D

_____   **1.** My friends and I spent many days romping through the woods and pretending the trees were the bad guys in our games.

_____   **2.** We would skip stones in the widest part of the stream.

_____   **3.** The summer after I had read *Huckleberry Finn*, we pretended to be Tom Sawyer and Huck Finn looking for treasure around our river.

_____   **4.** No matter how many stones we threw, the stream never filled up.

_____   **5.** I ruined many sneakers by wading in that stream, but I did not care since I did not buy them.

_____   **6.** The cool stream provided refuge from the trees.

_____ 7. Exploring the forest around my house ranked as my favorite activity as a child.

_____ 8. Only the advent of dusk brought us out of the forest.

PARAGRAPH E

_____ 1. Inside, bright posters decorate the walls.

_____ 2. Cigarettes butts, old fries, and hamburger wrappers cover the floor.

_____ 3. Rowdy teenagers, making fun of people as they pass, sit in a corner.

_____ 4. At the cashier, an old lady screams about her senior-citizen discount.

_____ 5. Yellow and red distinguish the garish sign.

_____ 6. Orange bricks and shiny yellow plastic form the building's exterior.

_____ 7. Billy Bob's, a fast-food restaurant, has its own characteristics.

_____ 8. All types of people patronize Billy Bob's.

_____ 9. A flustered mother tries to get her little children's orders.

_____ 10. The frantic atmosphere of Billy Bob's swirls around its clients.

_____ 11. A baby, covered with ketchup, throws his french fries to the floor.

SUMMARY

By recognizing primary and secondary supports, you can identify the development of a paragraph and can easily outline or diagram its major elements. Moreover, you have entered into a conversation with the author as you ask questions about the details used to support the topic sentence. This questioning makes you a conscious reader, one who is active in the reading process.

Read each of the following paragraphs carefully. Locate the topic sentence, its controlling idea, the primary supports, and the secondary supports. Label these elements.

1.   The most dramatic, commonly noted phenomenon of deserts is that they are ungodly hot and dry. This is certainly the case with the Sonoran Desert. Along the lower Colorado River, for example, there are places where surface temperatures approach 200 degrees F. and the average rain-fall is less than three inches, in some years nonexistent. Less obvious than these extreme conditions but at least as ecologically significant is the extraordinary diversity of climates and habitats in these areas: snow-capped peaks, swampy hollows, drifting dunes and scrub plains often exist in close proximity. At the same time environmental conditions can vary drastically from season to season, even hour to hour in the same small location. At noon, rocks on the sunny side of an outcropping can be too hot to touch, while those in the shade are coolish. At midnight the formation may be frosted and by morning submerged under the waters of a flash flood.

(Gilbert, Bil. "The Southwest's laid-back lizards." Smithsonian 18 (August 1987):79.)

2.   It is not quite true that no two lighthouses are alike. The first eight erected on the West Coast in the 1850s, and a number of others constructed there after that, followed the same basic New England design: a Cape Cod dwelling with the tower rising from the center, or standing close by. In New England and elsewhere, though, lighthouses reflected a variety of architectural styles, from Victorian to Second Empire. Since most stations in the Northeast were built on rock eminences and therefore had the advantage of height to begin with, enormous towers were not the rule. Some were made of stone and brick; others of wood or metal. Some stood on pilings and stilts; some were fastened to rock with iron rods. Still others, anchored to granite foundations or caisson-based structures in the middle of harbors and bays, appeared literally to ride the waves. Farther south, from Maryland through the Florida Keys, the coast was low and sandy. It was often necessary to build tall towers there—massive structures like the majestic Cape Hatteras, North Carolina, lighthouse, which was lit in 1870. At 190 feet, it is the tallest brick lighthouse in the country; it is also seriously threatened by erosion.

(Hanson, Dennis. "For lighthouses, a brighter future." Smithsonian 18 (August 1987):103.)

3.   Only within the last 30 years have instruments other than optical telescopes been used to study outer space. Radio telescopes have been developed to read the radio waves received from space. Astronomers use huge radio telescopes to listen to the sky. The weak radio energy from space is collected by one or more reflecting dishes. Then the energy is carried to a receiver. The receiver converts the radio energy into an electrical signal which can be recorded on a graph. In this way the radio telescope receives and records the radio signals from space. Radio maps have been drawn of the sky. Studies of these radio maps have revealed two types of radio energy sources never known to exist before radio telescopes were invented. These sources, quasars and pulsars, were discovered in the 1960's. Quasars, radio energy stars, are objects in space that emit strong radio signals. Pulsars are radio energy stars that emit energy in sharp, intense, and regular pulses. They were discovered in 1967. In 1960 there were two known radio energy stars. By 1979 more than 20,000 quasars had been identified, and more than 600 pulsars were known.

(Tillery, Bill. Earth Science. *Lexington, MA: Heath, 1987. p. 33.*)

4.   [Before the arrival of Columbus,] many Indian groups lived in the present-day lands of the United States and Canada. Each group had its own language, customs, and way of life. Along the northern Pacific coast, some groups fished for salmon, hunted for seals, and carved tall totem poles from giant evergreen trees. Along the Atlantic coast, Indian peoples farmed, hunted deer and rabbits, and made canoes of birchbark. The languages of the Indians were as varied as their ways of life. There were about 30 languages, with perhaps 2,000 dialects, spoken by Indian peoples.

(Jantzen, Steven, et al. World History. *Lexington, MA: Heath, 1988. p. 310.*)

5.   A [sports] referee must be strong physically and shrug off frequent pain. Occupational hazards include torn muscles, being cut by punches and spiked shoes when breaking up fights, being stunned by frozen pucks rocketing at 120 m.p.h. Baseballs, which often travel almost as fast as hockey pucks, have snapped the steel bars of umpires' face-masks, then knocked out teeth and broken jaws. In football, even an agile referee can be knocked down by gargantuan athletes charging full speed. To get into superb shape, each sports official must report to pre-season training camps at a stipulated weight. There he stretches, sprints, lifts weights, does calisthenics and other exercises needed especially for his sport. Hockey's officials, for instance, must run a mile in no more than seven minutes, do 80 situps within two minutes, and skate in relay races for two hours. Then, to stretch and strengthen their leg muscles, they practice alternately squatting and standing on

skates. Next comes the hand-wrestling needed to separate brawling players.

(Surface, Bill. "Referee: Roughest Role in Sports." Reader's Digest. 1976.)

6.   The digestive system has two main functions. The first function is to break down food. Food is broken down in two ways. First, large pieces of food are mechanically broken down into smaller pieces. Then, once the food is in tiny pieces, enzymes chemically change the large molecules of nutrients into smaller molecules. The second function of the digestive system is to absorb food. In this process, the simple molecules of food, along with water, minerals, and vitamins, pass through the walls of the intestines and into the blood. These substances are then delivered to all the cells of your body.

(Bierer, Loretta, et al. Life Science. Lexington, MA: Heath, 1987. p. 438.)

7.   Over the months that followed [the release of "We Are the World], the idea that brought about "We Are the World" influenced other fund-raising ideas to fight hunger. A group of Canadian singers and musicians formed Northern Lights and raised millions of Canadian dollars in 1985. In July 1985, the British group Band Aid and the American group USA for Africa organized and performed in a cross-continent concert, Live Aid, which raised more than 40 million dollars through ticket sales and a worldwide telethon. In May 1986, two events raised more millions to fight world hunger: Sport Aid, an athletic event; and Hands Across America, a human chain of Americans who had pledged money to stand in a nation-wide line. These events, plus hundreds of car washes, bake sales, "bikathons," and other small-scale fund-raisers, resulted in millions more dollars donated to fight hunger.

(Lewis, Mary. "The Song That Moved America," in Through the Starshine. Ed. Donna Alvermann et al. Lexington, MA: Heath, 1989. pp. 124–125.)

8.   No two cultures are exactly the same. The distinctions among cultures may be quite large or very small. Many cultural differences are seen in the buildings people construct, the clothes they wear, and the ways they make and transport goods. Some cultural differences can be heard in the ways people speak and the music they play. You can taste cultural differences too. Every culture has its own special foods and dishes. People of different cultures also have different points of view. Even when they act in similar ways, people may have different reasons for their actions. For example, a rancher on the pampas of South America protects and provides for cattle so that the animals will bring a good price when they are sold. Herding cattle is a way of earning a living for that rancher. In India, a follower of the Hindu religion protects cattle not because of the monetary value of cattle but because Hinduism teaches that these animals are sacred. An African herder on

the Serengeti Plain protects cattle for yet another reason. In this culture, cattle are a sign of status. They show one's importance in society.

(Gritzner, Charles. World Geography. Lexington, MA: Heath, 1989. pp. 126–127.)

9.   As the weeks went by, my interest in [Sherlock Holmes] and my curiosity as to his aims in life gradually deepened and increased. His very person and appearance were such as to strike the attention of the most casual observer. In height he was rather over six feet, and so excessively lean that he seemed to be considerably taller. His eyes were sharp and piercing, save during those intervals of torpor to which I have alluded; and his thin, hawk-like nose gave his whole expression an air of alertness and decision. His chin, too, had the prominence and squareness which mark the man of determination. His hands were invariably blotted with ink and stained with chemicals, yet he was possessed of extraordinary delicacy of touch, as I frequently had occasion to observe when I watched him manipulating his fragile philosophical instruments.

(Doyle, Sir Arthur Conan. "A Study in Scarlet," in The Complete Sherlock Holmes. Garden City, NY: Doubleday, 1930. p. 30.)

10.   All computers, from the smallest home computer to the largest supercomputer used by the military, are made up of the same basic components. Input represents the starting data, the raw facts, that are entered into the computer. The processor, or CPU for Central Processing Unit, is the data transformer. Inside the CPU, electronic circuits change the initial data in some way. Often, input data are combined with some other data in the CPU to produce information. All computer processors have some memory or storage. These are special electronic circuits that store data and the results of processing that will be needed later. Memory functions as an electronic storage cabinet. Information isn't useful if no one knows about it. Output is the result of processing. The ways in which we use the information produced by a computer depend on the form of the output. The form of the output depends, in turn, on the output device we use.

(Kershner, Helene G. Introduction to Computer Literacy. Lexington, MA: Heath, 1990. p. 5.)

Select and photocopy two passages of one to three paragraphs from two of your textbooks. Next, identify the topic sentence, primary supports, and secondary supports in each passage. Outline, map, or diagram these. Submit the photocopies and your outlines to your instructor.

Chapter 6

ORGANIZATIONAL PATTERNS

Objectives

1. To recognize transitional markers and their functions in sentences.
2. To recognize the organizational patterns writers use.

Key Concept

To help readers understand links between ideas, writers use *transitional markers*. These words or phrases define connections between ideas. These transitional markers also help readers determine an overall *organizational pattern* in paragraphs. By using these patterns, writers provide readers with specific sequences of supporting ideas and make their work more readable.

To reach goals, you make plans. Plans can be as simple as a shopping list or as complex as a college curriculum. Plans allow you to accomplish goals more easily. Without them, you lose time and waste energy. Writers, too, create plans as they compose. To help readers understand ideas quickly, writers use specific organizational patterns. Authors want to help you follow these patterns and understand the relationships between ideas. Therefore, authors use connecting words or phrases, called *transitional markers*, to link ideas. By recognizing these clues, you will be able to identify a writer's purpose, the development of supporting details, and the piece's overall structure.

TRANSITIONAL MARKERS

Transitional markers name relationships between ideas in a sentence or a group of sentences. Without these signs, you would be forced to determine the relationships yourself, and you may make the wrong connection. Consider the following sentence without a transitional marker between its two ideas:

> To rewire a light fixture, cut the wires; turn off the electricity.

If you were to follow this direction, you could be seriously injured. Next, read the revision of the sentence. It now includes transitional markers:

> To rewire a light fixture, *first*, turn off the electricity, and *then* cut the wires.

With its two transitional markers, *first* and *then*, this sentence is much clearer and will save you a shock. The instruction now emphasizes a sequence of steps. You will be able to perform the task without danger. The transitional markers in the sentence helped you to identify the relationship between the two ideas. These markers told you the chronological order of the steps you needed to know.

Different transitional markers stress different types of relationships. Consider this sentence:

> Hannah went shopping; Tom went fishing.

This sentence implies several relationships between the two ideas. However, you cannot be sure which relationship the writer intended without a transitional marker. Compare the sentence above to those below:

> Hannah went shopping, *and* Tom went fishing.
>
> Hannah went shopping, *but* Tom went fishing.
>
> Hannah went shopping, *for* Tom went fishing.
>
> Hannah went shopping, *so* Tom went fishing.

What differences in meaning do you find in these sentences? Each sentence provides a different interpretation of the two actions. In the first sentence, with *and* as the transitional marker, you can assume that the two people had different, but equal, interests. Hannah wanted to shop. Tom wanted to fish. In the second sentence, an opposition is stated by the transitional marker *but*. In this case, their actions are equal but opposite. You might conclude that these two people simply have different interests. In sentence three, Hannah's decision to go shopping is based on the fact that Tom went fishing. The transitional marker *for* shows a cause-effect relationship. Hannah went shopping *because* Tom went fishing. In the last sentence, Tom decided to go fishing because Hannah had gone shopping. In effect, the transitional marker *so* places the cause first and then states the effect. This example demonstrates the necessity of transitional markers and their importance in linking ideas.

In the practices that follow, combine the two sentences by inserting a word that links the ideas. Be able to explain your selection of connecting words.

1. Terry ordered a pizza. Quong preferred a French dinner.

    _____

2. Raoul spent all night studying. He had a final examination the next day.

    _____

3. The science-fiction movie won an Academy Award. The movie had new special effects and an interesting plot.

    _____

In sentence 1, you might have added one of the following words: *and*, *but*, *so*, or *yet*. In sentence 2, *because* or *for* would show the cause-effect relationship between ideas. In sentence 3, you might also have chosen *for* or *because* to show why the movie won an award. These are only some suggestions for transitional markers that would work in these sentences. What others could you have used? What relationships do they stress?

The following chart lists the most frequently used transitional markers and the relationships they stress. Review this list. As you discover new transitions, add them to the list.

Relationship	Transitional Words and Expressions	
Addition	again	in addition
	also	likewise
	and	moreover
	as well as	next
	further	similarly
	furthermore	too
Cause	because	for this reason
	for	since
Chronology	after	in the meantime
	always	meanwhile
	at last	next
	before	soon
	briefly	suddenly
	currently	then
	finally	until
	first (second, etc.)	when
	frequently	
Comparison	all	both
	and	like
	as	similarly

Relationship	Transitional Words and Expressions	
Conclusion	finally	both
	hence	thus
	so	to conclude
Contrast	although	nevertheless
	but	on the contrary
	conversely	on the other hand
	despite	though
	even so	unlike
	however	yet
Effect	as a result	so
	consequently	then
	for that reason	therefore
	hence	
Emphasis	above all	indeed
	especially	in fact
Example	for example	specifically
	for instance	such as
	in other words	to illustrate
Importance	finally	least
	first	next
	last	primarily
List	finally	least
	first	next
	last	primarily
Repetition	again	in summary
	as stated before	to reiterate
	i.e. (that is)	to repeat
Space	above	forward
	adjacent to	here
	alongside	in front of
	among	next to
	around	on top of
	below	over
	beside	there
	between	under
	beyond	where
	down	
Summary	finally	on the whole
	in brief	overall
	in short	

EXERCISE 1   Underline the transitional words and expressions in the following sentences. Identify the relationship between ideas the transition stresses, and write it in the blank.

1. Because Dana sings well, she has been invited to join the choir. _____

2. We had planned to purchase a new car; however, prices were too high. _____

3. Many people believe that the Gulf War will have a great impact on Middle East politics; moreover, the results of the war will be felt for some time. _____

4. Because good writing skills are imperative, you need to register for a composition course. _____

5. The university president believes that all faculty should teach courses; therefore, she is teaching a course in American history this semester. _____

6. Before you learn how to ski down a mountain, you should learn to stop on skis. _____

7. When the doctor saw the patient's pale face and stumbling walk, she immediately ordered more tests. _____

8. Businesses are interested in expanding their operations, yet the economy has slowed. _____

9. Next to the open field is a housing complex, which was built upon a battlefield. _____

10. Despite their efforts to negotiate a settlement, the two companies remained adversaries. _____

11. Jackson has been a professional athlete; currently, he is serving on the board of a sporting goods company. _____

12. The scientist stated the need for environmental legislation; indeed, he demanded immediate action. _____

13. Irene enjoyed her volunteer work at the hospital; as a result, she decided to enter medical school to become a doctor.

   _____

14. The linguist knows many languages; for example, he is fluent in Russian, French, Cantonese, and Italian. _____

15. The senator called for increased spending for space exploration; she primarily wanted to encourage manned space flights to Mars. _____

16. We were watching a scene from *Friday the 13th* when suddenly the doorbell rang. _____

17. Archaeologists recently discovered the remains of an ancient Indian mound; therefore, they requested funds to organize a dig. _____

18. To become a contestant on a game show, you must first apply and then be interviewed. _____

19. Cable television offers more channels and different types of programming; for those reasons, many people have subscribed to this service. _____

20. The strong wind was blowing steadily, and dark clouds were gathering; nevertheless, the foolhardy parachutist planned to jump from the plane. _____

EXERCISE 2   Insert transitional markers that indicate the relationships between ideas in the following sentences. Identify the relationships, and be prepared to explain your choices of transitional markers.

1. Frederick Douglass was born into slavery in 1817; _____, he escaped and later became a strong leader in the fight to end slavery.

   Relationship: _____

2. Charleston offers tourists a number of historical sites; _____, Fort Sumter, site of the first shots of the Civil War, is in Charleston's harbor.

   Relationship: _____

3. The Gulf Stream provides a warm, gentle current; _____ many types of marine life flourish there.

   Relationship: _____

4. During the first hundred years of the United States, seven presidents came from the South; _____, only one president in the 70s and 80s has been from this region.

   Relationship: _____

5. To run for a local political office, you must _____ file a notification of intent; _____, you must develop a campaign strategy and form a staff. _____, you must meet voters to learn their concerns and to become recognized.

   Relationship: _____

6. Many Americans live in urban areas; _____, they yearn for a return to small-town life.

   Relationship: _____

7. Los Angeles offers many attractions for tourists; _____, there is something for everyone to do. _____, there are national parks for hiking, beaches for swimming and surfing, film studios to tour, and museums to see.

   Relationship: _____

8. Good students share several characteristics. _____, they plan their semesters carefully by noting all due dates of examinations and papers. _____, they construct study plans for each week so that they never have to cram. _____, they prepare for each class by reading the assigned materials and completing assignments. _____, they take notes during each class and ask questions.

   Relationship: _____

9. The anthropologist has been studying Indian cultures for several years; _____, she is writing a book on her observations.

   Relationship: _____

10. Concord, Massachusetts, was home to many famous American authors. _____ you can see Thoreau's pond, Emerson's library, and the Alcotts' house.

    Relationship: _____

11. _____ we had finished studying for our

economics test, we headed to the closest restaurant;

_____ we had pizza and soda to celebrate.

Relationship: _____

12. _____ the military offers many benefits to

young adults, they have joined in great numbers. After their

tours are over, these military personnel reap the benefits.

_____, they are eligible to receive money for

college; _____, they have learned many

valuable skills.

Relationship: _____

13. _____ Americans enjoy a unified nation,

each ethnic group celebrates its heritage.

Relationship: _____

14. Ms. Thompson is a dedicated teacher; _____,

she has been named "Teacher of the Year."

Relationship: _____

15. To develop a lawn, you must _____ prepare

the ground by making sure that it is level. To do this, just fill

holes with topsoil. _____, spread fertilizer

and seed on the ground. _____, water each

day for approximately an hour. _____, sit

back and watch the grass grow.

Relationship: _____

16. _____ the Allies required that Germany pay

reparations after World War I and dismantle its army, Ger-

many suffered an economic depression and loss of national

pride. _____, the German people welcomed

a leader who promised to restore Germany to its greatness. This leader was Adolf Hitler.

Relationship: _____

17. Many of America's battlefields are under siege from a new foe—the developer. _____, some portions of sacred battlefields have been plowed under for shopping malls and housing complexes. _____, the Manassas Battlefield in Virginia was saved by an act of Congress from this fate.

Relationship: _____

18. The Smoky Mountains offer many attractions for vacationers; _____, tourists can go white-water rafting down some of the best rivers in the world. _____, they can test the wind currents off the mountains by hang gliding. _____, they can enjoy hiking on the Appalachian Trail.

Relationship: _____

19. Only two decades ago, medical doctors had only X rays to help them in diagnosing patients' problems; _____, today nearly every hospital is equipped with a CAT scanner, and doctors can use ultrasound imaging to diagnose problems. _____, patients receive a more accurate appraisal of their problems.

Relationship: _____

20. As an exercise, swimming offers numerous benefits. _____, swimming is a fun sport and does not cause the types of physical problems associated with other sports. _____, runners are plagued with shin

splints, barking and biting dogs, erratic drivers, sprained

ankles, and twisted knees. _____, swimming

is tranquil and peaceful. _____, swimming

develops all muscle groups; _____, it is the

perfect aerobic exercise.

Relationship: _____

Organizational Patterns

Writers support their ideas in several ways. They might describe, compare or contrast, or provide examples or reasons. They often use identifiable *organizational patterns*, sometimes called rhetorical patterns. These patterns allow readers to understand an author's message quickly.

Consider, for example, the following situation. If you were buying a new car, you would probably consider the features you want most. Next, you would organize this list according to your top priorities: for instance, price, efficiency, options, or performance. With this list in hand, you would visit car dealerships, read reports on cars, and scan the newspaper for car advertisements. As you complete this research, your list becomes increasingly important. The list will enable you to determine the make and model that best suits your needs. Arranged in order of importance, the list focuses your activity. Without such a list, however, you could wander aimlessly through new car showrooms and not be able to decide what to buy or why to buy it.

A similar situation could occur if a writer did not organize material according to a recognizable plan. Writers want their ideas to be understood. Therefore, they choose a particular plan of organization. This section will help you identify five major organizational patterns: chronology, classification, listing, comparison/contrast, and cause/effect. Your recognition of these patterns and their transitional markers enables you to predict the discussion of the main idea. You will have become a conscious reader who understands the relationships between ideas in a paragraph.

Chronology

Many types of writing are organized by time order. For example, the directions for a recipe or instructions for performing a task are arranged in chronological order. By structuring supports according to the sequence of tasks, writers trace actions and events easily for readers. Read the following passage and notice the italicized transitional markers that stress time.

> General James Oglethorpe established Fort Frederica, _now_ in ruins on St. Simon's Island [Georgia], in _1736_ as a fortified settlement to guard British North America's southern frontier. Oglethorpe's community drove back invading Spaniards during the Battle of Bloody Marsh in _1742_. _Then_ peace prevailed until the village burned in _1758_. _Today_ the tabby foundation (made of a concrete mixture of water, sand, lime, and oyster shells) stands in silhouette against the Frederica River while excavated house foundations line the original main street.

Transitional markers (words and dates)

("Coastal Forts Guard History." Southern Living 26 (Feb. 1991): 24.)

In this paragraph, dates serve as transitional markers to provide the history of the fort. In addition, words such as _now, then,_ and _today_ signal different time periods. Not all writers, however, use dates or specific times to indicate chronology. For example, a scientist might describe the steps or stages of a laboratory experiment by using _first, second, third, next,_ or _finally._

EXERCISE 3

Read each of the following paragraphs carefully. Underline the topic sentence. Circle the transitional words that signal the relationship between the details and the main idea of the paragraph.

1. Chinese history is marked by a succession of dynasties until dynastic rule was finally overthrown in the early 1900's. The first historic family to rule the Middle Kingdom (from about 1500 to 1027 B.C.) were the Shang kings. The last Shang king was overthrown by the first Chou king. The Chou dynasty, the longest in Chinese history, lasted for eight centuries (from 1027 to 221 B.C.). It was followed by the shortest and cruelest dynasty, the Ch'in, which in turn was followed by the mighty Han dynasty. These four dynasties—Shang, Chou, Ch'in, and Han—span the first 1,900 years of China's history.

   (Jantzen, Steven, et al. World History. Lexington, MA: Heath, 1988. p. 78.)

2. The population of the world is far greater today than ever before. Population has not expanded at a steady rate, however. For example, in A.D. 476—when Roman control over Europe and the Mediterranean region ended—there were about 200 million people on Earth. By the year 1700, over 12 centuries later, Earth's population had increased 3

times, to about 600 million. Yet, since the start of the
Industrial Revolution—less than 3 centuries ago—the
world's population has grown about 9 times. Today, there
are over 5 billion people in the world, an increase of over
4.4 billion since 1700.

(*Gritzner, Charles*. World Geography. *Lexington, MA: Heath, 1989,
p. 155.*)

Classification

Scientists group the vast number of life forms on this planet by
major characteristics. For instance, reptiles are cold-blooded creatures with scaly skins or hard plates to protect them. Within this
large category, scientists assign similar types of reptiles to smaller
subgroups. Lizards and snakes, for example, are considered as one
type of reptile. This act of dividing a large group of items into units
and then assigning individual elements to each unit is called
classification.

So useful is classification that we constantly employ it. Consider your last grocery list. More than likely, you grouped items by
major categories (such as vegetables, prepared mixes, meats, or
household products). Or you may have organized your list according
to the store's layout (fresh produce, then frozen foods, then dairy
products). With this classification, you would save time by going
down each aisle only once. In either case, you classified items. Read
the following paragraph carefully to learn which groups are
classified.

Classification
of
muscles

> Different kinds of muscles perform different jobs. Some
> muscles are directly under your control. You decide to raise
> your hand in class or to pedal your bicycle. The muscles that
> you control are called <u>*voluntary muscles.*</u> Voluntary muscles
> include nearly all the muscles connected to the bones in your
> arms and legs. Other muscles are not under your direct con-
> trol. These muscles are called <u>*involuntary muscles.*</u> Involuntary
> muscles work automatically. You do not make them move.
> The muscles in your heart and your digestive system are
> involuntary muscles.
>
> (*Bierer, Loretta, et al.* Life Science. *Lexington, MA: Heath, 1987. p. 426.*)

In this paragraph, muscles are classified by their functions: those
you control and those you do not directly control.

When you identify classified groups, look for the basis of the
classification. In other words, look for the distinguishing features
among the groups. These features will help you remember the
different categories.

✏️

EXERCISE 4   Read the following paragraphs carefully. In each paragraph, underline the topic sentence. Circle the different classifications.

1. There are three types of nuclear reactions. In the first
    type, a single nucleus spontaneously releases energy and
    particles are described as being radioactive. All the
    elements from atomic number 88, radium, to atomic
    number 109 are radioactive. In addition, the isotopes of
    many other elements are radioactive. In the second type
    of nuclear reaction, the nucleus of the atom is split. This
    type of reaction is used to provide energy in nuclear power
    plants. In the third kind of nuclear reaction, nuclei join
    together. Their joining releases a tremendous amount of
    energy. It is possible that this type of nuclear reaction
    may become a source of energy for the future. No matter
    what kind of nuclear reaction occurs, the result is always
    the same: One kind of atom is changed into another kind
    of atom.

    *(Nolan, Louise Mary. Physical Science. Lexington, MA: Heath, 1987.
    p. 235.)*

2. Computer systems are grouped into three types. The type
    that usually springs to mind is the mainframe computer—
    a roomful of whirring tape drives, blinking lights, and
    memory banks flanked by printers. A *mainframe* is a full-
    scale computer with large memory storage and complex
    capabilities. The Cray-1 computer (list price, $5 to $15
    million) is one of the world's largest, fastest, and most
    powerful mainframe computers. Such mainframe systems
    are used mainly by large firms and complex government
    and research organizations. A smaller computer system is
    much handier for most small firms. Such a *minicomputer*
    may be able to store enormous amounts of data and
    perform calculations in billionths of a second, just like a
    mainframe. Yet the actual hardware involved fits into the
    corner of a room. The third, and newest, type of computer
    system, the *microcomputer*, consists of a single unit hous-
    ing all memory, processing circuits, and wiring, as well as
    some input-output devices. The microcomputer's great
    advantage is its near-portability. In fact, the Osborne 1—
    pioneer in the field—and the Kaypro, Compaq, and
    Gavilan are truly portable.

    (Meggison, Leon, et al. Business. Lexington, MA: Heath, 1985. p. 429.)

Listing

Writers use lists to establish and prove their points. An author
might state that there are four major rights all American citizens
share or that education is important for three reasons. You can
predict that the author will provide examples for each right or
reason.

Usually, the topic sentence of a paragraph will identify the list an author will discuss. Often, writers will use transitional markers, such as *first, second,* or *third,* to introduce the separate entries in the list. These lists may be arranged in a number of ways. A writer might develop ideas from most important to least important. Or an author might reverse this method and go from the least to the most important. Other lists may be arranged by individual preference. A writer might choose to list examples of movies by their subject matter, their actors, or special effects. Finally, some lists may be random. In other words, no one item in the list is more important than the others.

Read the following paragraph. Note the italicized items in the list of reasons.

List of reasons

There are many reasons why insects are the most successful animals on earth. *First, insects reproduce often and in great numbers.* Suppose all the eggs from one pair of houseflies also reproduced at their fullest rate. The total number of flies descended from the first during one summer would completely fill a large high school, floor to ceiling! *Second,* because they are so varied in size, shape, and color, *some kinds of insects can be found everywhere,* from Antarctica to the African deserts. *Still another reason* for insect success is that different kinds of insects with their specialized mouthparts *can eat almost anything*—from clothing to plaster. Even though an exoskeleton limits their size, *small size is an advantage* to insects. Insects are able to hide easily from enemies, lay eggs in small places, and don't require much food.

(Bierer, Loretta, et al. Life Science. Lexington, MA: Heath, 1987. p. 233.)

In this paragraph, the author uses traditional transitional markers (*first* and *second*) to list reasons. In addition, the word *reason* signals the third item in the list. Finally, the word *advantage* identifies the last reason for insects' success. This list is arranged in an order from first to last. However, it is hard to determine the most important reason. More than likely, the insects' reproductive habits are more crucial to their success than their size, the last reason given. However, the author could have emphasized the order of importance of items in the list. In that case, transitional phrases such as *most important* and *least important* would have been used.

You can easily identify a numbered list. Sometimes, however, lists are not numbered. Writers often signal items in a list by referring to them directly. Read the topic sentence of the following paragraph—the first sentence—to learn what the author lists. You can predict that the author will list the "different consumption patterns" of "each age group." How might this list be developed in the paragraph?

Each age group has different consumption patterns, and marketing managers tend to design their marketing strategies accordingly. For example, <u>young children</u> need baby food, toys, and clothing. <u>School-aged</u> children purchase clothing, sports equipment, records and tapes, school supplies, and cosmetics. The <u>young-adult</u> and <u>middle-aged</u> groups purchase homes, second cars, new furniture, stereo systems, recreational equipment, and sports cars. And, although television commercials would make it appear that <u>golden-agers</u> are interested in only laxatives and high-fiber cereals, parents whose children have left home find themselves free to enjoy travel (including ocean cruises) and other luxuries they may formerly have denied themselves. They may be able to buy retirement homes in New England or the Sun Belt and engage in recreational activities. They're also good customers for goods and services for their children and grandchildren.

Items listed by age group

(Meggison, Leon, et al. Business. *Lexington, MA: Heath, 1985. p. 325.)*

From the controlling idea, you anticipated that the paragraph would discuss the age groups and their purchasing habits. As you can see, the supporting sentences in the paragraph do provide this information. The following age groups are discussed: young children, school-aged children, young-adult and middle-aged groups, and golden-agers. Notice that the entire list of groups and their purchases is introduced by the transitional marker *for example* in sentence two. After this marker, the names of the age groups introduce each new item in the list. Therefore, this list relies little on transitional markers. The list is arranged in a specific order—from those who need little (young children) to those who can spend the most (golden-agers). You can conclude that the list moves from the least important to the most important consumer.

EXERCISE 5   Read the following paragraphs carefully. Underline the topic sentence in each paragraph. Circle transitional markers that signal a list. Finally, determine the order of importance of items in the list. Does the list go from least to most important or from most to least important?

1. After the [Civil] war, the American economy expanded at a rate never before seen in the history of the world. There were three main reasons for this rapid growth. First, the United States had a wealth of raw materials. Second, it had a rapidly growing population to provide workers. (During the 1870s, immigrants arrived at the rate of nearly 2,000 a day.) Third, the nation had a democratic

political system that put few restraints on its business developments.

(Jantzen, Steven, et al. World History. Lexington, MA: Heath, 1988. p. 529.)

Order of Importance: _____

2. As with the civil rights movement for blacks, some of the goals of the 1960s women's movement have now been achieved and incorporated into the fabric of our society. Thanks to the women's movement most American women take for granted that they can control their own fertility. It is now also a part of our culture to see women in higher education, in Olympic sports, and in fields that used to be the exclusive domain of men, such as law, medicine, and engineering. In the holding of political office as well, women, along with blacks, have made great strides. In 1986 nineteen women ran for governor and over eleven hundred were state legislators. As improbable as it was for John Lewis, the former leader of SNCC [Student Nonviolent Coordinating Committee], to imagine that one day he would be a member of Congress and that the Reverend Jesse Jackson would be a presidential candidate, it was a major historic event for Geraldine Ferraro to be the vice-presidential candidate in 1984 on the Democrat ticket.

(Kosof, Anna. The Civil Rights Movement and Its Legacy. New York: Franklin Watts, 1991. p. 72.)

Order of Importance: _____

Comparison/Contrast

You analyze two automobile insurance policies, two or more brands of personal computers, three or more potential jobs. Doing so, you compare and contrast. In the situations above, you would probably look first at the *similarities* of the items to compare them, for many of these items share several similar features. Next, you would look at their *differences* to contrast them. Consider, for instance, two automobile insurance policies. Both would offer the same basic protection required by state law. However, the policies will differ in cost, in the reputation of each company, and in the quality of service. Unlike the comparison, this contrast will give you information that differentiates the policies so that you can choose between them.

Writers, too, analyze items by comparing and contrasting them. When writers compare two political parties, they stress the similarities. When writers contrast two theories of business management, they identify the differences. Often, writers will choose either to compare or to contrast items. Analyze the following paragraph to determine the transitional markers that signal a comparison or contrast.

> An orange grown in Florida usually has a thin and tightly fitting skin, and it is also heavy with juice. Californians say that if you want to eat a Florida orange you have to get into a bathtub first. California oranges are light in weight and have thick skins that break easily and come off in hunks. The flesh inside is marvelously sweet, and the segments almost separate themselves. In Florida, it is said that you can run over a California orange with a ten-ton truck and not even wet the pavement. The _differences_ from which these hyperboles arise will prevail in the two states even if the type of orange is the same. In arid climates, like California's, oranges develop a thick albedo, which is the white part of the skin. Florida is one of the two or three most rained-upon states in the United States. California uses the Colorado River and similarly impressive sources to irrigate its oranges, _but_ of course irrigation can only do so much. The annual _difference_ in rainfall between the Florida and California orange-growing areas is one million one hundred and forty thousand gallons per acre. For years, California was the leading orange state, _but_ Florida surpassed California in 1942, and grows three times as many oranges now. California oranges, for their part, can safely be called three times as beautiful.

Transitional markers

> (McPhee, John. "Oranges: Florida and California.")

In this paragraph, the transitional markers *differences* and *but* signal the contrasts between the oranges grown in the two states. In addition, the author uses the same points to contrast the two oranges. The writer first describes the skin and juice content of the Florida orange. Next, he describes the same features of the California orange and ends with a joke. He names water as the crucial element that causes the differences between these two oranges. Then, he contrasts the amount of water each crop receives. Note that he doesn't contrast the appearance of the Florida orange to the taste of the California orange.

From your analysis of this paragraph, you can identify two features of this organizational strategy. First, a writer will use traditional transitional markers to highlight comparisons and contrasts. Second, a writer will cover the same points about both items.

EXERCISE 6

Read the following paragraphs carefully. In each paragraph underline the topic sentence and number the points made about the items compared or contrasted. Next, circle the transitional markers. Finally, label the organizational pattern as either a comparison or a contrast.

1. The difference between an American cookbook and a French one is that the former is very accurate and the second exceedingly vague. American recipes look like doctors' prescriptions. Perfect cooking seems to depend on perfect dosage. You are told to take a teaspoon of this and a tablespoon of that, then to stir them together until thoroughly blended. A French recipe seldom tells you how many ounces of butter to use to make *crepe suzette*, or how many spoonfuls of oil should go into a salad dressing. French cookbooks are full of unusual measurements such as a *pinch* of pepper, a *suspicion* of garlic, or a *generous sprinkling* of brandy. There are constant references to seasoning *to taste*, as if the recipe were merely intended to give a general direction, relying on the experience and art of the cook to make the dish turn out right.

    (de Sales, Raoul de Roussy. *"Love in America."* Atlantic Monthly. 1953.)

Comparison or Contrast: _____

2. The difference between a brain and a computer can be expressed in a single word: complexity. The large mammalian brain is the most complicated thing, for its size, known to us. The human brain weighs three pounds, but in that three pounds are ten billion neurons and a hundred billion smaller cells. These millions of cells are interconnected in a vastly complicated network that we can't begin to unravel yet. Even the most complicated computer man has yet built can't compare in intricacy with the brain. Computer switches and components number in the thousands rather than in the billions. What's more, the computer switch is just an on-off device, whereas the brain cell is itself possessed of a tremendously complex inner structure.

    (Asimov, Isaac. *"The Difference Between a Brain and a Computer,"* in Please Explain. *Boston: Houghton Mifflin, 1973.*)

Comparison or Contrast: _____

Cause/Effect

When scientists trace the reasons a new disease has emerged, they search for *causes*. For example, a doctor in Lyme, Connecticut, noticed that several of his patients suffered from arthritic conditions. These patients had no previous symptoms of arthritis. Then, the doctor looked for the causes. Eventually, the patients' neighborhoods—all lived near wooded areas—provided the clue to the disease. Deer in these areas carried a tick, the deer tick. This tick, in turn, harbored a virus. This virus was transmitted to people when the ticks bit them. Once the cause of the illness, called Lyme Disease, was identified, doctors could look for cures.

In contrast, environmentalists survey an area contaminated by an oil spill. They look for the results, or *effects*, of the spill on animal and plant life. Oil from refineries was released into the Persian Gulf during the war. Environmentalists noted the immediate effects. Birds coated in oil were unable to survive. Waves of oil blackened beaches and destroyed life there, and the slow-moving tides allowed the oil to remain on the surface. Scientists concluded that these effects would last for years.

Causes lead *to* a situation. Effects come *from* a situation. These actions occur in a chronological order. A writer will often present causes or effects by using transitional markers that indicate time. Other writers may choose to list causes or effects in order of importance. Analyze the following paragraph to determine whether the author names causes or effects. Look at the topic sentence carefully. It will give you a clue to the writer's purpose.

Key term ———→   Many people doubt that they could possibly be _affected_ by television violence. Yet studies show that the _average person becomes more angry_ and irritable when watching television

Effects   violence and experiences a change in mood for the better when the violence stops. _Murders and rapes are likely to be more common,_ and people's _general anxiety and tension higher,_ when they are watching violent programs. The _amount of fighting and beatings around the home and in the world increases._ And many _criminals admit to having gotten their ideas from television._

(Berger, Gilda. Violence and the Media. *New York: Franklin Watts, 1989.* p. 61.)

The topic sentence, the first one in the paragraph, states that television violence affects people. The key word in the opening sentence is *affected.* This word tells you that the author will concentrate on the results of viewing television violence. The rest of the paragraph shows the effects of this violence. People become angry. They feel more tension. Violent crimes and domestic conflict increase. Criminals use television as an educational tool. Using information from studies, the author demonstrates that changes in mood and increases in crime are caused by television violence. The chart on the following page indicates the cause and its effects.

Cause	Effects
violence on television	people grow more angry
	crimes increase
	people are more anxious and tense
	violence gives criminals ideas

To analyze a paragraph that develops causes or effects, look first at the topic sentence. It should point to the development of the paragraph. Look carefully, too, at the organization of causes or effects. Determine whether they are arranged in order of importance or in chronological sequence.

EXERCISE 7

Read the following paragraphs carefully. Underline the topic sentence and circle the transitional markers that signal a cause or an effect. Finally, determine whether the paragraph focuses on causes or effects.

1. On December 1, 1955, an attractive Negro seamstress, Mrs. Rosa Parks, boarded the Cleveland Avenue Bus in downtown Montgomery. She was returning after her regular day's work in the Montgomery Fair—a leading department store. Tired from long hours on her feet, Mrs. Parks sat down in the first seat behind the section reserved for whites. Not long after she took her seat, the bus driver ordered her, along with three other Negro passengers to move back in order to accommodate boarding white passengers. By this time every seat in the bus was taken. This meant that if Mrs. Parks followed the driver's command she would have to stand while a white male passenger, who had just boarded the bus, would sit. The other three Negro passengers immediately complied with the driver's request. But Mrs. Parks quietly refused. The result was her arrest.

(King, Martin Luther, Jr. "A Momentous Arrest," in Stride Toward Freedom. *New York: Harper & Row, 1958. p. 43.*)

Causes or Effects: _____

2. [F]or all its benefits, cholesterol has emerged as a major public-health menace. It is the principal component of plaque, the fatty, yellowish deposit inside the arteries that can build up like rust accumulating in iron water pipes; eventually it may narrow the arteries enough to reduce the flow of blood seriously. The resulting disorder is call atherosclerosis, from *athera* and *sklerosis*, the Greek words for gruel and hardening. When plaque blocks the coronary arteries, often the first result is the intense pain of angina. If the blockage is severe enough, or if a narrowed artery is

totally obstructed by a blood clot, the consequence may be a sudden—and possibly fatal—heart attack. (When plaque blocks arteries in the head and neck, it can cause a stroke, the brain's equivalent of a heart attack.)

(Langone, John. "Cholesterol Is the Culprit." Reader's Digest 125 (June 1984): 180. Condensed from Discover (March 1984).)

Causes or Effects: _____

Mixed Patterns

Many paragraphs develop only one organizational pattern. However, some paragraphs combine patterns. For instance, a paragraph that contrasts two movies might also provide reasons or causes for the differences between the movies. Or the paragraph might list the major differences in order of importance and provide examples. In either case, you may find that transitional markers for all of these patterns—comparison/contrast, cause/effect, and listing—are present. You must then decide on the main pattern for the paragraph.

The paragraph's topic sentence should provide the key. The topic sentence should inform you of the author's purpose. The author may compare or contrast, list information, provide causes or effects, classify, or offer a chronological sequence. By knowing the paragraph's purpose, you should be able to determine the *main* pattern for the paragraph.

Read the following paragraph carefully. Notice the transitional markers and the type of pattern they suggest. What is the main pattern for the paragraph?

Mexico's two most pressing problems are population growth and foreign debt. . . . Nowhere is population growth more visible than in Mexico City. Hoping to find jobs, more than 2,000 people move to the city each day. The metropolitan area is one of the world's largest. It had 18 million residents by the mid-1980's. Experts predict that it will have 26 million residents by the year 2000. Joblessness, vast slums, dense smog, and tangled traffic jams are among the city's problems. The rapid economic growth experienced during the 1970's has slowed. Much of this income came from foreign oil sales. At the time, the nation borrowed heavily from other nations to pay for the development of new industries. It expected that future oil income would help pay these debts. When world oil prices dropped in in 1980's, Mexico found it hard to repay its loans. Today it suffers from one of the world's highest foreign debts.

(Gritzner, Charles. World Geography. Lexington, MA: Heath, 1989. p. 248.)

This paragraph has a number of transitional markers and ideas that signal different organizational patterns.

1. The markers *by the year 2000*, *at the time*, and *today* stress a *chronological* order, as do the dates included in the paragraph.

2. A *cause* is given for the population growth in Mexico City: "Hoping to find jobs, more than 2,000 people move to the city each day."

3. The *effects* of the crowded conditions are listed: "joblessness, vast slums, dense smog, and tangled traffic jams."

4. In addition, *causes* and *effects* of Mexico's foreign debt are discussed.

With these different transitional markers, it may seem hard to determine one main organizational pattern. However, if you analyze the topic sentence, the first one in the paragraph, you learn that Mexico has "two pressing problems." From this topic sentence and its controlling idea, you should conclude that the author will provide a list of those two problems and an explanation of each. Therefore, the main pattern is *listing*.

Use this method of locating transitional markers and the topic sentence when you need to determine the main pattern of a paragraph.

SUMMARY

Writers use transitional markers to ensure that readers understand the connections between ideas or sentences. In paragraphs, writers often use organizational patterns to structure supporting examples and details. By identifying these transitional markers and organizational patterns, you can determine a paragraph's purpose, development, and structure. Thus, you become a conscious reader who understands how ideas are presented.

Read the following paragraphs carefully. In each paragraph, underline the topic sentence and circle all transitional markers. Next, determine the use of the transitional markers in the paragraph. Finally, in the blank at the end of each paragraph, identify the main organizational patterns: chronology, classification, listing, comparison/contrast, or cause/effect. Be prepared to explain how the transitions reinforce this strategy.

1. The first systematic use of animals for handicapped persons was guide dogs for the blind developed in Germany early in this century. More recently dogs are being trained to aid the deaf. Some 30 years ago, in England especially, word began to spread that riding horses offered more than just recreation to physically disabled, retarded or emotionally damaged people. Then, spontaneously, here and there in Europe and North America, animals began to be used in therapeutic situations for the emotionally and mentally handicapped.

   (Curtis, Patricia. "Man's Best Friend . . . And Then Some." Reader's Digest 121(June 1983):23, 25. Condensed from Smithsonian (July 1981).)

Organizational Pattern: _____

2. Mankind is only one species living on earth. Yet we continue to destroy the natural habitat around us, habitat that has provided a home for countless other species for thousands or even millions of years. The prairies of the Great Plains once consisted of many different species of grasses, herbs, and animals. Now, grass, corn, and wheat plus perhaps a few hogs and cattle dominate the ecosystem. Marshes have been filled in to make housing tracts, shopping centers, and industrial parks. Streams have been altered, land has been strip-mined, highways have been constructed, and urban sprawl continues at a frightening rate. All this development removes land from the natural habitat that preceded it.

   (Herda, D. J., and Margaret Madden. Land Use and Abuse. New York: Franklin Watts, 1990. p. 101.)

Organizational Pattern: _____

3. The advent of television, in the decade from 1950 to 1959, presented a major challenge to Hollywood. The industry had to find a way to draw fans away from the novelty of home TV sets and bring them back into the movie houses. The solution involved putting an end to the old image of screen gangsters and introducing new, even more violent heroes. Among some typical examples are the following: the sadistic thug in *The Big Heat* (1953); the violent prisoner in *Riot in Cell Block II*

(1954); the detective more brutal than the criminals he pursues in *Kiss Me Deadly* (1955); and the old-time hood in *Al Capone* (1959).

(Berger, Gilda. Violence and the Media. *New York: Franklin Watts, 1989. p. 81.*)

Organizational Pattern: _____

4. If we think back to the time when our fuel was wood, we gain some appreciation of the benefits fossil fuels have brought. They have also led to vast global industries with immense financial and political power—not just the oil, gas and coal conglomerates but also subsidiary industries dependent on them wholly (autos, airplanes) or partially (chemicals, fertilizers). This dependence means that nations will go to extreme lengths to preserve their sources of supply. Fossil fuels were important factors in the conduct of World Wars I and II. The Japanese aggression at the start of World War II was explained and justified on the grounds that she was obliged to safeguard her sources of oil.

(Sagan, Carl. "Tomorrow's Energy." Parade Magazine (Nov. 25, 1990):10.)

Organizational Pattern: _____

5. The perfectionist [Paul] Simon, 49, and the primitivist [Neil] Young, 45, show just how far a couple of guys from similar backgrounds can diverge. Both were middle-class city kids: Simon's father was a college English teacher in Queens, N.Y., Young's a Toronto sportswriter. Both played rock and roll in their teens: Young's band (like hundreds of others) was called the Squires; Simon and boyhood friend Art Garfunkel, calling themselves Tom and Jerry, had a song called "Hey Schoolgirl" on the national charts when they were still in high school. Both Young and Simon took up acoustic guitar and quasi-poetic songwriting under the influence of Bob Dylan. By the mid-'60s, both were folk-rock stars: Simon and Garfunkel's string of hits began with "The Sound of Silence" in 1965; Young joined the influential band Buffalo Springfield in 1966. And both still love the dumb, innocent rock and roll they grew up on. Simon performed the Del Vikings' 1957 doowop hit "Whispering Bells" with Ladysmith Black Mambazo on his "Graceland" tour and hopes to do the Dells' 1956 "Oh, What a Night" with

his new group; on "Ragged Glory," Young covers Don &
Dewey's 1958 garage-band standard, "Farmer John."

*(Gates, David. "In Praise of Midlife Crisis." Newsweek (14 January
1991):48–49.)*

Organizational Pattern: _____

6. Some people really like chili, apparently, but nobody can
   agree how the stuff should be made. C. V. Wood, twice
   winner at Terlingua [Texas] uses flank steak, pork chops,
   chicken, and green chilis. My friend Hughes Rudd of CBS
   News, who imported five hundred pounds of chili powder
   into Russia as a condition of accepting employment as
   Moscow correspondent, favors coarse-ground beef. Isadore
   Bleckman, the cameraman I must live with on the road,
   insists upon one-inch cubes of stew beef and puts garlic in
   his chili, an Illinois affectation. An Indian of my acquaintance, Mr. Fulton Batisse, who eats chili for breakfast
   when he can, uses buffalo meat and plays an Indian drum
   while it's cooking. I ask you.

   *(Kuralt, Charles. "Chili," in Dateline America. New York: Harcourt
   Brace Jovanovich, 1979:110–111.)*

Organizational Pattern: _____

7. Among other interesting distinctions, coyotes are one of
   the most primitive of living dogs. Also they are, unlike
   ourselves, absolutely native American animals. According
   to fossil remains, a close relative of the contemporary
   coyote existed here two million to three million years ago.
   It in turn seems to have descended from a group of small
   canids that was widely dispersed throughout the world and
   that also gave rise to the jackals of Eurasia and Africa.
   One to two million years ago, a division occurred in
   North America between the coyote and the wolf. Time
   passed. Glaciers advanced and receded. Mammoths, saber-
   toothed tigers and dire wolves (aptly named canids that
   had enormous heads) came and went. Native horses left
   the continent over land bridges, and others returned on
   galleons. Through it all, coyotes remained basically the
   same—primitive in evolutionary terms but marvelously
   flexible, always progressive and innovative—riding out,
   adjusting to and exploiting the changes.

   *(Gilber, Bil. "Outfoxed, So to Speak, by the Wily Coyote." Smithsonian
   21 (March 1991):69.)*

Organizational Pattern: _____

8. [T]he benefits of animals to the handicapped have been
   established, but are pets good for all of us? Interesting
   findings are emerging. For instance, most people with pets
   talk to them. And while there is a rise in blood pressure
   when people talk to each other, there is no rise when they

talk to their pets. This suggests that animal companionship—uncritical, nonjudgmental—has soothing results. Another point: men seem to fondle their pets as much as women do—possibly because they find it one of the few socially acceptable forms of caressing available to them. Such findings will not surprise those of us who are close to our pets, but will perhaps give credibility to what many of us know in our bones.

(*Curtis, Patricia. "Man's Best Friend . . . And Then Some."* Reader's Digest *121 (June 1983):28. Condensed from* Smithsonian *(July 1981).)*

Organizational Pattern: _____

9. The fact is that millions of American women are not doing so well. There is still a major discrepancy in wages. According to the U.S. Census Bureau, women still earn only sixty-one cents for every dollar paid to men. Most gainfully employed women still cluster in the low-paying, sex-segregated jobs like nursing, teaching, or secretarial positions, sometimes called the "pink collar ghetto" jobs. Women and children are the poorest segment of our society, and their number is growing. Three out of five adults officially designated as below the poverty line are women. Half of the poor families in America are headed by a woman. Minority women and their children are the most disadvantaged group in America. Two-thirds of the children in black and Hispanic communities come from households headed by a single woman.

(*Kosof, Anna.* The Civil Rights Movement and Its Legacy. *New York: Franklin Watts, 1991. p. 73.)*

Organizational Pattern: _____

10. To a New Yorker the city is both changeless and changing. In many respects it neither looks nor feels the way it did twenty-five years ago. The elevated railways have been pulled down, all but the Third Avenue. An old-timer walking up Sixth past the Jefferson Market jail misses the railroad, misses its sound, its spotted shade, its little aerial stations, and the tremor of the thing. Broadway has changed in aspect. It used to have a discernible bony structure beneath its loud bright surface; but the signs are so enormous now, the buildings and shops and hotels have largely disappeared under the neon lights and letters and the frozen-custard facade. Broadway is a custard street with no frame supporting it. In Greenwich Village the light is thinning: big apartments have come in, bordering the square, and the bars are mirrored and chromed. But there is still in the Village the lingering traces of poesy, Mexican glass, hammered brass, batik, lamps made of whiskey bottles, first novels made of fresh

memories—the old Village with its alleys and ratty one-room rents catering to the erratic needs of those whose hearts are young and gay.

(White, E. B. "Here Is New York," in Essays of E. B. White. New York: Harper & Row, 1977. p. 130.)

Organizational Pattern: _____

APPLICATION II

Choose two movies or television programs that you like. On a sheet of paper, list your reasons for liking each one. Next, consider the similarities and differences between the two. (You might want to consider the topics each covers, the types of humor, and the variety of characters.) Finally, write a paragraph that compares and contrasts these two movies or programs and submit it to your instructor. Underline your topic sentence and circle any transitional markers you used in the paragraph.

Chapter 7

PREVIEWING AND SKIMMING

Objectives
1. To understand the advantages of previewing.
2. To learn how to preview a textbook.
3. To understand the advantages of skimming.
4. To learn how to skim.

Key Concept
Previewing is not the same as reading. Previewing is a separate, distinct step in the reading process. Likewise, skimming is not a substitute for reading. However, in some situations, skimming is more effective and efficient than reading.

Conscious readers read to learn. When doing so, they must perform some extra tasks. These extra activities improve their comprehension of the material. Previewing and skimming can help readers learn more from written material.

PREVIEWING

It may be difficult to believe that adding another set of actions to your reading can actually improve your understanding. However, one of the added activities, previewing, *does* indeed improve comprehension. At first, previewing material will take you a few extra minutes. Eventually, though, it will make your reading and learning more efficient and effective. Therefore, that extra time will definitely be well spent.

As its name suggests, previewing is looking ahead, a "preview." A movie preview gives the audience a general idea of the movie's plot. It does not summarize the whole movie. Similarly, a textbook preview gives you a general idea of the book's structure and contents. It shows you the ways the text can help you learn about the topic. In effect, a preview gives you control of your learning situation. By recognizing key elements of the topic and understanding the author's purpose, you will know where the course is headed. Therefore, you will be able, to a certain extent, to control your progress through the material.

When to Preview

Preview *before* you begin working on a textbook's individual chapters. Ideally, you should preview the book as soon as you acquire it. A preview familiarizes you with your textbook: its content, structure, and possible study aids. If you preview the whole book before you focus on a specific chapter, you will become accustomed to its format, theme, and purpose. This familiarity will help you deal with each chapter.

When you are comfortable as you read, you are in control. You are not overwhelmed by the material. Previewing gives you control of your learning. Therefore, it is important for you to preview the entire text before you read a single chapter. You want to feel comfortable and confident as you deal with the new information each chapter presents. Your confidence will, in turn, increase your comprehension and learning. So be sure to preview each textbook as soon as you can.

How to Preview

Previewing involves looking ahead at a few key parts of the book. This examination does not require detailed reading of any particular part. Previewing simply helps you to become aware of the book's important elements and its study aids. By examining the book before reading it, you can understand its general topic. You can also recognize the usefulness of some generally overlooked elements. This overall understanding of your text will help you later as you read and analyze each chapter.

When previewing, examine the following major parts of the textbook.

Title Page. Some students ignore this page because they think they already know it. After all, they know the book is their "history text" or "psych text." Unfortunately, simply classifying the text according to its subject area overlooks much information. You should spend a minute examining the title page.

Note the complete title and subtitle. They reveal the subject matter and the author's perspective. Next, notice the author's name and any biographical information, such as academic degrees and university affiliations. Such information can help you decide whether the author is an expert in that field.

Consider the following information from two title pages and the questions that follow.

Earth's Oceans, by Desmond Otaru, B.A., Suffolk Falls Central College

Denizens of the Deep: An Examination of Deep-Ocean Dwellers,
by Priscilla Smith-Jones, Ph.D., Tuscaloosa State University

1. Which book would probably be used in an introductory environmental science course? Why?

2. Which book is more suited to a graduate marine biology course? Why?

3. Which author is probably more knowledgeable about the subject matter? Why?

4. Which author is more likely to be recognized as an expert in the field? Why?

By directing you to the text that suits your needs, your preview can help you be an efficient reader. For expert analysis of a particular life form, you will read Smith-Jones's book. For a general discussion of an ecosystem, you will read Otaru's book. The title page can also give you a clue about your instructor's plan for the course. You can make an educated guess about the topics to be covered and the level of detailed discussion.

Copyright Page. This page follows the title page. Note the date of publication. In some fields, it is essential to learn current ideas and trends. Consider the following texts. Which would be more useful to a student who is a computer science major?

Computers: The Newest Technological Wonders. Copyright 1970.

Pascal and COBOL Programming. Copyright 1991.

Obviously, the student should use the more recent text. Because computer technology has changed so much in the last two decades, the older text is outdated and useless to someone who will work with the current generation of computers.

Preface, Introduction, Foreword, or Abstract. Reading the author's introductory material will probably take two or three minutes. However, the rewards are worth the time. In such introductory material, authors generally explain their reasons for writing the book, their approaches to the topic, and their expectations for readers. By spending a few minutes looking at the introduction, you will gain insight into a text's purpose and ultimate goal. By inference, then, you can recognize your teacher's purpose. Finally, your understanding will help you as you read each chapter and learn more about the topic.

EXERCISE 1   Read the following preface, and then answer the questions.

Preface

My purpose in writing *Introductory Psychology* was to create a highly effective teaching text, a book that supports the efforts of instructors to help their students master the rapidly expanding field of psychology. As a teacher of introductory psychology for many years, and as an educational psychologist concerned about the learning skills of college students, I recognize the importance of textbooks as teaching tools. Even the most experienced teachers need the support of effective textbooks, for college teaching is more challenging today than ever before. I have thus worked hard to write a book that would achieve breadth and depth of coverage, that would be clear and highly readable, and that would stimulate student interest.

An effective teaching text must offer comprehensive, detailed, and accurate coverage. *Introductory Psychology* covers the full range of important topics—from motivations and emotion to attribution theory, from the superego to the brain chemical called endorphin, and from classical conditioning to cognitive restructuring. Each major academic area is surveyed in depth, and important theories and recent findings are discussed.

An effective teaching text must not only cover essential material but also promote mastery of that material. This book was written to help students at all levels master the important facts, concepts, and theories of psychology. It was designed to be easy to read, with clear definitions, explanations, and examples. Chapter glossaries, chapter summaries, and interim summaries aid student learning. Finally a unique chapter on academic learning and retention helps students identify their study problems and teaches them how to apply basic psychological principles, in order to become more efficient and independent learners.

An effective teaching text must stimulate the natural interest of students in human behavior, so that they will want to read about it on their own. I believe students will find this book meaningful because of its discussion of research and principles on topics of great personal and social significance—for example, career choice, consumer psychology, crime, sex, and the psychology of energy conservation. In addition, checklists and inventories are placed throughout the book to help students connect the textual material to their own lives.

Introductory Psychology is intended for use in courses in introductory or general psychology and for students who are psychology majors as well as for students who will never take another psychology course. It was designed to be a flexible text, one that can fit a variety of courses and course organizations. The order of chapter assignments can be altered to fit an instructor's own preferred sequence of topics. For those instructors who teach courses with an experimental emphasis, research methods and statistics are presented in the Appendix.

No book stands alone, unrelated to previous works. This book has benefited from my earlier text, the second edition of *Psychology: An Introduction to Human Behavior*; some of the chapters of the current book are based on chapters of the earlier one. However, the present book is distinctly different and has an identity of its own. *Introductory Psychology* has much more depth and breadth of coverage, a much stronger research base, and a more traditional organization.

(Holland, Morris K. Introductory Psychology. *Lexington, MA: Heath, 1981.*)

1. What is the author's purpose in writing this text?

   _____

   _____

2. List three characteristics of an effective teaching textbook.

   _____

   _____

3. In which courses can this textbook be used?

   _____

   _____

4. What learning aids are included in each chapter?

   _____

   _____

You can see by your answers to the exercise questions that reading the preface provided a thorough introduction to the text. This preface emphasizes the qualities of an effective textbook. The author stresses learning from the material. So he has included several learning aids in each chapter. The author obviously wants his readers to be able to understand the material easily and to remember it. Likewise, the teacher (who, after all, selected the book) wants the material to be understandable to the students.

Be sure to read any introductory material when you preview a textbook. As you discovered from Exercise 1, that material can give you a sense of purpose for the course. It can also help you to understand your instructor's goal.

Table of Contents. Never omit a text's table of contents from your preview. The table of contents outlines the book for you. It provides complete information on what material is covered, in what order, and in how much detail. It gives you useful knowledge about the book's structure and contents. By looking at the table of contents, you can anticipate and later recall the important topics and essential material. You can also use it to help you structure your notes.

EXERCISE 2

Examine the table of contents on pages 181–182, and then answer the following questions.

1. Through how many stages do children progress as they develop?

   _____

   _____

   _____

2. What kind of factors influence life before birth?

   _____

   _____

   _____

3. Which five aspects of child development are studied during infancy and the preschool years?

   _____

   _____

   _____

4. Why do you think language development is omitted during the middle childhood years and adolescence?

_____

_____

_____

5. Does this text focus only on typical children? Explain your answer.

_____No_____

_____

_____

BRIEF CONTENTS

Zigler and Finn-Stevenson. Children: Development and Social Issues.
Lexington, MA: Heath, 1987. pp. v–vi.

Study Aids. Be aware of additional study aids as you preview the text. Not all books have them, but you can be on the lookout for the following aids:

1. *Lists of charts, graphs, maps, or illustrations.* These lists direct you to the visual aids offered in each chapter. They can help you locate specific items quickly. You do not have to read through the lists. Simply note whether or not your book provides them.

2. *Index.* The index, located at the back of the book, lists all the topics discussed in the text and tells their page numbers. While you preview, check to see if your text has this study aid. If it does, you can use the index to identify specific pages on which a useful piece of information can be found. You can also use the index as a source for a research topic.

3. *Glossary.* A glossary is a dictionary of important terms. It identifies and defines key terms and concepts used in the text. Text glossaries are usually found either at the end of each chapter or at the end of the book.

4. *Bibliography.* The bibliography is the list of sources the author used when writing. It may also include books and articles related to the text subject and recommended by the author. Obviously, you do not need to read each citation. Merely note whether your text has a bibliography and its location. In some books, the list is at the end of each chapter. In others, it is at the end of the book. You can use your textbook's bibliography as a starting point for a research paper. Use the author's list and check the sources because some of the material may be useful to you. If it is, then you can save time and effort.

5. *Appendix.* This material, added or "appended" to the end of the book, contains supplementary information. This material is important, but not relevant to any one specific chapter. For instance, an appendix might contain additional charts, graphs, and tables. Another might provide intriguing biographical information about central characters. Examine the appendix carefully to determine its contents and usefulness.

Previewing a textbook will probably take no more than ten minutes. That time is well invested. Previewing directs you through the text. It gives you control over the reading material. With direction and control, you can improve your understanding of the material. Therefore, be sure to preview each of your textbooks as soon as you can. (Definitely preview before you begin working on an individual chapter.)

EXERCISE 3   The following pages (pp. 185–198) contain the title and copyright pages, preface, and table of contents from a business writing textbook. Preview these key parts, and answer the following questions.

1. a. Complete title: _____

   Based on the title, what do you think is the purpose of the

   book? _____

   _____

   _____

   b. Authors: _____

   c. Qualifications of the authors: _____

   _____

   d. Publisher: _____

   e. Copyright date: _____

2. a. What perception provides the first breakthrough to effective

   communication? _____

   _____

   _____

   b. What is the basic premise of this text? _____

   _____

   _____

3. Based on the preface, list some unique features and innovative

   approaches of this book. _____

   _____

   _____

   _____

COMMUNICATING IN BUSINESS TODAY

RUTH G. NEWMAN

with

MARIE A. DANZIGER
Massachusetts Institute of Technology

and

MARK COHEN
Digital Equipment Corporation

D. C. HEATH AND COMPANY
Lexington, Massachusetts   Toronto

Published simultaneously in Canada.

Printed in the United States of America.

International Standard Book Number: 0-669-06344-4

Library of Congress Catalog Card Number: 86-81357

Acquisitions Editor: Paul Smith
Developmental Editor: Holt Johnson
Production Editor: Holt Johnson
Designers: Victor A. Curran, Bruce Terzian
Production Coordinator: Michael O'Dea
Photo Researcher: Martha Shethar
Text Permissions Editor: Margaret Roll

Acknowledgments

Russell Baker, "Little Red Riding Hood Revisited."
From *The New York Times*, January 13, 1980. Copyright
© 1980 by The New York Times Company. Reprinted
by permission.

Dianna Booher, "You Are What You Write—
Model Memos for All Occasions." *From Send Me A
Memo* by Dianna Booher. © 1984 by Dianna Booher.
Reprinted by permission of Facts on File, Inc., New
York.

Jerr Boschee, "The Anatomy of an Interview."
From IABC Communication World, April 1985. Re-
printed courtesy of The International Association of
Business Communicators and Jerr Boschee.

David W. Ewing, "A Sinister Disease Invades the
Business World." *Los Angeles Times*, January 12, 1979.
Reprinted by permission.

Gail Godwin, "The Watcher at the Gates." *New
York Times Book Review*, January 9, 1977. Copyright ©
1977 by The New York Times Company. Reprinted by
permission.

Carol A. Gosselink and Suzanne J. McKinley,
"What You Don't Say." From *Communicator's Journal*,
March/April 1964.

Carole Howard, "When A Reporter Calls . . ."
From *Communicator's Journal*, May/June 1984.

Terry Marotta, "Speechless." From *The Boston
Globe*, April 17, 1985. Reprinted by permission of Terry
Marotta, a syndicated columnist whose work appears in
newspapers throughout New England.

Eugene McCarthy and James Kilpatrick, "The
Gobbledegook." From *A Political Bestiary* by Eugene Mc-
Carthy and James Kilpatrick. Copyright © 1978 by
McGraw-Hill Book Company. Reprinted by permission.

Jonathan Newman, "Today, Tomorrow, and Always: Office Automation." Reprinted by permission.

Ruth G. Newman, "Case of the Questionable
Communiqués." From *Harvard Business Review*,
November/December 1975. Reprinted by permission.

Herbert Popper, "Six Guidelines for Fast, Func-
tional Writing." Reprinted by special permission from
Chemical Engineering, June 30, 1969. Copyright © 1969
by McGraw-Hill, Inc., New York, NY 10020.

Ralph Proodian, "A Strong Voice Is a Valuable
Managerial Asset." Published in *The Wall Street Journal*,
January 31, 1983. Copyright © 1983. Reprinted by per-
mission of Ralph Proodian, Ed.D., Assistant Professor of
Speech, Brooklyn College, CUNY.

Carl B. Rogers and Richard E. Farson, "Active
Listening." The University of Chicago, Industrial Relations Center.

The Royal Bank of Canada, "Imagination Helps
Communication." The Royal Bank of Canada 1960.
Reprinted with the permission of the Royal Bank of
Canada.

Susan E. Russ, "A Bureaucrat's to Chocolate Chip
Cookies." Special to *The Washington Post*.

William Safire, "The Fumblerules of Grammar."
From *The New York Times Magazine*, November 7, 1979.
Copyright © 1979 by The New York Times Company.
Reprinted by permission.

Paul S. Swensson, "Keys to Good Writing." From
Women in Communications Journal, *Matrix*, fall 1977.
Reprinted with permission of Women in Commu-
nications, Inc. from the *Matrix* magazine.

Marvin H. Swift, "Clear Writing Means Clear
Thinking Means . . ." From *Harvard Business Review*,
January/February 1973. Reprinted by permission.

PREFACE

During the past twenty years or more, I have been a student, a teacher, a writer, manager of several communication functions within business firms, and more recently an entrepreneurial consultant in business communication. For most of my professional life, therefore, while preoccupied with words and their effects, I have shuttled between two separate worlds. The first of these is the academic world of students, teachers, and scholarship; the second is the world that students, and even some teachers, call the "real world" — the marketplace where business transactions take place.

For most students and for many employees, however, the latter world is not very *real* at all. They harbor an abiding and contagious suspicion that business has a special mystique. They expect that the business environment will require them to put on hold their commonsensical perceptions about how to make people respond well to their ideas and words. If they are industrious and ambitious, they are prepared at the outset to master a whole new set of rules about writing, speaking, and even thinking. For the most part, they are wrong in this expectation.

The first breakthrough in learning to communicate well is achieved with the perception that communication begins with knowing who one is, whom one is addressing, and what one hopes to accomplish. Further success is almost guaranteed if one aims to be as logical, persuasive, and personable as one's personal endowments permit . . . and then some.

A basic premise of this text is that all writers must work hard to master the traditional tools of their trade. And even when they have the requisite knowledge in place, the writing process is always highly individualized, filled with starts and stops, and pressing endlessly towards a moving goal. In a real sense, writers must rediscover a successful writing process with each new effort to communicate.

Communicating in Business Today makes no bones about the fact that confidence and skill in communicating are acquired through study, strenuous effort, and constant practice. And it makes it clear that for student writers, adding to their arsenal can be a strenuous and time-consuming enterprise. But, through many realistic cases and examples, it also strongly implies that the business environment rewards those individuals who possess these skills in abundance.

Key Features

In designing this text we have aimed to provide students with pathways to learning that, while strenuous, are also interesting and compelling. We have tried to challenge and motivate students to discover their best selves and to exert their individual powers to resolve problems that they typically will encounter in the workplace. Moreover, because *Communicating in Business Today* avoids cookbook solutions and stresses the uniqueness of each writer and each business situation, it challenges instructors to help students develop their special abilities.

Among the text's distinctive features are the following:

Process/Product Case Method. A new approach to the case method stimulates rapid learning:

- Although many opportunities are provided for students to think independently, they are first carefully trained in audience and situation analysis. At frequent intervals, both an appropriate process for resolving the case problem and examples of the resulting memo, letter, or report are discussed in detail.
- Cases mirror real workplace tasks; moreover, they place readers in roles that are appropriate to the professional aims and aspirations of entry-level employees across a broad spectrum of industries and business functions.

Readability and Accessibility. This text is written in a style that aims to emulate what it teaches:

- We have tried to speak directly to our readers in a clear, candid, conversational style.
- Both style and content reflect a close analysis of our reading audience; an important objective has been to help our readers perceive that they are in touch with an instructor who understands and to a great extent shares their attitudes and perspectives.

Exceptionally Broad Coverage. Along with close attention to all aspects of business writing, the text provides extensive coverage of the following critical topics:

- *The job campaign,* from preliminary brainstorming, résumés and cover letters, through the acceptance letter.
- *The preparation and use of graphics* for business writing and speaking, with multiple examples.
- *Collaborative writing efforts,* in a full chapter devoted to "The Politics of Report Writing."
- A detailed list of *business research sources,* with discussion of available on-line data bases.

- *Planning, preparing, and delivering the spoken presentation.*
- *Business meetings,* from the perspective of both leader and participant.
- *International communications.*
- *Office automation technology* and its benefits.

Realistic, Practical Discussion Problems and Tasks. The text includes an extremely broad selection of chapter-end exercises.

- *Discussion Problems*
  These do not simply invite students to regurgitate the chapter's content. Many are case related; others help students to share their own communication strategies with their peers.
- *Tasks*
  Many are related to the preceding discussion problems—allowing students to implement the strategies they have defended in discussions. Others provide opportunities for practicing the techniques demonstrated in the chapter.

Innovative Approaches. Although there are many innovations in our text, the following are perhaps most notable:

- *The Dialogues*
  Four dialogues, or short plays, vividly reveal how writers tackle business communication. Based on actual recorded transcripts, they show a group of students analyzing each other's writings. Their discussions provide exceptional insights into the minds of writers and editors. Each dialogue is based on an interesting and challenging case. Each is followed by additional student letters or memos to discuss and revise.
- *Dynamic Treatment of Proposals and Reports*
  In confronting an important contemporary issue, an entry-level employee helps resolve a critical problem at his company. As he masters essential communication skills, the text covers in detail research techniques (including use of on-line data bases), letter proposals and formal proposals, formatting, and all topics relevant to preparing a major report.
- *Unique Application of Rhetorical Modes to Business Writing*
  The "Patterns of Relationship" chapter provides new insights into methods by which writers create logical structure. Using real-world examples, the text clearly shows that the relationships we deal with most frequently in business writing are natural and familiar: space, time, comparison, analysis, cause/effect, and problem/solution.
- *Traditional and New Techniques for Prewriting and Planning*
  Not only the traditional outline but also modern methods taught to executives by business consultants and trainers are explained. Students are helped to see planning as a natural and inevitable part of the writing process.

CONTENTS

**DIALOGUE III
Applying for a Job**

**13   The Politics of Report Writing:
Roles and Responsibilities**   328

**14   Report Writing I, Process & Product:
The Proposal**   344

15 Report Writing II, Process & Product: The Report 380

16 Graphic Aids for Reports and Presentations 428

4. Do the authors provide any additional readings on topics of concern or interest to the business community? If so, list them.

   _____

   _____

   _____

5. What study aids does this text include? _____

   _____

   _____

SKIMMING

Like previewing, skimming is a survival skill for college. Skimming is another form of surveying, a way of getting an overview of material before actually reading it. Sometimes skimming can be used as a middle step in the reading process, between previewing and reading analytically. It can also be an independent process, used for its own purposes.

Look at these different situations:

1. For a research paper, you have selected five books and several articles.

   Will you be able to read them all?

   Should you analyze them all?

2. You haven't yet read the two chapters your sociology instructor assigned for the next class. You have 45 minutes until class begins, but no one can read 95 pages in that time.

   What can you do?

   What should you do?

3. An A student in high-school math, you are just beginning a college calculus course. The first unit of the textbook reviews algebra, geometry, and trigonometry.

   Should you read that unit carefully and analytically?

In each of the above examples, your best course of action would be to *skim* the material.

Purpose of Skimming

Whether you're dealing with a chapter, a unit, or a whole book, skimming quickly provides an outline of the material. In other words, you skim to gain a general understanding of reading material in a short amount of time. When you skim, you do not carefully analyze the chapter or article. In fact, you will not completely understand it. Complete understanding is the goal of analytical reading. Skimming simply *familiarizes* you with the material in the shortest amount of time.

Imagine that you want to attend a town meeting about the proposed construction of a nuclear-power plant in your area. After skimming an article on nuclear power, you will not be qualified to present a logical argument concerning the proposed construction. However, you will be able to listen to and understand both sides of the controversy. Your skimming will enable you to relate each speaker's comments to the general concept of the proposed construction.

When to Skim

Skimming's goal is familiarity with the material, not detailed understanding. When you skim, you make a trade: complete comprehension for speed. You should skim under the following conditions:

1. You need to know the general outline of the reading material.

2. You need to recognize the material's topic, thesis, and supporting ideas.

3. You need the information fast.

After skimming the article, you can then decide whether you need or want to read it analytically.

Look again at the three situations mentioned earlier:

1. *The research paper.* You should skim all your possible sources first because they might not be relevant to your thesis. Then, you can read and later note any useful source.

2. *Two chapters in 45 minutes.* Although skimming will not help you participate in a class discussion, it will help you understand the teacher's lecture. It will enable you to be an active listener.

3. *High-school math review.* Because you understood high-school math so well, you probably just need to review some general concepts. You do not need a thorough discussion of the subject. Therefore, skim Unit One.

Remember: Skim when you need to understand the material quickly. If the material is important, you can read it analytically at another time.

Skimming and Previewing

How does skimming differ from previewing? Actually, skimming is an extension of previewing. An intermediate step in the reading process, skimming provides more information than previewing does. Skimming gives a general outline of a piece. After skimming an essay, you should recognize the author's thesis and reasons for the opinion. Although skimming does not give a complete analysis of material, it allows you to process information more thoroughly than does previewing.

Advantages and Disadvantages of Skimming

To skim, you read less. You do not read the entire article or chapter; you read only selected parts. Because you are "reading" less, you are "reading" faster. This speed is the primary advantage of skimming. Ideally, your skimming rate will be twice your average reading rate. For example, if you read at 250 words per minute, then you should skim at 500 words per minute.

Unfortunately, skimming does have a disadvantage: decreased comprehension. Because you do not read the entire piece, you can not understand the whole essay. Some details, some fine points of an argument, and some statistics or examples must be omitted during skimming. Consequently, you will not be able to use these details. You will not be able to answer questions about them. When skimming, you will probably comprehend only about 50 percent of the material. Usually, when you read, you comprehend 70 to 80 percent. However, when you skim material, you obviously believe that the increased speed is worth the decreased comprehension. For instance, if you skim a chapter just before class, you have decided that it is better to understand a little about some of the material than to be totally unfamiliar with it.

How to Skim

The skimming process requires you to read completely, and as quickly as possible, the following parts of the material:

1. The introductory paragraphs (usually the first and second ones in an essay or chapter),

2. The first sentence in each body paragraph (usually the paragraph's topic sentence, which identifies its main idea), and

3. The concluding paragraphs (usually the last two in an essay).

Because your goal is to understand the article's general ideas and organization, you need to recognize its thesis and supports. Therefore, you read the introduction. The author usually states the main idea there. Likewise, in the conclusion, the writer will generally restate the thesis or summarize the message. By reading these two parts, you will be using the essay's structure to help you understand the writer's arguments.

In a well-written essay, the body paragraphs provide support for the author's thesis. Consequently, by reading each paragraph's topic sentence, you can recognize the essay's overall organization. You can also notice how the author develops and supports the main idea. Admittedly, this technique assumes that the first sentence of each body paragraph functions as its topic sentence. This is not always so. However, do not spend time determining whether each first sentence is actually a topic sentence. Such indecision wastes time and defeats your purpose. Just assume that the topic sentence of each body paragraph is its first sentence—in most cases, it will be.

Skimming Check

After skimming, you should be able to accomplish three tasks:

1. State the author's thesis and major supporting ideas. (You should be familiar with the selection even if you cannot refer to its statistics and examples.)

2. Understand the author's viewpoint.

3. Decide whether you need to read and analyze the material. The decision to read or not will be based on the reason you skimmed the piece in the first place. For instance, if an article is a possible source for a research paper, you skim to determine its relevance to your topic. If it is relevant, then you should read, analyze, and take notes on it. If it is not relevant, then it would be inefficient to read the entire selection. In such a case, skimming will have saved you from reading unnecessary material. You can be a more efficient reader by skimming another source as you continue your research.

Skimming is a useful reading technique. There are many times when you will need to become familiar with new material quickly. After skimming the selection, you will know enough about its ideas and arguments to understand discussions on the topic and to respond to general questions. Consequently, skimming can truly help you survive at college.

EXERCISE 4   To practice this skill, skim the essay "The Nazca Drawings." Then answer the questions that follow the reading.

The Nazca Drawings

DANIEL COHEN

No one knows who first discovered the huge drawings in South America's coastal desert. Travelers walking through the drab and inhospitable region would have notice strange "lines" in the sand. But they could make nothing of these lines.

When airplanes began to fly regularly over the coastal desert, the pilots noticed that the desert floor seemed to be covered with huge drawings. Some were geometric figures like rectangles and squares. More fantastic were the figures of birds, spiders, monkeys, whales, and a host of strange-looking creatures that it has been impossible to identify. There were also straight lines that ran for hundreds of meters, but seemed to begin and end nowhere. It looked almost as though a giant had been carelessly doodling on the desert floor.

The "lines" that had been seen by people on the ground were a part of these drawings. The drawings themselves were so large that their true shape could not be made out from the surface. Thus the existence of the drawings had gone unnoticed for centuries.

These colossal drawings are located in the desert some 400 kilometers south of Lima, the capital of Peru. They are scattered in an area about 95 kilometers long and between 8 and 16 kilometers wide. Most of the drawings are found on plateaus between two valleys, the Ica and the Nazca. Practically every flat spot in this region contains some sort of drawing.

Before we can discuss who made these drawings, why and how, we have to take a closer look at the place in which they are located. The desert runs for some 3,200 kilometers along the coast of South America. It covers much of the coastline of Peru. It is quite narrow, varying in width between one and 40 kilometers.

The desert, made up of high plains and low hills, rolls back from the coast of the Pacific Ocean. The great chain of the Andes mountains rises steeply from its eastern edge.

A unique set of geographical circumstances has created this desert. A cold ocean current flows along part of the South American coast. The current is like an icy river cutting through the tropical waters of the Pacific. It effectively blocks rain from falling along the coast. Only when the moist ocean air is pushed up over the mountains is it able to dump its accumulated moisture as rainfall. The eastern slopes of the Andes which face away from the ocean are covered with a lush tropical rain forest. But on the coast is the desert, in which it almost never rains.

For much of the year this desert is cloudless and extremely hot. One traveler noted that it was "hot enough to boil your brains." Between May and November the cold current in the Pacific runs even colder. This creates a fog which often shrouds the desert. But still no rain falls. It is because it almost never rains in this desert that the lines and drawings have survived at all, for they are quite fragile. The actual construction of the lines and figures was simple.

The floor of the desert is covered by a layer of dark rocks and pebbles. To make the lines the surface pebbles were removed to expose the lighter rocks and soil beneath them. The surface material was then piled in a uniform way on both sides of the line. From the air the figures might seem etched by a light colored line, which itself is outlined by two darker filaments. When the sun is low the little piles of pebbles cast long shadows which make the outlines of the drawings clearer.

If there were heavy rains on the Peruvian coast these figures would have been washed away centuries ago. But scientists have estimated that they have lasted some 1,500 years already. . . .

Some people have said that these lines are "Inca roads." The region in which they lie was at one time part of the great Inca Empire. But they are not roads at all because they do not lead anywhere, and they were made centuries before the Incas ever appeared in Peru. In fact, an Inca road runs right through some of the figures. The Incas apparently were not interested in them. The descendants of the people who made the lines were probably subjects of the Incas. . . .

So we only know in a general way who built the lines and when. We say that they are at least 1,500 years old. Scientists got that date through a lucky accident. At the end of one of the lines they found an old tree stump. No trees grow in this region, so the stump obviously was brought there. Its placement at the very end of a line made scientists believe that the line builders used it as some sort of marker when they were making the lines.

The age of a piece of wood can be determined by a technique called radio-carbon dating. The tests indicated the tree had been cut 1,500 years ago, probably while the lines were being built. An age of 1,500 years also fits in with other things that we know about the people who lived on the fringes of the desert.

About 2,000 years ago a number of peoples flourished near the desert. They lived mostly in the valleys on the desert's eastern side. These valleys were formed by rivers and streams carrying water down to the sea from the torrential storms that drench the rain forests on the other side of the Andes. The water deposits fertile silt in the valleys. By employing painstakingly careful methods of irrigation, crops can be grown in these valleys.

Racially and culturally all the people who settled in these desert valleys came from the same basic stock. But the valleys were separated from one another by long stretches of desert, so people did not go back and forth too often. As a result each region developed its own individual way of life.

In the northern valleys were a people we call the Mochicas. They were experts at making pottery. In the center valleys were the Paracas, who were superbly skilled at embroidery and weaving. In the South between the Ica and the Nazca valleys were the people scientists call the Ica-Nazcas. They made excellent pottery and fabrics, but they are now most well-known for the lines and figures they made in the desert. Some of the designs found in their pottery and weaving have been repeated on a gigantic scale in the desert figures.

As we have seen, the lines and figures themselves were fairly easy to etch into the surface of the desert. But first the figures would have to have been drawn as scale models, then traced in final form on the desert floor. So the moving and piling of all those rocks and stones, not to mention the time that it took to lay out the figures in the first place, must have involved thousands of hours of work in the broiling sun.

These figures must have been important to those who made them. They were important enough for the Ica-Nazca people to take a large number of laborers away from the hard job of growing food and send them into the desert to create these giant figures. What could their significance have been?

An interesting, but controversial, theory was advanced by Dr. Paul Kosok, a historian from Long Island University. Dr. Kosok was studying the peoples of ancient Peru. He and his wife went to Peru in 1941. On June 22 the couple happened to be in the desert looking at the lines and figures. In the southern hemisphere, June 22 is the day of the winter solstice, the shortest day of the year. Dr. Kosok and his wife followed one of the lines up a small mesa. As they stood pondering the significance of the lines the sun began to set.

To their surprise the setting sun touched the horizon right over one of the lines at whose base they stood. Quite suddenly Dr. Kosok had an inspiration that these lines were part of a gigantic system of astronomical calculation. Later he wrote, "the largest astronomy book in the world seemed spread out before us." He assumed that if the Ica-Nazca priests stood at certain spots on the lines and watched where the sun set or rose they would be able to tell what time of year it was, just as he and his wife had seen the sun set right over a particular line on the shortest day of the year.

Dr. Kosok was pressed for time, and he had to leave Peru before he could do much work on his theory. He had always planned to return to continue his work, and he did so briefly years later. But he died long before his project was completed. Others have taken up this theory and attempted to work it out more exactly.

Some of the things that we know about the civilizations of ancient Peru make the desert calendar theory attractive. First the ancient Peruvians were farmers, so exact knowledge of the change of seasons would have been important to them. Still they would not have needed such an elaborate method of telling the seasons to know when the proper planting time was.

Another possible reason for building a vast desert calendar was that the Ica-Nazca people probably lived in a theocracy—a society that was ruled by priests. In most Native South American civilizations the main duty of the priests was to study the movements of the sun, moon and stars. The people of South and Central America were fascinated by time. The date upon which an event took place was of paramount significance. These Native Americans developed a calendar that was better than any used by the civilizations of Europe and Asia. So if any people in the world were going to lavish a great deal of time and effort on building a great calendar, the civilizations of South America were the ones.

Not all of the scientists who have studied the lines and figures of the Nazca region agree that they were part of a desert calendar. They raise many of the same objections that were raised to a similar theory regarding Stonehenge.

No astronomical theories can possibly account for all of the tracings in the desert. Some of these lines may really have been the outlines of roads, or more accurately ceremonial avenues along which religious processions passed. The rectangles and some of the other geometric figures could have been sacred enclosures, in which the rituals of this deeply religious society were performed.

Most puzzling of all are the drawings of surrealistic spiders, whales, birds, monkeys, and other figures. What could their purpose have been? Even if people stand upon a high platform, they can get only a partial glimpse of the drawings. Usually they would be completely unable to make out what these figures were supposed to be. Only with the invention of the airplane have people been able to see the huge figures in their entirety.

The probable answer is that the figures were not meant for the eyes of humans. They were meant to be seen only by the gods of the Ica-Nazca people who lived in the sky.

Cohen, Daniel, "The Nazca Drawings" in Time and Beyond *by Robert B. Ruddell and Sam Leaton Sebesta. (Boston: Allyn and Bacon, 1978) Excerpts from pp. 21–31.*

1. What are the Nazca drawings? _____

_____

_____

2. Why are the drawings interesting or intriguing? _____

_____

_____

3. Where are the drawings located? _____

_____

_____

4. Name one theory that tries to explain the purpose of the

drawings. _____

_____

5. What is a theocracy? _____

_____

_____

6. Does any one theory adequately explain all the drawings?

_____

_____

_____

7. According to the author, for whom were these drawings most

likely made? _____

_____

_____

EXERCISE 5

To practice this skill further, skim the section of a history chapter reprinted on pp. 210–218. Then answer the questions that follow the selection.

1. India flourished under whose rule? _____

_____

2. Name a famous dramatist. _____

_____

3. List some scientific advances made in India. _____

_____

4. Did the Hindus and Muslims meet peaceably? _____

_____

5. Who destroyed Delhi? _____

_____

6. Who founded the Mughal dynasty? _____

_____

7. Name two flaws associated with the Mughal dynasty.

_____

8. Explorers from which country first reached India by a sea route? _____

_____

Chapter **13**

300 - 1700

Civilizations of India and Southeast Asia

Although the Taj Mahal was built by a conquering dynasty in the 1600's, it has become a symbol of India. The four outer towers are minarets, from which leaders call Muslims to prayer.

1. **India flourished under the Guptas.**

2. **Mughals ruled India in splendor.**

3. **Kingdoms arose in Southeast Asia.**

Shah Jahan, the ruler of northern India, was one of the wealthiest kings in the world. He was also a heartbroken man. In 1631, after 19 years of marriage, his beloved wife, Mumtaz Mahal (moom-**TAHZ** mah-**HAHL**), had died. She had given her husband 13 children but died giving birth to the fourteenth. The grieving monarch commanded that a tomb be built "as beautiful as she was beautiful."

Those events were the beginning of the romantic story of the Taj Mahal. Fine white marble and jewels were gathered from many parts of Asia and brought to a spot near Agra. For 22 years, 20,000 workers labored on Shah Jahan's last gift to his queen.

The ivory-white beauty of India's greatest monument is difficult to describe. Artists have praised it for its perfect proportions. Visitors have marveled at the way the towering dome and four minarets seem to change colors as the sun moves across the sky. Inside are thousands of carved marble flowers inlaid with tiny sapphires, bloodstones, rubies, and lapis lazuli.

Shah Jahan dreamed of building an identical tomb of black marble for himself nearby. The two tombs were to be linked by a bridge of polished silver, a symbol of the royal couple's love. However, the black tomb was never built. One of Shah Jahan's sons revolted and imprisoned his aged father not far from the Taj Mahal. When the old emperor died in 1666, a mirror was found in his prison room. It was angled so that the dying man could gaze at the reflection of the Taj Mahal. When he died, Shah Jahan was buried in the Taj Mahal next to the bejeweled casket of Mumtaz Mahal.

During their lives, Shah Jahan and Mumtaz Mahal prayed to Allah, the Muslim name for God. In the 1600's, Islam was fairly new to India. The religion of ancient India had been Hinduism (pages 70–72), not Islam. At the point where Chapter 4 ended, with the fall of the Maurya dynasty in 180 B.C., the prophet Muhammad (founder of Islam) had not been born.

In this chapter, we must go a long way back in time to a dynasty of Hindu rulers called the Guptas. These powerful kings lived more than 1,000 years before the building of the Taj Mahal. We will see how Hinduism developed during this early period. Then we will see how Islamic Turks swept in from central Asia, slaughtering Hindus and destroying their temples. These conquerors brought the Muslim religion to India.

In the 1,400 years described in this chapter, there was much violence. However, there was also much splendor and beauty. The marble domes and minarets of the Taj Mahal stand as a monument to the achievements of these years.

India flourished under the Guptas. 1

In India, 500 years of disunity followed the end of the Mauryan dynasty (page 76) in 180 B.C. In northern India, waves of invaders continued to arrive from Persia, Afghanistan, and the plains

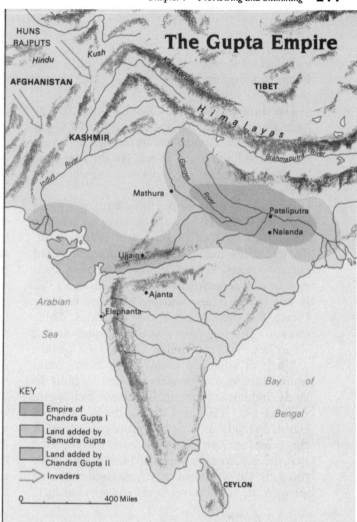

Map Study

What river valley formed the heartland of the early Gupta empire? Under what ruler did the empire reach its greatest size?

of central Asia. These newcomers set up many warring states and kingdoms. Southern India was not affected by those invasions. Politically, the south remained a land apart.

The Gupta dynasty ruled the north.

In A.D. 320, a Hindu prince named Chandra Gupta (CHUHN-druh GOOP-tuh) was crowned king of the upper Ganges valley. (He was no relation to the long-dead Chandragupta Maurya.) The new king was the first in a line of remarkable rulers who brought a golden age to India.

The Gupta dynasty ruled a mighty empire for nearly 150 years (320–467). After the founder of the line, Chandra Gupta I, came Samudra Gupta, called the Poet King. Samudra Gupta extended his kingdom to the mouth of the Ganges River, winning another nickname—"exterminator of all other kings."

The third Gupta ruler, Chandra Gupta II, was both a man of learning and a conqueror. During his reign, the Gupta empire stretched across northern India from sea to sea. For the first time in 500 years, northern India was united under one government.

Indian scholars in Gupta times left few written histories. To a Hindu, the passage of worldly time from past to present was unimportant. Therefore, few Indian scholars bothered to record current events. Instead, Indians celebrated their past in oral accounts called *itihas* (meaning "so it was told"). These oral records were very accurate, but they do not emphasize dates. Thus, modern historians have problems pinpointing when key events in Indian history took place.

Much of what we know about India comes from Chinese monks who traveled to India to study Buddhism in the land where it had begun. Around A.D. 405, the Chinese monk Fa-Hsien traveled widely in India and greatly marveled at the peace and prosperity he saw. He reported that the government supported free hospitals for the sick. He was especially impressed that as a stranger, he could travel freely and without fear.

Science and learning advanced.

Learning thrived during the Gupta period. Young Hindus of the priestly (Brahmin) castes attended school from the age of 9 to 30. The university at Nalanda on the Ganges River was famous throughout Asia and attracted students of philosophy from faraway kingdoms. Gupta scholars made many advances in science. The following list details only a few.

Inoculation Indian doctors were the first to give injections. Cowpox injections helped to stop epidemics of the deadly disease smallpox. In India's free hospitals, inoculation was widely used 1,000 years before Europeans first tried it.

Surgery Indian surgeons were remarkably advanced. They sterilized their cutting tools. They knew how to set broken bones. They repaired injured ears and noses by techniques of plastic surgery.

Number system Hindu mathematicians were the first to use a system of numbers based on ten. (Muslims of Baghdad adopted the system and passed it along to Europe, so Europeans called these numbers Arabic numerals.) Hindu philosophers understood the concept of zero and wrote it as a number. They also had a symbol for infinity.

Kalidasa wrote great drama.

The greatest literature of India's golden age was drama. Imagine an Indian actor wearing a sparkling, richly embroidered costume and the jeweled crown of a king. Standing beside him is an actress in the plain cotton gown of a poor hermit's daughter. The actress is playing the title role in one of the most famous plays in world literature, *Shakuntala*. The plot involves an unfortunate accident by which the king, though married to Shakuntala, loses all memory of her.

Shakuntala was written by the poet and dramatist Kalidasa (KAH-lih-DAH-suh), whose genius has been compared to Shakespeare's. Unlike Shakespeare, however, Kalidasa wrote no tragedies. There might be moments of sorrow during the play, but all his plays ended happily.

Emotion is the key to Indian drama. Audiences at the Gupta court recognized eight pure emotions known as *rasas*. One scene might make them feel the emotion of laughter, another sadness, a third pride. The other five rasas were love, anger, fear, loathing, and wonder. Then the final scene of a drama swept the audience up in an overpowering emotion that combined all the others.

Huns destroyed the Gupta empire.

The last Gupta rulers faced the same frightening challenge as the last Roman emperors. During the 400's, the Huns rampaged across Asia and Europe. While Attila was terrifying Rome, other Hun chieftains crossed the rocky passes of the Hindu Kush into India. Under constant attack from the Huns, the Gupta empire shrank. The Gupta dynasty disappeared from history during the 600's.

For the people of northern India, the next six centuries (650–1250) were ones of turmoil. First, several proud, warlike tribes from central Asia crossed the Hindu Kush mountains and settled in northwestern India. The local Hindus called this new ruling group Rajputs, a name that meant "sons of kings."

The Rajputs built new kingdoms.

In the 800's and 900's, northern India once again became a land of small kingdoms, ruled by Rajput warrior-kings. Soon after coming to India in the 500's, the Rajputs converted to Hinduism. They claimed membership in Hinduism's second highest caste, the Kshatriyas (or warriors).

Like European knights and Japanese samurai, Rajput men lived by a code of honor and bravery. Women were respected and had some property rights as well. However, both poetry and drama stressed that a woman's highest virtue was devotion to her husband. If her husband died, a faithful wife could show her love by a Hindu rite known as *suttee*. As her husband's body burned on a funeral pyre, she would remain at his side and die honorably in the flames.

An *age of great temples* By the 800's, three gods had risen to new importance in Hinduism: Brahman the Creator, Shiva the Destroyer, and Vishnu the Preserver. Poems, tales, and songs honored these gods and told of their deeds.

The 800's and 900's were a great age of temple building. Hindus could worship at a temple dedicated to the energetic Shiva, or they might become devotees of Vishnu, a loving god. (The creator-god, Brahman, though greatly honored, was seldom worshiped directly.) Among the great temples were those on the island of Elephanta, off India's west coast. Here, towering sculptures of Hindu gods fill caves that were cut into solid rock.

Decline of Buddhism During the Rajput centuries, Buddhism almost ceased to exist as a separate faith. Indians still worshiped figures of the Buddha, but they now worshiped him in Hindu temples. Hindu priests taught that the gentle Buddha had come to earth as an incarnation of the loving god, Vishnu. Thus, Indian Buddhism slipped quietly back into Hinduism.

Hindus and Muslims met in war.

In the 700's, Hinduism was one of the oldest religions in the world. Islam was the newest. The fierce conflict between Hindu and Muslim that began in this century has been called "probably the bloodiest story in history."

Arab Muslims conquered a major portion of the Indus River valley in 712, just as other Arab armies were conquering Spain. This first Muslim invasion, however, was mild compared to what followed.

In 997, a Turkish chieftain named Mahmud (muh-**MOOD**) became sultan of a little state in eastern Afghanistan called Ghazni. Mahmud of Ghazni was no barbarian. He loved Persian poetry and the Koran. He also loved gold and silver, and he made a solemn vow to plunder India

The Buddhist temples at Ajanta were hollowed out of granite cliffs between 100 B.C. and A.D. 500. Within the caves, the walls are covered with magnificent paintings.

every year. For 17 successive years, Mahmud's troops sacked India's cities and destroyed Hindu temples. They massacred and enslaved thousands. The Rajputs resisted bravely, but their slow-moving war elephants were no match for the lightninglike attacks of the Turkish cavalry. Mahmud of Ghazni died in 1030, leaving behind a legacy of hatred between Hindu and Muslim.

Muslim sultans ruled from Delhi.

About 160 years later, in 1191, another Turkish sultan named Muhammad Ghuri (GOO-ree) rode into India bent on conquest. A desperate stand by the Rajputs defeated him. The next year he returned and took a terrible revenge. His armies conquered city after city. At Nalanda, he destroyed the famous university. Much of northern India was conquered by Turkish armies and ruled by Turkish generals from the city of Delhi.

Thus began what is called the Delhi sultanate. For over 300 years (1200–1526), northern India was ruled by Turkish sultans from their courts in Delhi. These Turkish rulers were Muslims, and they treated the Hindus as a conquered people. Hindu kingdoms survived as independent states only in the Deccan, to the south.

The conquest of the Muslim Turks, though cruel, may have saved India from the Mongols. Although the Mongols raided and threatened India, the Turkish rulers were strong enough to turn them back.

Section Review 1

Define: (a) itihas, (b) caste, (c) inoculation, (d) rasa, (e) suttee, (f) sultan
Identify: (a) Shah Jahan, (b) Mumtaz Mahal, (c) Taj Mahal, (d) Chandra Gupta, (e) Gupta

Voice from the Past · *The Harshest of Sultans*

The most powerful of the Delhi sultans was the harsh Ala-ud-din (ah-LAH-ood-DEEN), who took the throne by murdering his uncle in 1296. A Muslim historian wrote the following account of Ala-ud-din's cruel measures.

The people were pressed and [taxed] and money was exacted from them on every kind of pretext . . . The people became so absorbed in trying to keep themselves alive that rebellion was never mentioned. Next [Ala-ud-din] set up a system of espionage so minute that nothing done, good or bad, was hidden from him . . . Nobles dared not speak aloud even in thousand-columned palaces, but had to communicate by signs. In their own houses, night and day, dread of spies made them tremble . . .

The Hindu was to be [made so poor] as to be unable to keep a horse, wear fine clothes, or enjoy any of life's luxuries. No Hindu could hold up his head . . . "I am an unlettered man," [Ala-ud-din] said, "but I have seen a great deal. Be assured that the Hindus will never become submissive and obedient till they are reduced to poverty. I have therefore given orders that just enough shall be left to them of [grain], milk, and curds, from year to year . . . Although I have not studied the science or the Book, I am a Muslim of the Muslims. To prevent rebellion, in which many perish, I issue such ordinances as I consider to be for the good of the State and the benefit of the people."

1. (a) What measures did the sultan use to prevent the nobles from plotting against him? (b) To prevent the common people from rebelling against him?
2. (a) What was the religion of the sultan? (b) What did he mean by "the Book"?
3. What was his policy toward Hindus?
4. What justification did the sultan give for his policies?

dynasty, (f) Arabic numerals, (g) Kalidasa, (h) Huns, (i) Rajputs, (j) Turks

Answer:

1. (a) How did Gupta rule affect northern India? (b) What were some of the key achievements in the arts and sciences under the Guptas?
2. What brought the Gupta empire to an end?
3. (a) In the Rajput kingdoms, what virtues were expected of a man? (b) Of a woman?
4. What changes in religion took place in Rajput times?
5. (a) What was the Delhi sultanate? (b) How did it come into being? (c) What was its effect on the Hindu population?

Critical Thinking

6. Briefly summarize the status of each of the following religions in northern India about the year 1200. (a) Hinduism (b) Buddhism (c) Islam

Mughals ruled India in splendor. 2

The greatest menace to the Delhi sultans came from their own homeland, the steppes of central Asia. Late in the 1300's, a fearsome conqueror rode out over the dusty steppe of Turkestan. He was Timur the Lame, or Tamerlane.

Tamerlane destroyed Delhi.

Tamerlane boasted descent from Genghis Khan, even though he was more Turk than Mongol. He led his forces westward into Persia, northward into Russia, and westward again into Mesopotamia and Asia Minor. From his capital in Samarkand, Tamerlane terrorized all of western Asia. To mark his victories, he erected heaps of human skulls where villages had been.

In 1398, Tamerlane led his armies south through the mountain passes into India. Within a few months, he had taken Delhi itself. Although he was a Muslim, he massacred Muslims and Hindus alike. About 100,000 people were sold into slavery. A witness wrote, "The city was utterly destroyed . . . for two whole months, not a bird moved in the city."

Unlike Genghis Khan, Tamerlane failed to build an empire that outlasted his own life. After his death in 1405, nothing remained of his conquests. Delhi was rebuilt, but the Turkish sultans who ruled there for the next century were weaker than their predecessors. To the west, Rajput princes strengthened their Hindu states. No single ruler was able to dominate India. Wars among the rival states and kingdoms were frequent.

Babur founded the Mughal dynasty.

In 1526, another Turkish-Mongol conqueror from central Asia ended the feeble Delhi sultanate for good. His name was Babur (BAH-buhr), which meant "the tiger." He traced his descent from Genghis Khan on his father's side and from Tamerlane on his mother's side. Babur was a hulking, broad-shouldered, big-bellied man. As his son testified, "He never hit a man whom he did not knock down." He was also a wily politician, a skilled general, and an educated man who wrote an autobiography.

Babur conquered India with cannon and firepower. His troops carried a supply of gunpowder, muskets, and several hefty cannon across the mountain passes from Afghanistan into northern India. Soon Babur captured Delhi and Agra in north-central India. The Delhi sultanate was thus overthrown after 320 years (1206–1526).

The new empire established by Babur came to be known as the Mughal (MOO-gahl) empire. (*Mughal* was another form of the name *Mongol.*) Mughal rule became a byword for wealth and splendor.

Akbar enlarged the Mughal empire.

By far the greatest and most talented of India's Mughal monarchs was Babur's grandson. Though his Muslim name was Muhammad, he was known as Akbar, which means "most great." Akbar was 13 when his father (Babur's son) had a fatal fall down a flight of palace stairs. Akbar ruled the Mughal empire with wisdom and fairness from 1556 to 1605.

Early in his reign, Akbar added new lands to the Mughal empire. Dressed in golden armor and mounted on an elephant, he fought countless battles against tough Rajput challengers. By the end of his reign, the Mughal empire covered almost all of northern India and much of the Deccan.

Like the Delhi sultans, the Mughal rulers were Muslims. However, Hindus in Mughal lands outnumbered Muslims by at least four to one. To unify his empire, Akbar decided that he needed Hindu support. Therefore, after defeating the Rajput princes, he did not seek revenge. Instead, he spared the Rajputs' lives and invited them to help rule. He married a Rajput princess and entrusted Hindus with high government offices. Akbar also removed the special taxes that Hindus had paid their Muslim rulers. His tax system stressed fairness. For example, in years of famine, taxes were dropped.

Akbar's wise policy toward Hindus was based on his personal religious tolerance. In his adult years, he ceased to believe that Islam was the only true faith. What Hindus taught might also be true, he thought. He was interested, too, in the teachings of Christian missionaries.

After learning about all these faiths, Akbar concluded that a new religion could embrace them all. He called his new religion *Din Ilahi* (Divine Faith) and made himself its leader. He made few converts, however, and his religion died with him in 1605.

Splendor disguised a weakening empire.

Under Akbar's successors, the strong empire he had built began to weaken. Later rulers were neither as tolerant nor as skilled in administration as Akbar had been.

A *strong queen* Akbar's son was named Jahangir (juh-HAHN-geer), meaning "world-grasper." He was sadly misnamed, however. Addicted to

Footnote to History

Akbar was an intelligent and cultured man who was eager for all kinds of knowledge, but he never learned to read or write. He mastered many fields of knowledge, from science to poetry, through conversation with scholars at his court. Some recent historians suspect he had the learning disability known today as dyslexia, which makes it difficult for a person to perceive letters and words.

both wine and opium, he played little part in governing. His reign (1605–1627) might have been an even greater disaster for India if he had not married an able woman.

In 1611, Jahangir married a Persian princess whom he called Nur Jahan ("the light of the world"). Nur Jahan was probably the most powerful woman in India's history before modern times. For many years, she was the true ruler of the empire.

Religious intolerance You have already read about the next Mughal monarch—Shah Jahan, the builder of the Taj Mahal. In his 30-year rule (1628–1658), Shah Jahan was as cruel toward his enemies as he had been loving toward his wife. He was followed by his even more ruthless son, Aurangzeb (OH-rung-zeb), who imprisoned his aging father as you have read.

Shah Jahan and especially Aurangzeb turned away from Akbar's policy of treating Hindus and Muslims as equals. Aurangzeb tried to make his empire an Islamic state. In 1669, he ordered the destruction of Hindu temples. He also returned to the policy of taxing non-Muslims more heavily than Muslims. No longer did Hindus serve the empire in high positions. By his intolerance, Aurangzeb weakened his government.

Extremes of wealth and poverty During Shah Jahan's reign, the Mughal empire was at its peak. Its glittering treasures amazed European visitors. For example, at the Red Fort at Agra (one of three royal residences built of red sandstone) the Mughal treasury contained these items:

> *750 pounds of pearls, 275 pounds of emeralds, 5,000 gems from Cathay (China) . . . 200 daggers, 1,000 gold studded saddles with jewels, 2 golden thrones, 3 silver thrones, 100 silver chairs, 5 golden chairs, 200 most precious mirrors . . .*

The list goes on and on. And it was said that the treasury at Lahore, the Mughals' third capital, was three times the size of Agra's.

India's poor, however, had few comforts. A European traveler left a description of a poor family's house that was not far from the great treasury of Agra:

> *Their houses are built of mud with thatched roofs. Furniture there is little or none except some earthenware pots to hold water and for cooking and two beds . . . Their bed*

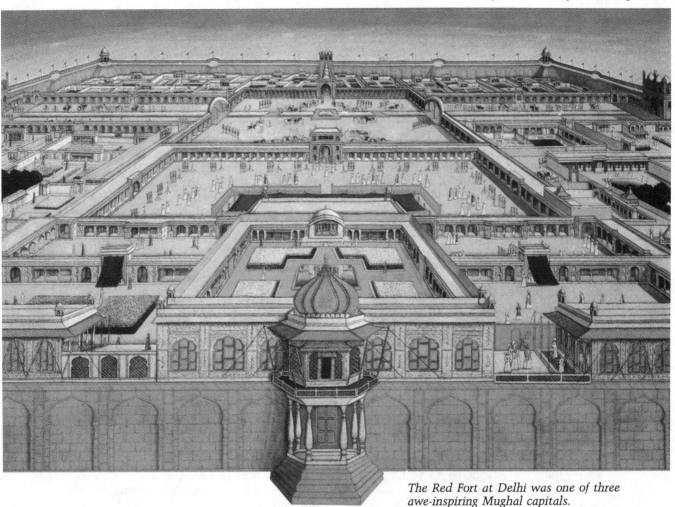

The Red Fort at Delhi was one of three awe-inspiring Mughal capitals.

cloths are scanty, merely a sheet or perhaps two . . . This is sufficient in the hot weather, but the bitter cold nights are miserable indeed . . .

In 1630 (during Shah Jahan's reign), a Dutch merchant visited northern India during one of the region's frequent famines. He wrote, "As the famine increased, men abandoned towns and villages and wandered helplessly . . . wherever you went, you saw nothing but corpses."

Hinduism and Islam were rivals.

All India's earlier conquerors had eventually blended into the Hindu system, but the Muslims did not. Their strong monotheism kept them from being absorbed by the Hindu majority.

Yet Hinduism and Islam did affect each other. For example, Hindus began to dress in the same styles as Muslims. Hindu women in northern India began to veil their faces as Muslim women did. Northern Hindus also adopted the idea of **purdah**. Purdah was a Muslim practice of keeping women in seclusion. Women were not allowed to go out in public or meet socially with any man outside the family.

Some Hindus converted to Islam. Islam's idea of the equality of all believers had a strong appeal to lower-caste Hindus and to untouchables.

A few thinkers tried to blend the ideas of Hinduism and Islam. One such thinker was Nanak, who lived from 1469 to 1539. Nanak became the *guru* (religious teacher) of a new religion. His teachings combined the strict monotheism of Islam with the Hindu idea of a mystical union with God. Followers of Nanak became known as Sikhs (seeks), meaning "disciples."

The Mughal rulers persecuted the Sikhs and killed two of their gurus. As a result, the Sikhs became a community of soldiers, ready to defend themselves or to attack. Many Sikh men took the last name Singh, meaning "lion," while women took the name Kaur, meaning "lioness." When Mughal rule weakened, the Sikhs set up an independent military state in northern India.

Europeans reached India's coast.

While Shah Jahan concentrated on building lavish tombs and palaces, Europeans were increasing their influence in Asia. In 1498, a Portuguese captain and adventurer, Vasco da Gama, arrived in India after sailing all the way around Africa. He reached India in 1498. For the first time, powerful newcomers had arrived in India by sea rather than through the mountain passes of the Himalayas to the north.

Da Gama's voyage marked a great turning point in India's history. After 1500, control of the seas around India became the key to controlling India itself. The Mughal rulers, however, took little interest in building warships. In the end, the weakness of their navy proved fatal to both the Mughal empire and the smaller Hindu kingdoms to the south.

The spices Da Gama took back from his voyage sold in Europe for 27 times their cost in India. Obviously, there were fortunes to be made in the Indian Ocean. Portuguese merchants were quick to go after them.

The Portuguese did not try to conquer India or the spice-producing islands south of China (the East Indies). Instead, they set up strong bases at strategic points all along the major Asian sea lanes.

A Portuguese sea captain named Alfonso de Albuquerque (al-buh-KEHR-kay) seized the western Indian port of Goa in 1510. In 1511, his fleet sailed to the East Indies and occupied the strategic port of Malacca (muh-LAK-uh) on the Malay peninsula. (See map on page 293.) In 1515, he captured his last great prize, the Muslim city of Hormuz (hor-MOOZ). It lay at the entrance to the Persian Gulf. From these three bases and the East African city of Zanzibar, the Portuguese dominated the Indian Ocean trade for the remainder of the 1500's. For the time being, however, the Europeans were not a serious threat to the Mughal emperors.

Section Review 2

Define: (a) purdah, (b) guru
Identify: (a) Tamerlane, (b) Babur, (c) Mughal dynasty, (d) Akbar, (e) Aurangzeb, (f) Sikhs, (g) Da Gama
Answer:
1. (a) How was the Delhi sultanate affected by Tamerlane? (b) By Babur?
2. List two major achievements of Akbar.
3. Compare the home of a poor family with the royal residences of the Mughals.
4. What are some customs that Hindus adopted from Muslims?
5. (a) What important change was marked by Da Gama's arrival in India? (b) How did the Portuguese come to control trade in the Indian Ocean?

Daily Life · *Cloths of Many Colors*

Indian farmers raised cotton to make cloth as early as 3000 B.C. By 300 B.C., Indian clothmakers were printing unique designs on their fabrics. Although European merchants at first were dazzled by India's jewels, they soon found that they could make even greater fortunes in the cloth trade. From Indian looms came cloth of many different weights and patterns. In Europe, each type of cloth came to be known by the name of the Indian city or region where it was woven. For example, the fabric madras takes its name from the Indian city Madras, calico from the city Calicut, cashmere from the region Kashmir. *Chintz* comes from a Hindi word whose root means "bright" or "many-colored." Even the word *dungaree* comes from the name of a section of Bombay where sturdy blue denim was woven.

The Brooklyn Museum

9. Did the coming of Europeans present an immediate threat to

the Indian rulers? _____

_____

_____

10. For what is Shah Jahan famous? _____

_____

_____

SUMMARY

Previewing is a type of survey reading. When you preview a text-book, you look only at certain helpful parts—parts that will help you to understand and learn the material in the text and, by extension, in the course. Skimming is another kind of survey reading, one that combines speed and adequate, but not extensive, comprehension. You should skim to discover quickly an author's thesis and main supporting arguments. Although skimming cannot replace analytical reading, it can be a useful supplement to the reading process.

Preview one of your textbooks and answer the following questions.

1. a. Complete title of the text: _____

    b. Based on the title, what do you think is the theme of the
        book? _____

        _____

        _____

    c. Author's name: _____

    d. Author's qualifications: _____

    e. Copyright date: _____

2. Summarize the introduction, preface, or foreword in one or two
    sentences. _____

    _____

    _____

3. Use your preview of the table of contents to describe the
    structure and organization of the text. _____

    _____

    _____

    _____

    _____

4. List all the study aids you located in the text. _____

    _____

    _____

    _____

    _____

In this application, you will both skim and read the following article. After each activity, answer the appropriate comprehension questions.

1. *Read the title.*

2. What do you guess this article will be about?

3. Now *skim* the article.

4. Based on your skimming, write a brief preliminary summary of the article.

_____

_____

_____

_____

_____

Don't Know Much About History?

JEAN GRASSO FITZPATRICK

Your fifth grader has an assignment to write an essay about Christopher Columbus. He asks you to decide: Was Columbus a) an invader; b) a conqueror; c) an explorer?

Your seventh grader is writing a report on Cleopatra and asks you what race she was. You answer: a) Asian; b) Caucasian; c) Black.

Your sixth-grader's homework asks him to identify prominent people in history, one of whom is described as a "popular Jewish teacher who told parables during the first century." You answer: a) Moses; b) Jesus; c) David.

Unless you are privy to one of the new multicultural history textbooks being adopted by some states—California and New York among them—your answers to these questions may be very different from what your child is learning in school today. According to some educators, Columbus may be labeled an invader, Cleopatra may have been Black, and Jesus is part of the teachings of secular history.

As multicultural curricula gain popularity, our nation's schoolchildren are being exposed to a dizzying diversity of customs, religions and historical perspectives. For example, instead of learning that the Pilgrims' first Thanksgiving was a harmonious celebration, children are being taught that it was a far less joyous occasion for the Native American, due to the destructive effects of Colonial culture.

The trend is attracting plenty of controversy. Traditionalists voice concern that kids won't learn the "essentials" of Western history and values, while African American, Native American, Hispanic and Muslim critics charge that multicultural teaching often trivializes their cultures, presenting them as "quaint" and irrelevant to present-day life.

Others claim that multicultural education will fragment American culture and replace solid, historical scholarship with "feel-good" curricula aimed solely at bolstering the self-esteem of minorities. Yet according to Hugh J. Scott, Ed.D., dean of the division of programs and education at Hunter College in New York City: "If you believe in teaching your child the truth, multicultural learning can present the world more realistically. Many parents fear it, but we've actually been doing it for years. The history books will not be rewritten; heroes will not be demeaned."

As parents, we may be tempted to shrug and assume this is one more educational fad we'll never figure out. (Remember how *our* parents reacted to the new math?) But as our children look toward life in the 21st century, with Caucasians predicted to be a minority in major U.S. cities, and with Asia and Africa occupying increasingly important roles on the world stage, multicultural learning is nothing less than a passport to the future.

Even if you were raised on John Smith, Pocahontas and "manifest destiny"—and wish every time you turn on the TV news that you had a better background on the Middle East—as a parent you have a key role to play both at home and in the classroom. At its best, educators say, multicultural learning is a family/school affair.

Here are three ways you can insure that multicultural education is an enriching experience for your child and your whole family.

KNOW YOUR CHILD'S CURRICULUM

Not all multicultural education is the same. An innovative multicultural classroom offers not only a change in the *material* covered, but also in the *way* events and groups are studied. Instead of getting a smorgasbord of heroes and holidays from different ethnic and racial groups—what educators have derisively called a "tourist curriculum"—your child should be learning new approaches to social studies.

By reading firsthand accounts of events and learning to evaluate them, students should begin to develop an understanding of history as a complex weave of narratives told from different perspectives and influenced by geography, religious beliefs and values. A 1950's textbook describes plantation life in the Old South like this: "The older colored people work on the great farm or help about the plantation home. The small black boys and girls play about the small houses." Compare that passage with this description found in the 1991 textbook *America Will Be* (Houghton Mifflin): "Most slaves lived in drafty, one-room cabins with dirt floors. Many times two or more families would live together in one cabin. They slept on the ground on mattresses filled with cornhusks."

A 1991 Houghton Mifflin seventh-grade text includes two contrasting descriptions of the Crusaders. There is a 13-year-old Christian girl who sees them as "men whose faces were full of good humor and zeal for their righteous cause." The Muslim leader Saladin, on the other hand, calls them "raiders, the voracity of whose harm could not be contained and the fire of whose evil could not be quenched."

In the new approach to history, events are seen from the point of view of both winners and losers. Long before they read about Columbus's arrival in the Americas, students get an inside look at daily life, architectural achievements and religious beliefs in the Incan, Aztec and Mayan empires. Traditionally, the Alamo, site of the 1836 battle between the Mexicans and U.S. forces, has been viewed as a shrine to Texan independence and statehood. Multiculturalists want to incorporate the positive Hispanic influences on the area as well.

Instead of being barraged with opposing viewpoints, however, your child should be learning to apply critical thinking and creative problem-solving skills to the information being acquired. In a multicultural approach to the Hudson River, for example, social studies teacher Carl Oechsner of the Anne M. Dorner Middle School in Ossining, New York, takes students back in time with slides of old photographs and contemporary accounts of everyday life by early African-Americans in the community, the Irish immigrants who built the railroad, and the Irish and Italians who worked on nearby Croton Dam.

Students investigate the vital role the river has historically played in the lives of the people who have lived along its banks. They take trips to the river to find fossil remains, visit the old Indian middens (refuse heaps) and explore the wine cellars of a founding family. "I tie together historical material by bringing in a current issue—getting the kids to apply what they've learned to a real-life problem *today*," says Oechsner.

Once they have an appreciation of the multicultural heritage of life on the river, Oechsner assigns groups of students to design a revitalized waterfront that will benefit a variety of community groups. The top five student plans are then presented to the village board and televised on local cable.

SHARE YOUR TALENTS AND HERITAGE

Offering your child a rich foundation of your own family's beliefs and traditions is one way to help him appreciate diversity. "Multiculturalism is knowing how different cultures express their ideas about common human experiences," says Sharon Robinson, Ph.D., director of the National Education Association's National Center for Innovation. She cites rites of passage—a wedding, say, or a christening or a bar mitzvah—as obvious examples. A child who has first-hand experience with the ritual and lore of his own particular tradition is better able to understand how important these things can be for another person.

An innovative teacher will provide classroom opportunities for parents and children of different backgrounds to share their cultural heritage with members of the student body. For example, the teacher might invite students or parents to prepare their traditional dishes for United Nations Day, or show the class national costumes, or recount popular folktales.

If you're unhappy with the way your ethnic, racial or religious group or holiday is being presented at your child's school, Dr. Robinson suggests that you write a note to the teacher as a first step. "Say, 'I would love to come in to discuss a way of observing the holiday that would enhance students' knowledge about that part of the world.'" (After several years of hearing how my son's teachers made a green dessert for St. Patrick's Day, my husband—a native Irishman—now packs up a bag of taped traditional music and real soda bread, which my son takes in for an authentic celebration.)

Beyond getting involved in your child's classroom, as a parent you have influence at the policy-making level.

REINFORCE THIS KIND OF LEARNING AT HOME

You can help your child integrate the variety of groups and traditions he is learning about in school by making the exploration of different cultures a family activity at home. At breakfast or dinner, perhaps, talk about events reported in the newspaper, suggests Donna Hupe, a fifth-grade teacher in Pennsylvania's Seneca Valley School District. Conversations like these help kids make the connections between the problem-solving they're learning in the classroom and the conflicts in our society and world today.

If your son comes home with a question or comment you find personally upsetting—such as "Columbus didn't really do much, did he, Mom?"—try to stay calm and use it as an opportunity to help him hone his critical-thinking skills. "Offer to do some research together with your child," suggests Keith Zook, technology coordinator for the Connections Project of Grosse Ile., Michigan, schools, "but keep in mind that each generation is going to view history in a different way. If your child's textbook seems to provide too narrow a perspective on a particular event in history, look for additional material on the subject at your public library. Focus on learning more together, not on winning a debate."

But long before controversy arises, you can lay the groundwork for shared exploration. Pay a visit to the local historical society or museum with your child; you may discover military uniforms worn by African-American troops, for instance, or dollhouses crafted by German immigrants, or daguerreotypes of the Italian neighborhood that was razed during urban renewal. Plan occasional dinners featuring simple dishes from different national cuisines (check your public library for international cookbooks) and let your child share in the preparation and serving. Give your child a deeper understanding of different religions by attending a service at the house of worship of a faith not your own. Look through an international catalog for crafts, games, toys and musical instruments you can enjoy together.

Read aloud folktales and literature from different cultures. Watch the TV news together—or documentaries like the widely acclaimed PBS specials on the Civil War and on Christopher Columbus—and use these occasions as opportunities for each of you to bring up your own questions and comments.

At its best, multicultural learning is a *celebration* of diversity and an exploration of how people with conflicting ethnic, religious, and geographic interests can live and work together. By teaching the positive side of differences—freedom from oppression and the importance of roots—the "new" multicultural curriculum reinforces the old-fashioned values that make up the American dream.

Family Circle; March 10, 1992; pp. 81–84.

5. Answer these questions to check your comprehension. Remember—because you have only skimmed the article, you are not expected to know all of its details.

a. Has there been any controversy surrounding the introduction of multicultural education into the curriculum?

_____

_____

b. Is multicultural education standardized? Is it all the same?

_____

_____

c. Can family beliefs and heritage be incorporated into a multicultural curriculum? _____

_____

_____

d. Should the home be involved in promoting multicultural education? _____

_____

_____

e. Is multicultural education intended to be a celebration of diversity? _____

_____

_____

f. Explain the contrasting views of the Crusaders.

_____

_____

g. Is having a green dessert on St. Patrick's Day a good example of multicultural education? _____

_____

_____

h. Why should parents offer to do research with their children? _____

_____

_____

i. Is occasionally celebrating a special event, such as Black History Month, multicultural education?

_____

_____

6. Now *read* the article.

7. Based on your reading, revise your preliminary summary by adding any important information that might not have been available to you when you skimmed.

8. Answer these questions to check your comprehension. Since you have both skimmed *and* read the article, you should be able to answer most of them accurately.

a. Has there been any controversy surrounding the introduction of multicultural education into the curriculum?

_____

_____

b. Is multicultural education standardized? Is it all the same?

_____

_____

c. Can family beliefs and heritage be incorporated into a
multicultural curriculum? _____

_____

_____

d. Should the home be involved in promoting multicultural
education? _____

_____

_____

e. Is multicultural education intended to be a celebration
of diversity? _____

_____

_____

f. Explain the contrasting views of the Crusaders.

_____

_____

g. Is having a green dessert on St. Patrick's Day a good
example of multicultural education? _____

_____

_____

h. Why should parents offer to do research with their
children? _____

_____

_____

   i. Is occasionally celebrating a special event, such as Black

       History Month, multicultural education?

       _____

       _____

APPLICATION III

Choose an article or chapter that you are required to read for one of
your classes. First, skim the material. Then, list its main ideas and
supports. Next, read the material carefully. In a paragraph, summarize the article or chapter. Finally, discuss with your fellow students
how skimming the article or chapter made reading it easier. Explain
how skimming helped you to anticipate the author's supporting
ideas and conclusions.

Chapter 8

APPROACHING TEXTBOOKS

Objectives
1. To read a textbook chapter efficiently.
2. To analyze a textbook chapter effectively.
3. To use the chapter's structure as an aid to learning.
4. To be able to use information from the chapter.

Key Concept

Reading a textbook chapter should be a learning experience.

Does this scene seem familiar to you? Your teacher assigns a textbook chapter to be read in preparation for the next class. That same night, you sit down and read the whole chapter in one hour. However, two days later when the teacher begins discussing the chapter in class, you cannot participate because you don't remember what you read about the topic. Most of the material is not familiar to you. What happened? You obviously did not "read" the chapter very effectively.

READING A CHAPTER

Reading a textbook chapter requires more than just letting your eyes flow across each line of print. Really "reading" a chapter means analyzing the material and learning from it. Anything else is just a waste of time and effort.

At this point in your educational career, you should be a conscious reader. You are no longer reading to develop your ability to decode words. You are not reading to improve your ability to read. You are reading to learn. You want to be able to extract information from your textbooks. As a conscious reader, your emphasis is on the information contained in the chapter.

How can you gain access to that information? How can you extract it? Merely reading the text is not sufficient because that is just an exercise for your eyes. Since you need to learn from the chapter, you must involve your mind in the reading process. Involving your mind demands a conscious effort on your part; thus, you must be a *conscious reader*.

Conscious Readers

What do conscious readers do? How do conscious readers differ from other readers?

First, *conscious readers focus their attention.* These readers have a purpose for their activity. They know that they must learn from the chapter. Therefore, they concentrate as they read in order to remember what they have learned. *Second, conscious readers analyze the chapter.* They do more than just look at the whole chapter. They examine each of its parts in order to understand the topic. *Third, conscious readers know that they must be able to recall the information* whenever they need it. Consequently, they make an effort to work with the information, to manipulate it, in order to make the ideas easier to recall. Remember that knowledge is based on understanding, remembering, and recalling information.

Exercise 1

The energy crisis has been discussed and debated for more than a decade. Many experts believe that greater reliance on renewable energy sources, such as wind and water, would resolve the energy crisis. What do you know about renewable energy? Brainstorm for three minutes and jot your ideas in the space provided.

Analytical Reading

Conscious readers, who want reading a textbook chapter to be a learning experience, read *analytically*. What does that mean? How can a reader "analyze" a chapter? In fact, what is *analysis*? Think of the last time your blood was tested. What happened to it? The lab technician separated your blood into its components: white cells, red cells, platelets, serum, HDL/LDL levels, antibodies, and on and on. Then, the technician closely examined each of those parts and looked for signs of well-being and disease. In other words, your blood was analyzed. The blood test is an example of a thorough analysis. Like a technician, you can and should analyze each and every textbook chapter.

Benefits of analytical reading. Why should you analyze each chapter? Your goal is to understand the material and learn from it. Consider these advantages of analytical reading:

1. *Efficiency*—Sometimes learning about a topic requires three steps:

   a. reading the textbook,

   b. listening to the lecture, and

   c. reading the text for greater understanding.

   If you can grasp the chapter's key points by reading the first time, then you can eliminate the last step. Furthermore, during the lecture, you can concentrate on understanding the subject's details. This makes you an efficient reader.

2. *Control*—Learning from reading gives you more control of the learning situation. If you must rely on the instructor's explanation in order to understand the textbook, then a missed class can be disastrous. However, by analyzing the text, you can keep pace with the course contents even when you must be absent from class.

Making changes. What changes should you make in your reading habits in order to analyze? For the most part, you can perform many of the same reading actions as before but in a more focused way. You will emphasize *the reasons* for your actions, instead of the actions themselves. You will process the chapter's contents in order to learn, not just to complete the assignment.

What does analytical reading require? How should you do it? There are five steps in the process:

1. Surveying

2 Questioning

3. Reading

4. Recording

5. Reviewing

These steps are abbreviated as SQ3R. The analytical process is *developmental.* This means the usefulness of each step depends on the successful completion of the previous step. No step should be omitted or considered more important than another. Your reading goal should be to analyze thoroughly each chapter you read and gain as much understanding as possible. In order to do this, you should follow SQ3R each time you read. The rest of this chapter will show you this process.

STEP ONE: SURVEY

The survey is the first step. It provides a foundation for understanding and analyzing the chapter. A survey offers an overview, a general idea of the chapter's contents and structure. The survey also reveals the topic and emphasizes its major elements. Finally, the survey helps you to focus your attention when you get to the third step of the process: reading.

All too often, students turn the pages in their textbooks, but they misdirect their energy. When assigning a chapter to be read, the teacher intends that the students should *read and understand.* Instead, many students read just to finish the chapter and be done with the assignment. This is a waste of energy and time.

Why does this happen? Frequently, the cause is a lack of direction. The students do not know the topic. Furthermore, they do not know how to determine what is important about the topic. Consequently, they do not know where to focus their attention.

Surveying helps to solve the problem. By surveying, you can recognize each chapter's key points and begin to learn them. Later, as you read the chapter, you will recognize each important part. Then you can concentrate as you read key ideas.

How to Survey

When you survey a piece, you preview the topic and its major elements. Note that the survey does not provide a detailed analysis of the material, so it can never substitute for actually reading the chapter.

To survey a chapter, you should look at the following parts:

1. *Title, Subtitle, and Subheads.* Read them because they outline the chapter and organize its contents. In addition, the title and subheads can provide a framework for your notetaking.

Look at the example on the following page:

THE HUMAN IMPRINT IN THE MODERN WORLD

POPULATION AND SETTLEMENT

Growing Numbers of People

Medical Advances
Improved Public Health
Increased Food Supplies

Keeping Track of Population

Migration

Where the World's People Live

Mapping Population Distribution
Urban Growth
The Outward Spread of Cities

POLITICAL PATTERNS

From Frontiers to Borders

The Political Map

Unitary versus Federal Government

Authoritarian versus Democratic Government

(Gritzner, Charles F. World Geography. Lexington, MA: Heath, 1989. Chapter 6.)

2. *Chapter Introduction, Summary, and/or Conclusion.* In the
opening and closing remarks, an author usually emphasizes the
chapter's main points. Although every chapter does not have an
introduction, summary, and conclusion, most well-written texts will
have at least one in each chapter. Do not skip over them. Instead,
look for them and read them because they *highlight* important information that you should remember.

Exercise 2

Read the following introduction from a science textbook chapter as
part of your chapter survey. Then answer the questions that follow.

The perfect energy source would be cheap, plentiful, efficient,
easy to use, and would not cause pollution. Is there such an
energy source? Maybe not, but there are things in the environment that do supply energy without showing signs of ever
running out. What gives off heat and light every day? What
causes a sailboat to move over the water? How does a raft get
downstream?

People have used energy from the sun, wind, and water for
centuries. Before the extensive use of fossil and nuclear fuels,
these sources of energy were very important. Now the problems associated with fossil and nuclear fuels are becoming
better known. As a result, people are beginning to think about
using other energy sources.

In this chapter you will find out how the sun, the wind, and water are being used as sources of energy. You will also learn about other energy sources that are minor now but might become more important in the future.

(Nolan, Louise Mary. Physical Science. Lexington, MA: Heath, 1987. p. 475.)

1. Describe the perfect energy source. _____

    _____

2. Have people just recently begun to use the wind as a source of

    energy? _____

    _____

3. Why are people looking for other energy sources now?

    _____

4. What are the main ideas of this chapter? _____

    _____

As you can see by your answers to the exercise questions, reading the introduction *did* provide a preview to the topic. The next step in the reading/learning process is to analyze the whole chapter. When you do this, you will recognize that you already have developed from your survey some familiarity with the chapter's key points. This familiarity will increase your understanding enormously.

3. Charts, Graphs, Tables, Pictures, and Visual Aids. These study aids are tremendously helpful. Do not skip over them. Visual aids are not space-*fillers*, as many students think. They are actually space-*savers*. They provide a great deal of detailed information in an easy-to-understand, but condensed, form. With graphics and illustrations, you can *see* as well as read ideas. The bold-faced print, italicized words, maps, and diagrams are designed to clarify difficult and boring material. Take advantage of their special design to aid your learning.

Analyze the timeline on the following page, a chart that portrays events in a time sequence:

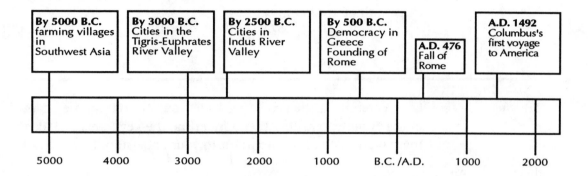

| By 5000 B.C. farming villages in Southwest Asia | By 3000 B.C. Cities in the Tigris-Euphrates River Valley | By 2500 B.C. Cities in Indus River Valley | By 500 B.C. Democracy in Greece Founding of Rome | A.D. 476 Fall of Rome | A.D. 1492 Columbus's first voyage to America |

5000   4000   3000   2000   1000   B.C./A.D.   1000   2000

(*Gritzner, Charles F.* World Geography, *Lexington, MA: Heath, 1989. p. 134.*

If the author had presented all of the material from the timeline in sentences, the writing would have been a boring jumble of dates and events. Instead, the visual aid makes it easier for readers to understand and follow the course of events. So, as a conscious reader, you should deliberately look for each chapter's visual aids and take note of their information.

4. Review Questions. Surveying this study aid is basic to your learning the chapter's material. Authors write review questions specifically to test each student's understanding of important ideas and facts in a chapter. Each question usually focuses on a specific aspect of the topic. So you should read each question as part of the surveying process. Then, when you actually read the chapter, you will have advance information about its key elements, and you will know which topics require concentration and attention.

The following review questions test a reader's understanding of an American history chapter:

Checking Up

1. Who was Stephen Austin?
2. How did the United States get Texas and California?
3. Why did the population of California increase between 1848 and 1849?
4. What answers would you give to the key questions at the beginning of this chapter?
5. How were traders and trappers important to the settling of the West in the early 1800s?

(*Our United States.* Allyn and Bacon, Inc. *1986. p. 198.*)

As you read each section of the chapter later, the review questions you surveyed will remind you about which information you must remember from that part. Try to answer the questions. If you can, then you have understood that section's main point, and you can continue reading.

Exercise 3

Look carefully at the preceding review questions from the chapter in the American history text. Underline the key terms and ideas that you think will be important to your understanding of this chapter.

5. *List of Key Terms, or Glossary.* Sometimes, textbooks will provide a list of important terms and their definitions. This list can be called a *glossary*. A glossary may be found at the end of each chapter or at the end of the whole text. Sometimes key terms are listed at the beginning of a chapter, to alert students to their significance. If there is a glossary or word list, look it over. If you do not understand a term, read its definition. Later, as you are reading, you will not be distracted by an unknown word, and your concentration will not be broken as you look up its meaning. The following is the first page of an end-of-book glossary from an economics text.

Glossary of Economic Terms

Most of the terms in this glossary are found in the text. For a more extensive treatment of any term concisely defined here, use the index to find the location of the term in the text.

ability-to-pay principle: justification for taxing people with larger incomes a greater percentage of their income, based on the principle of diminishing marginal utility.

absolute advantage: an advantage that one nation has over another in trade by being able to produce a good more efficiently (at less cost).

acceleration principle: a change in sales at the consumer level will bring about a greater change in sales of producer goods.

acceptability: a characteristic of money that allows it to be accepted by individuals and businesses as a medium of exchange in a wide market.

administered price: price set under conditions of imperfect competition, where the individual firm has some degree of control.

ad valorem tax: tax applied according to the value of what is being taxed, particularly imports.

agency shop: work place in which all employees in a particular bargaining unit are required to pay union dues even though they may not want to join the union.

aggregate demand: total spending in the economy; the sum of personal consumption expenditures, business investment, and government spending.

aggregate supply: the total retail value of goods and services produced and available in a given period.

alternative cost: *See* opportunity cost.

antitrust: describes an act or a policy designed to curb monopolistic tendencies or power.

arbitration: method of settling a labor dispute in which both parties agree to accept the decision of a third party.

assessment: for taxation purposes, the official valuation of property or income.

asset: anything of value that is owned.

automatic stabilizer: tool that compensates for changes in the business cycle without requiring action by a public official or agency.

avoidance: a legal way to reduce tax payments.

balance of payments: statement listing all financial transactions that a nation and its people have with all other nations.

balance of trade: the difference between the total value of goods and services exported to other countries and the total value of goods and services imported.

balance sheet: itemized statement showing a business's assets, liabilities, and net worth on a given date.

bank reserves: amount of money a bank holds in order to meet the requirements of the Federal Reserve Bank or of a law, or the demands of its depositors. In addition to these reserves, a bank holds secondary reserves in the form of securities that can be easily converted into money.

base period: a time in the past against which changes are measured. It is used to measure price index.

benefit principle of taxation: justification for taxing people according to the benefits they received from government.

bill of exchange: written claim for foreign currency. It is the same as a foreign exchange check.

blacklist: list of workers, usually union organizers, circulated by employers in order to prevent those on the list from getting jobs.

bond: security representing indebtedness, frequently issued in $1000 denominations, and bearing a fixed rate of interest. Both governments and business firms issue bonds.

Gordon and Dawson, Introductory Economics, *6/e. Lexington, MA: Heath, 1987. p. 459.*

6. Bibliography. The bibliography is a list of books and articles the author consulted while writing. As you survey, you should merely note whether or not the chapter provides this study aid. If it does, the bibliography could offer you a useful starting point for a research paper. In effect, the author has provided you with some titles that are particularly appropriate to the chapter's topic. Can you tell the chapter topic from the following chapter reading list?

BOOKS TO READ

In the Days of Dinosaurs, by Roy Chapman Andrews, Random House, Inc.

The Caves of the Great Hunters, by Hans Baumann, Pantheon Books, Inc.

Archeologists and What They Do, by Robert J. Braidwood, Franklin Watts, Inc.

The Story of Archeology in the Americas, by Mary Elting and Franklin Folsom, Harvey House, Inc.

About Cave Men of the Old Stone Age, by Bettina Leonard Kramer, Melmont Publishers, Inc.

(*Schreider, Hymen and Nina.* Science for Today and Tomorrow. *Lexington,* MA: *Heath, 1968. p. 99.*)

Not all textbooks nor all chapters offer each of these study aids. However, you should look for each of them as you survey. Take advantage of the ones provided. Surveying a chapter takes approximately ten minutes, but that time is well spent. Because surveying highlights important ideas and emphasizes key concepts, it begins the learning process. Surveying also improves your reading by making it more efficient and effective. It lets you direct your concentration and focus your energy on the chapter's important elements, so you understand and learn. Conscious readers know that the benefits derived from surveying justify the extra time.

Exercise 4	In Exercise 1, you brainstormed to see what you know about renewable energy resources. What do you know about alternative energy sources? Can society get energy only from oil and natural gas? Spend about three minutes brainstorming about alternate energy sources. Write your ideas below.

Exercise 5	Survey the sample chapter, "Energy Alternatives," which appears at the end of this chapter, pages 249–264.

Exercise 6	Based on your survey, answer the following questions.

   1. Name three renewable sources of energy. _____

       _____

   2. Is solar energy currently being used to produce electricity?

       _____

   3. Name the two forms of water energy currently being used.

       _____

4. Is Niagara Falls used to produce hydroelectric power? _____

_____

5. Name one form of biomass energy. _____

_____

STEP TWO: QUESTION

Most students are used to answering questions because academic life is filled with them. You answer questions on applications and in interviews. You respond to questions in class and on tests. You may even ask yourself questions as you study in order to check your understanding of the material.

Questions are an expected part of the academic environment. In other words, the question-and-answer format is familiar to you. Asking questions jogs your memory and helps you to retrieve information that might otherwise have remained buried. Simply asking a question forces you to focus your attention and search your memory for the answer. Because questions help you to concentrate, they should be part of the learning process, not just the review process.

How to Question

How can you make questions part of learning? How can you create questions to focus your attention when you do not know where your attention should be focused? If you have not yet read a chapter, how can you develop any questions about its important elements? Think about that last question for a moment. What did your survey of the chapter reveal to you? The survey provided you with an outline of the chapter. Its title and subheads highlighted the chapter's key elements. So use those chapter parts to focus your attention by turning the title and subheads into questions.

For example, look at the sample title and subheads on the following page. See how each can be turned into a useful question.

Title and Subheads	Questions
HUMAN IMPRINTS OF THE PAST	What are the human imprints in the past?
	How did humans imprint themselves?
Culture: The Human Difference	How do humans make a difference?
Human Habitats and Cultures	What is a habitat?
	What is culture?
Every culture is unique.	Why is every culture unique?
Cultures Have Common Elements	What are their common elements?
Cultures Change	How do cultures change?

(Gritzner, Charles F. World Geography. *Lexington, MA: Heath, 1989. pp. 124–127.)*

After developing questions, you should be able to recognize key ideas as you read the text. Asking questions, therefore, comes *before* reading because it makes your reading more purposeful. You have a goal as you read. You are not reading just to finish the chapter and complete the assignment. You are reading to find the answer to each of your questions, and each answer helps you to understand the material.

Exercise 7

Reread the title and subheads in the sample chapter, "Energy Alternatives." Develop at least one question from each heading. List your questions in the following space.

STEP THREE: READ

Surveying and questioning are prereading steps in the reading process. They help you to learn from your reading. This is the goal of every conscious reader. However, these steps cannot substitute for reading and analyzing the material. Analytical reading is an essential part of the learning process.

Surveying introduced you to the topic and its major parts. Questioning helped you to recognize the ideas you needed to know and understand in the text. Analytical reading will give you that needed knowledge and understanding.

How to Read and Analyze

How do you analyze the text? Where do you begin? What should you do? You should read the material, but do not think of your task as "reading the whole chapter." Instead, your task is to read section by section. In this way, your task is not overwhelming; it is manageable.

Benefits of Analyzing

Why should you read the material one section at a time?

1. Analyzing each part separately lets you concentrate on the information. Your job will be to find the answers to only two or three questions; that is manageable.

2. It will be easy to decide whether or not the material answers the questions you developed. If it does not, you might want to ask those questions of your teacher.

3. Analyzing each section lets you quickly locate any problem areas, any material you are having trouble understanding. Then, you will be aware of your need to pay attention in class as your instructor discusses that troublesome topic.

The Last Analysis

Finally, after reading and analyzing all the parts of the chapter, take some time to consider the whole chapter and its ideas.

1. Review the chapter's thesis. Think about its supporting ideas.

2. Decide whether the material explains the topic or whether there are some gaps in the information presented.

3. Be able to identify and explain the relationships between the thesis and the rest of the chapter's material. After all, the assignment was to read the whole chapter, so you must be able to discuss the topic in its entirety, not just bits and pieces of it.

The few minutes it will take you to consider the entire chapter and to recognize the usefulness of its parts will be time well spent.

Exercise 8

Read and analyze the chapter, "Energy Alternatives," beginning on page 249. Read to answer the questions you developed in Exercise 7. When you have finished, spend a few minutes thinking about the ideas presented in the chapter. Finally, determine the relationship of each aspect to the general topic.

STEP FOUR: RECORD

Think of the last time you attended a lecture or discussion. Ideally, the topic was interesting, the presenter was knowledgeable, and the question-and-answer session was thought provoking. Later, as you talked about the event with a friend, you may have recognized that, although you remembered an outline of the topic, you could not recall its fine points. Why did that happen? You were interested; you had paid attention; you understood the discussion. Why, then, did you forget most of the material?

Probably you forgot most of the lecture material because you did not take notes. *Taking notes is essential to learning.* Although you may understand a topic thoroughly, if you cannot remember the ideas and recall them whenever you need to use them, then you have not really learned the material. You have understood it for a short time, but you have not learned it for future use. As you may suspect, that type of understanding is absolutely useless to you.

Information Your Notes Should Contain

To make sure that you *learn* new ideas, not just understand them, you must take notes on chapters. That is the meaning of the recording step: taking notes.

1. You should record the topic, its main ideas, and their supporting details.

2. You should make the relationships between the ideas clear.

3. You should try to connect the new material with the ideas you have already learned. The more connections between topics you can form, the easier it will be to recall the ideas when required.

Chapter 2 discusses several formats for notetaking. You can choose whichever one seems most appropriate for the material and most comfortable to you. How you take notes is not important; taking notes is. Use your chapter analysis to help you determine which ideas should be recorded. Try to be brief and visual. Your goal is to record the key ideas in written form so that you can learn the material.

Exercise 9

Take notes on the sample chapter, "Energy Alternatives." Use whichever notetaking format you find suitable.

STEP FIVE: REVIEW

Think of some of the math concepts you studied a few years ago. Can you still solve a quadratic equation? Most likely you cannot because you have not practiced that skill regularly. Contrast that with some of the math skills you learned many years ago in elementary school. You can still add, subtract, multiply, and divide because you use those skills daily. Learning is not an event that occurs once, and then the idea is fixed forever in your mind. Learning is a continuous, lifelong process. If a concept or skill is important to you, it must be renewed. Otherwise, it will become rusty and unavailable to you when you need it. Reviewing helps to renew key ideas, and keep them fresh in your mind.

Review means "to look over again." Reviewing reinforces ideas and emphasizes concepts in order to ensure their storage in your long-term memory.

When to Review

You should not review as soon as you have finished taking notes. In fact, it is usually better to wait a day or two before reviewing. Immediate review becomes a mechanical process. If you wait, it is more likely that you will review to reinforce ideas and emphasize concepts. At that point, it will also be easier for you to recognize any idea that you cannot easily recall. For example, you may remember that the text discussed five causes of the Civil War, but you can only remember three. In that case, you must do more studying.

How to Review

Your review style depends on your learning style. If you prefer, you can review by yourself. If you enjoy a team approach to most situations, you can organize a study group. The other members can improve your understanding and help you develop different viewpoints. If you are more comfortable working with a partner, try to find one. Then you can ask each other questions. The format of the review is not important; the review itself is. Although reviewing is the final step in the study/learning process, it is not the least step. Without constant review, information becomes inaccessible and useless.

Exercise 9

Review the key concepts from the sample chapter.

Learning is a lifelong task. Your knowledge grows by a series of steps that are always based on previously learned material. In order for it to be useful to you, you must be able to comprehend, keep, and remember information you have learned. Applying the SQ3R method as you "read" each chapter will help you to learn, in the true sense of the word.

SUMMARY

Applying SQ3R to each of your textbook chapters will make you a more efficient and effective reader. SQ3R lets you learn and study as you read. Therefore, it saves you both time and effort. As a conscious reader, use your reading skills as an aid to learning. SQ3R should definitely be one of your learning tools.

Application I

Choose a chapter that has been assigned by one of your instructors. Survey it first. Next, develop questions about its content. Then, read the chapter and look for answers to your questions. After reading the chapter, take notes on its key elements. (Use the format you prefer.) Finally, set up a review session, either with a partner or a study group from the class.

Application II

Use SQ3R whenever you have to deal with lengthy, unfamiliar material. The process will help you grasp the material's key elements.

Chapter 23
Energy
Alternatives

Lesson Titles
23.1 Solar Energy
23.2 Energy from Water
23.3 Wind and Other Sources of Energy

The perfect energy source would be cheap, plentiful, efficient, easy to use, and would not cause pollution. Is there such an energy source? Maybe not, but there are things in the environment that do supply energy without showing signs of ever running out. What gives off heat and light every day? What causes a sailboat to move over the water? How does a raft get downstream?

People have used energy from the sun, wind, and water for centuries. Before the extensive use of fossil and nuclear fuels, these sources of energy were very important. Now the problems associated with fossil and nuclear fuels are becoming better known. As a result, people are beginning to think about using other energy sources.

In this chapter you will find out how the sun, the wind, and water are being used as sources of energy. You will also learn about other energy sources that are minor now but might become more important in the future.

Figure 23.1 An apartment building that has been modified to use solar energy

23.1
Solar Energy

You will find out
- why people are interested in solar energy;
- what devices are being used to collect solar energy;
- how solar energy can be used.

The idea of using energy from the sun, or **solar energy**, to answer people's energy needs is not a new one. Solar energy has been used to dry and bake foods for centuries. In the early 1600's, a French inventor reportedly used solar energy to heat air in an engine that pumped water. The Pueblo Indians built their homes out of adobe, a mixture of mud and sand. The adobe absorbed heat from the sun during the day and gave off that heat at night. Clearly, use of solar energy is not new. What is new, however, is an increasing and intensified interest in solar energy.

Why are people suddenly so interested in solar energy and other energy alternatives? They have come to recognize that while fossil and nuclear fuels can and do effectively answer their energy needs, these fuels are nonrenewable. They are also becoming more and more expensive. In addition, the use of fossil and nuclear fuels

Figure 23.2 The walls of these adobe homes absorb solar heat during the day and release that heat at night.

Figure 23.3 A solar home

creates some serious environmental problems. The question people are asking now is whether there is another energy source that could answer their energy needs without presenting the same serious problems. Many people believe that solar energy is the answer or, at least, part of the answer.

Solar energy is a **renewable** energy source. A renewable energy source is one that can be replaced. Every day the earth receives an enormous amount of solar energy. The use of solar energy does not appear to threaten the environment. Scientists and engineers are working on ways to collect, store, and change solar energy into other forms of usable energy. As ways to do these things become more practical, efficient, and affordable, more businesses and individual home owners are choosing to use solar energy.

The simplest way to use solar energy to heat a building is to allow sunlight in through windows or glass panels. If you have ever entered a car that had been closed up while sitting in the sun, you have surely noticed the results of this kind of solar heating. The temperature of a greenhouse can also be dramatically affected in the same way. This use of solar energy, while simple and relatively inexpensive, only affects areas that receive direct sunlight.

Do You Know?
If the sun's energy came from coal, it would shine at its present brightness for less than 5,000 years. By that time, all the coal would have been burned up.

Do You Know?
The average amount of solar energy that falls on a square meter in the United States in one year is equal to the amount of energy produced by the burning of one barrel of oil.

Scientists have devised ways to collect solar energy in one area of a building and carry it to other areas. **Solar collectors** collect and change solar energy into heat energy. These devices are positioned on a building in a place that allows for maximum exposure to sunlight. Some can even be moved or tilted to follow the sun. Many collectors are flat metal plates painted black. They are painted black because a dark surface absorbs solar energy better than a light one. Water or air passing in pipes behind the plates is heated. The warm water or air is then pumped to places where it is needed. The same water or air can be used over and over to absorb and transport heat. Other solar collectors have curved mirrors that direct sunlight onto tanks or pipes carrying water or air. Like the flat plates, the tanks and pipes are often painted black for better absorption of solar energy.

Solar cells are used to collect solar energy and change it into electric energy. These devices are used on spaceflights. Large panels covered with thousands of solar cells provide electric power for the spacecraft. On Earth, solar cells are in use in homes and businesses. However, they are not in widespread use. One reason for this is the current high cost of making and installing the cells.

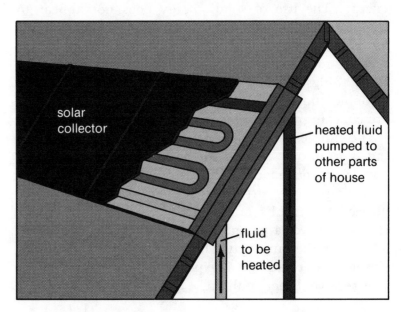

Figure 23.4 Using solar collectors in a solar home

Buildings using solar cells or solar collectors or both exist today. It is probable that more will be built in the future. However, the conversion of already existing buildings to solar energy is not realistic in most cases due to the expense involved. Also, most existing buildings are not located or positioned for maximum exposure to sunlight. Still, the use of solar energy to answer the energy needs of a single building is growing.

Activity

How Can You Make a Solar Collector?

Materials
shoe box
newspaper
black spray paint
rubber or plastic
    tubing with a
    small opening
    (about 1 m)
funnel to fit
    into tubing
tape
plastic wrap
2 beakers
graduated cylinder
thermometer

Procedure
1. Half fill the shoe box with crumpled newspaper. Spray paint on the newspaper and the inside of the box.

2. Punch a hole wide enough for the tubing at each end of the box. Arrange the tubing as shown in the diagram. Tape it in place. Cover the box tightly with plastic wrap.

3. Put 100 mL of water in a beaker. Measure and record the temperature of the water.

4. Place the box in direct sunlight. Rest one end on a thin book to slightly tilt the box. Set an empty beaker under the lower end of the tubing. Insert the funnel into the other end.

5. Pour the water into the funnel. Allow it to flow through the tubing and collect in the empty beaker.

6. Repeat step 5 fifteen times. After every fifth trial, measure and record the temperature of the water and the trial number.

Questions
1. Make a line graph to show the temperatures you measured.

2. How does the water temperature change?

3. How could you make your solar collector produce hotter water?

Figure 23.5 Collecting solar energy in a New Mexico desert

What about using solar energy on a larger scale to provide electricity, not just for a single home, but for a whole community? The problem here is that the sun's energy, although plentiful, is spread out over an enormous area. Suppose solar cells were being used to produce as much electricity as the amount currently being produced in the United States by other means. Experts estimate that this would require solar cells covering from 25,000 to 70,000 square kilometers of land! Where is there an area of land this size that is available? Not any area of land will do. The land must receive a consistently large amount of solar energy.

The most appropriate areas for collecting solar energy in large amounts are in the desert areas of the world near the equator. Within the United States, the desert areas of Arizona and New Mexico are most appropriate. However, the use of large areas of these states to collect solar energy would probably conflict with other interests.

Experts have suggested two possible ways to collect solar energy without taking over large land areas. One way would be to construct solar collection stations in ocean areas. The second way is to use solar collection satellites. As a satellite orbited Earth, the satellite would receive a constant, reliable supply of solar energy. This energy could then be sent down to Earth.

As the use of solar energy grows and is further investigated, more practical and effective applications of it will be developed. Although it does not seem to have a negative effect on the environment, there is a possibility that the widespread use of solar energy might bring about some change in the overall distribution of heat from the sun. However, at the present time, solar energy does appear to be a promising energy alternative. People should also remember that once they have paid the price for the purchase and installation of solar energy devices, the sunlight is free.

Figure 23.6 A solar music box

Study Questions for 23.1

1. What makes solar energy a desirable energy source?
2. What is a solar collector?
3. What is a solar cell?
4. What problem has prevented the use of solar energy to produce electricity for whole communities rather than single buildings?

23.2
Energy from Water

You will find out
- how hydroelectric power is produced;
- how hydroelectric power is related to solar energy;
- why hydroelectric power is not more widely used;
- how tidal energy is used.

For years people have used moving water to carry logs downriver to sawmills and paper mills. Rivers have also moved rafts of goods and people from place to place. The major application of moving water as an energy source, however, has been in the generation of electricity. When falling water strikes the blades of a turbine, a rotational motion is produced. This motion is used to generate electricity. The electricity generated by the use of moving water is called **hydroelectric power.**

Figure 23.7 Falling water can be used to generate electricity.

Do You Know?
One of the earliest hydroelectric power plants was built in Niagara Falls, New York, in 1896.

In order to produce hydroelectric power at a steady rate, the water in rivers is dammed up to make waterfalls. The largest hydroelectric power plant in the United States is at the Grand Coulee Dam across the Columbia River in the state of Washington. Although many states in the United States have hydroelectric power plants, the most productive ones are in Washington, Oregon, and California.

Water vapor condenses

Water falls to Earth

Water evaporates from Earth

Water from above sea level flows toward ocean

Figure 23.8 The water cycle

Hydroelectric power is related to solar energy. The sun heats water and causes it to evaporate from the surface of the earth. That water eventually falls back to the earth as rain or snow. If the water falls on a place that is above sea level, it runs downhill. It may eventually enter a river and flow to the ocean. While in a river, that water may be used to produce hydroelectric power. As long as there is sunlight to evaporate water so that it can fall back to earth and form rivers, the production of hydroelectric power will be possible.

Figure 23.9 A hydroelectric power plant at the Bonneville Dam on the Columbia River in the state of Washington

Hydroelectric power is renewable and does not cause pollution. Why, then, is it not more widely used? Not all rivers are appropriate for the production of hydroelectric power. Also, the damming up of rivers causes drastic changes in the environment. Plant and animal life both in and along a river are threatened. In some areas, plans for hydroelectric power plants have been considered and finally canceled due to environmental concerns.

Many of the world's large rivers are in undeveloped areas of South America, Africa, and Asia. The potential for hydroelectric power in these areas is high. But, so far, the countries with that potential have not made use of it.

Another kind of energy that involves water is **tidal energy.** Gravitational forces involving the earth, the sun, and the moon cause ocean tides. Tidewaters can be used to turn turbines that generate electricity. The Rance tidal power plant in France has been producing electricity since 1966.

Tidal energy is renewable and does not cause pollution. However, the tidal areas that are involved may suffer some of the same changes in their environment as the river areas around hydroelectric power plants. This problem has limited the development of tidal power plants. Another limiting factor is the availability of coastline areas that are suitable for tidal power plants. A suitable coastline would be a narrow bay or inlet where there is a great difference in the water levels at high and low tides.

Figure 23.10 The Rance tidal power plant

1. How is hydroelectric power produced?
2. What is the relationship between hydroelectric power and solar energy?
3. How do the dams associated with hydroelectric power plants affect the environment?
4. How is tidal energy used?

23.3
Wind and Other Sources of Energy

You will find out
- how wind energy is used;
- what is meant by geothermal energy;
- what is meant by biomass.

The wind is a source of energy that people have been using for centuries. Wind once filled the sails of ocean-going ships. It also turned windmills to grind grain and pump water.

Wind is the movement of masses of air from one place to another. This movement is the result of temperature differences in the atmosphere. The temperature differences come from uneven heating of the atmosphere by the sun. Wind energy, like solar energy, is a renewable energy source. Also like solar energy, the use of wind energy does not appear to threaten the environment.

Today, windmills are being used to generate electricity. The blades of a windmill act like a turbine. Wind strikes the blades, causing them to turn. This rotational motion is used to generate electricity.

Figure 23.11 *left:* Wind results when warmer, less dense air rises and cooler, denser air moves in to replace it. *right:* Using wind energy to generate electricity

In some areas, one windmill provides the electricity for a single home or business. In other areas, a large number of windmills generate enough electricity to service many homes or businesses. There is, of course, one obvious limitation to the large-scale use of windmills to generate electricity. Many areas do not receive enough wind on a regular basis to make windmills practical.

Activity

How Can You Measure Wind Speed?

Materials
protractor
long needle
thread
Ping-Pong ball
wood (30 cm by 2 cm)
glue

Procedure

1. Make a handle by gluing the wood to the corner of the protractor at the 180° mark.

2. Thread the needle and push it through the Ping-Pong ball. Pull the thread through the ball and tie a knot at one end.

3. Glue the free end of the thread to the center of the straight side of the protractor. When the protractor is held level, the thread and ball should hang at exactly 90°.

4. Use your device to measure the wind speed in five different areas near your school. Compare the protractor reading in degrees with those on the chart to determine approximate wind speed.

Questions

1. Make a bar graph to show the wind speed in the areas you visited.

2. To be useful in generating electricity, wind must have a constant speed of at least 13 km/h. Could the wind in any of the areas you visited be used to generate electricity?

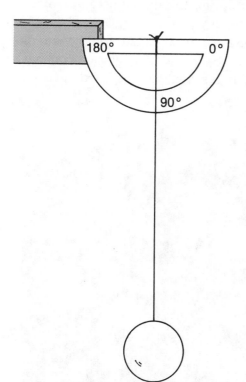

Angle	km/h
90°	0
80°	13
70°	19
60°	24
50°	29
40°	34
30°	42
20°	52

The interior of the earth is very hot. This fact may surprise you since people generally find basements and underground caves cool or even cold. However, this situation exists only in areas very near the earth's surface. If, for example, you were to go way down in the shaft of a deep coal mine, you would find it hot.

The high temperatures inside the earth can heat underground water supplies. This hot water and the steam it produces may come to or near the surface. It may erupt forcefully in geysers or flow into pools known as hot springs. The heat energy that comes from inside the earth is called **geothermal** [JEE-oh-thur-muhl] **energy.** Steam from geothermal energy can be used to spin turbines to generate electricity. Geothermal energy can also heat buildings and cook food.

Geothermal energy is renewable and does not appear to seriously threaten the environment. However, the waters in geysers and hot springs do contain many minerals. In significant amounts, the distribution of these minerals could affect the environment.

Only certain locations are appropriate for the use of geothermal energy. Those areas have geysers or hot springs at or near the earth's surface. The Lardello area

Do You Know?
The steam wells tapped by The Geysers power plant are 2.5 km deep.

Figure 23.12 The Geysers power plant uses geothermal energy to generate electricity.

Figure 23.13 Wood, a form of biomass, is a renewable energy source.

of Italy has been using geothermal energy since 1904. Many areas of Iceland also rely on geothermal energy. In the United States, The Geysers power plant in California has been using geothermal energy since 1960.

Living things provide an energy source called **biomass** [BY-oh-mas]. Biomass includes all the materials in living things, their wastes, and their remains. Probably the most obvious use of energy from biomass is the burning of wood for heat. Other kinds of plant material can also be burned. In addition, efforts have been made to use garbage and other wastes for fuel.

Biomass is a renewable energy source. As long as there are living things there will be biomass. However, the burning of biomass does contribute to air pollution. Also, the careless cutting down of thousands of trees can drastically change the environment. Even if new trees are planted, it takes many years for them to grow. In the meantime, the area may lose topsoil due to the action of wind and running water. Food and shelter for animals are also lost when trees are cut down.

Study Questions for 23.3
1. How is wind energy used?
2. What is geothermal energy?
3. What is biomass?

CHAPTER REVIEW

Main Ideas

- Solar energy is renewable, and its use does not appear to threaten the environment.
- Solar collectors collect and change solar energy into heat energy.
- Solar cells collect and change solar energy into electricity.
- Some individual buildings use solar energy for heating and electric power. Large areas of land are needed to gather solar energy for communities.
- The electricity generated by the use of moving water is called hydroelectric power.
- To produce hydroelectric power, rivers are dammed to make waterfalls.
- Hydroelectric power is related to solar energy because hydroelectric power is a result of the water cycle.
- The dams involved in the production of hydroelectric power can cause drastic environmental changes.
- Tidal energy can be used to run turbines that generate electricity.
- Wind energy can be used to generate electricity through the use of windmills.
- Geothermal energy is heat energy that comes from inside the earth. It can be used to generate electricity and to heat buildings.
- Biomass includes all the materials in living things, their wastes, and their remains. Biomass is a renewable energy source.

Using Vocabulary

On your paper, write a magazine article about alternative energy sources in which you use each of the following terms. Underline the terms in your article.

solar energy	solar cells	geothermal energy
renewable	hydroelectric power	biomass
solar collectors	tidal energy	

Chapter 9

CRITICAL READING

Objectives

Objectives
1. To distinguish between facts and opinions.
2. To make inferences from passages.
3. To recognize and draw conclusions.
4. To recognize and form judgments.

Key Concept
As a conscious reader, you must be able to respond critically to a passage from any source. Your critical response is based on your ability to identify opinions, make inferences, draw conclusions, and form judgments. These skills and those you have developed throughout this book make you a conscious reader who enters a dialogue with an author.

Every day you use your critical skills. You determine whether it is a fact or an opinion that the food in the cafeteria is wholesome and tasty. You make inferences about new people you meet based on your observations of their clothing, behavior, and attitude. You draw conclusions about students on your campus. You make judgments about the merits of studying or going to a movie. Now, you must use these same skills in your reading.

Throughout this book, you have developed your reading abilities by analyzing material. Using thoughtful analysis, you can look at separate parts of a passage: its main ideas, its topic sentence, and its types of supporting details. This information gives you access to the literal meaning of a passage. Here, the author states ideas in a straightforward manner. Now, you must develop your critical reading abilities to complete your growth as a conscious reader. As a conscious reader, you must identify opinions, make inferences, draw conclusions, and form judgments. With these skills, you enter into a conversation with the writer of a work and understand the message more completely.

FACTS AND OPINIONS

Facts can be proven or disproven through objective means. You can easily check facts by referring to sources, using sensory experience, or measuring. For instance, it is a fact that a triangle has three sides. It is a fact that sodium and chloride atoms form salt. It is a fact that

Richard Wright wrote *Native Son*. Each of these facts can be proven by senses or sources.

Unlike facts, opinions are personal beliefs. These beliefs can never be proven or disproven. For example, it is an opinion that California has the best national parks in the country. It is an opinion that Mexican food is better than Italian cuisine. It is an opinion that the federal government should provide health services for its citizens. However, each of these opinions can be *supported* by facts. A writer could compare the number, size, and services of national parks in California to those elsewhere. A restaurant reviewer could provide examples of Mexican dishes that are more nutritious, flavorful, or attractive than Italian dishes. A senator could cite statistics that many Americans do not have health coverage and cannot afford to buy it. However, this evidence does not *prove* these opinions. At best, the factual evidence *suggests* that the statements might be correct.

To distinguish facts from opinions, examine the following pairs of statements. What differences do you notice?

Fact: Most of the students at State University are commuters.

Opinion: Commuters do not participate in campus activities.

Fact: The Indiana Jones films have many special effects.

Opinion: The Indiana Jones films are the most exciting adventure films.

Fact: Television newscasters cover major events in brief, five-minute segments.

Opinion: Television newscasters give incomplete accounts of major events.

Each of the above facts can be proven. The number of commuters at the university can be counted. The special effects in the Indiana Jones films can also be observed and counted. Watching the nightly news will confirm that events are given only a few minutes each. However, the opinions cannot be proven true or false. Although some college commuters may rush home after classes, others do participate in activities. You may believe that the Indiana Jones films are exciting adventure stories. However, many other movies could also be considered exciting. Finally, newscasters do focus on a brief summary of events. However, they provide enough information for viewers who want only the bare facts.

As a conscious reader, you need to distinguish between facts and opinions. Frequently, we accept opinions as factual statements. Analyze the following statements. Are they facts or opinions?

Nike shoes are the best.

Georgia O'Keeffe's paintings are the best of modern art.

The National Gallery in Washington has the finest collection of painting and sculptures.

E. M. Forster was the most skillful British novelist of the twentieth century.

Each of these statements, similar to ones you hear in conversations, can be supported by factual evidence. Others are likely to agree with these statements. However, these statements remain opinions. Because we willingly accept many statements like these as absolutely true, we fail to distinguish between facts and opinions. Hence, we allow others to guide our thoughts. If you fail to distinguish between facts and opinions when you read, then the same problem can occur. You allow the writer to influence your thoughts.

EXERCISE 1

Read each of the following sentences carefully. If the sentence can be proven or disproven by using objective evidence, label it as a fact (F) in the blank. If the sentence reveals a personal opinion that cannot be absolutely proven or disproven, label it as an opinion (O) in the blank.

_____ 1. Nuclear power plants provide a safe, environmentally clean form of energy.

_____ 2. Brazil's rain forests are being destroyed at a rapid rate.

_____ 3. Advertisements shape consumers' buying patterns.

_____ 4. The Louvre Museum holds the most amazing collection of art.

_____ 5. The Boston Symphony Orchestra is the best in the United States.

_____ 6. All thoroughbred horses have the same official birthday, January 1.

_____ 7. Horse racing is a fast-growing, exciting sport.

_____ 8. America's trade deficit improved during the past year.

_____ 9. The average American household has two televisions.

_____ 10. A well-designed garden provides enjoyment and recreation.

EXERCISE 2   Read the following advertisements for GM and Canon carefully. Label all facts and opinions in the margin.

We drive cars through sand storms or ice storms. At 120° in the Arizona desert and 40° below in the Canadian tundra.

We run cars over cement blocks, gravel, cracks, potholes and pits. Again and again and again.

We use a machine to batter in roofs. Or we slowly crush front ends in a powerful vise.

Last year we willingly put cars—ours and others—through 27 million miles of test driving.

And it's all for you. Because it takes repeated analysis of wear and tear at these extremes to find new ways to make your car last longer and perform better in normal use.

We believe in taking the extra time, giving the extra effort and paying attention to every detail. That's what it takes to provide the quality that leads more people to buy GM cars and trucks than any other kind. And why GM owners are the most loyal on the road.

That's the GM commitment to excellence.

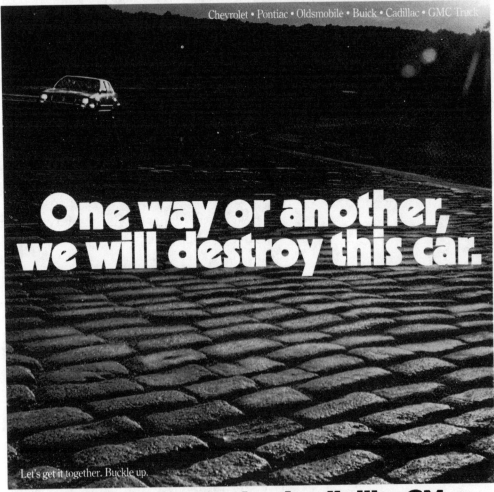

Chevrolet • Pontiac • Oldsmobile • Buick • Cadillac • GMC Truck

One way or another, we will destroy this car.

Let's get it together. Buckle up.

Nobody sweats the details like GM.

GM-PAP-P40300
7 x 10 page
National Publications

NW Ayer Incorporated
DETROIT

(*Smithsonian 15 (April 1984):127.*)

WILDLIFE AS CANON SEES IT

Bare-necked Umbrellabird

Genus: *Cephalopterus*
Species: *glabricollis*
Adult size: 36-41 cm
Adult weight: 320-450 g
Habitat: Tropical rain forests in Costa Rica and Panama
Surviving number: Unknown
Photographed by Michael and Susan Fogden

The male bare-necked umbrellabird descends to the lower canopy of the cloud forest to perform its courtship display. There, on a selected perch, it spreads its "umbrella" crest and emits resonating calls as its throat sac inflates and turns a vivid scarlet. Like many other tropical birds, the bare-necked umbrellabird is threatened by the destruction of its forest habitat. To save endangered species, it is essential to protect their habitats and understand the vital role of each species within the earth's ecosystems. Photography, both as a scientific research tool and as a means of communication, can help promote a greater awareness and understanding of the bare-necked umbrellabird and our entire wildlife heritage.

EOS 1
The New Classic

(National Geographic. Jan. 1991. Frontmatter.)

EXERCISE 3

Read each paragraph below carefully. Identify each sentence as either a fact or an opinion.

1.   To prevent the greenhouse effect from increasing still further, the world must cut its dependence on fossil fuels by more than half.¹ In the short term, while we're stuck with fossil fuels, we can use them much more efficiently.² With 5 percent of the world's population, the United States uses nearly 25 percent of the world's energy.³ The U.S. is the world's worst CO_2 polluter.⁴ Your car emits more than its own weight in CO_2 each year.⁵ Clearly, if we can get more miles per gallon of gasoline, we'll be putting less carbon dioxide into the atmosphere.⁶ All experts agree that huge improvements in fuel efficiency are possible.⁷ If we can drive at 40 miles per gallon, we'll be injecting only half as much CO_2 into the air as when we drove at 20 miles per gallon; at 80 miles per gallon, only a quarter as much.⁸ This issue is typical of the emerging conflict between short-term maximizing of profits and long-term reduction of greenhouse warming.⁹

(Sagan, Carl. "Tomorrow's Energy." Parade (25 November 1990):11.)

2.   The many wars that have erupted in Africa since independence have further accelerated the slaughter of animals.¹ With the accompanying breakdown of law, it has become open season on wildlife in many places.² An African peasant living at the subsistence level near a game park can get up to $500 for the horns of one rhino or a pair of small elephant tusks, more cash than he otherwise would ever see in his lifetime.³ And some rangers earning only about $50 a month stand to realize nearly a year's pay from shooting one elephant or rhino.⁴ Matters are made worse by African judges who tend to be lenient with poachers.⁵ Their attitude is: "The man is poor and has a big family to feed."⁶ Sentences are often only three to six months in jail.⁷ Usually, however, poaching is not the work of hungry peasants.⁸ Rather, it has become big business.⁹ Gangs of sometimes as many as 60 men, riding in trucks, cover vast areas.¹⁰ Crooked dealers, in league with the poachers, then smuggle their booty into world markets.¹¹

(Reed, David. "Africa's Wildlife: Countdown to Zero." Reader's Digest 121 (July 1982):138–139.)

INFERENCES

An inference is an opinion based upon factual evidence. Inferences rely on the *suggestions* of factual evidence. However, inferences cannot be proven or disproven based upon the information given. Analyze the cartoon on the following page. What can you infer about Weevil Bumstead's political career?

THAT'S WEEVIL BUMSTEAD, THE POLITICIAN

WHAT DID HE RUN FOR?

WELL, THE LAST TIME ANYBODY SAW HIM...

HE WAS RUNNING FOR THE BORDER

(Young and Drake. "Blondie." Baltimore Sun *(18 May 1991).)*

If you inferred that Weevil had been involved in shady, unethical politics, then your inference is correct. The fact that he was last seen running for the border indicates that he had to get out of town quickly. However, since no facts are presented to confirm this opinion, it is an inference.

Although we may not recognize them, we make inferences all the time. We make inferences about a person's social standing, wealth, taste, and behavior. Consider, for instance, the inferences you might make if you were to see someone elegantly dressed, perfectly groomed, driving an expensive car. You might immediately assume that the person is wealthy. In another case, if you were to see a group of people gathering around city hall, you might infer that these are angry protestors who will picket the mayor. However, these inferences based on slight factual evidence—clothing and a car and a mass of people—cannot be proven as facts. Instead, you may find later that your inferences are incorrect. For instance, the person in the expensive car might have only rented it for a special dance. The crowd of people might be assembled to hear the mayor's speech. Other possibilities also exist. Your inferences are based upon your knowledge of people, situations, and society. Unless you have further information, however, these inferences remain only reasonable guesses.

We make inferences easily. In fact, many advertisers rely on our ability to make inferences in order to sell their products. For instance, if you buy a certain brand of tennis shoe endorsed by a professional athlete, then you infer that you will gain some of the athlete's ability. This ability to make inferences quickly is helpful in a number of situations. For example, your inferences about the quality of consumer goods allow you to make quick decisions. In this way, you do not take weeks to decide on the perfect coat or cassette player to buy. In addition, your inferences about situations can help you save time. If you were to see a long line of cars ahead of you, then you might infer that there is a traffic jam. You might then choose a different route.

However, too often we overlook the steps that lead us to a particular inference. Our own backgrounds, beliefs, and opinions help us form inferences. Look at the differences between cultures as an example. In the United States, many brides wear white as a symbol of purity. However, in China, white is a symbol of death, so Chinese brides wear red, the color of life. However, many Americans would be surprised to see a bride dressed in red. Consequently, your inference about the wedding would depend on your cultural background.

Conscious readers use inferences to enable them to understand an author's implied meaning. Analyze the following sentences. What inferences can you draw from these facts?

Over 60 percent of newspaper readers turn to the section on local news first.

Only 10 percent of the federal budget is spent on health care.

Both of these factual statements suggest a number of inferences. For example, the first sentence suggests that people are more interested in the news of their town or city in terms of their daily lives. It might suggest further that many newspaper readers get their national news from television reports. The second sentence might imply that the nation spends billions on health care for its citizens. On the other hand, the same figure could suggest that health care receives only a small portion of the billions the government spends each year. Additionally, health care may receive less money than the defense department or some other division of the federal bureaucracy. More information will allow you to determine the correct inference.

EXERCISE 4   Analyze the following advertisements for RCA and Hyatt resorts. What inferences can you draw from these advertisements about the values, beliefs, or types of people who will use these products?

"Your wish is our command."

"Whatever you say, boss."

At last, technology that serves man.

Must a VCR be so darn hard to program? Must a remote have seven thousand buttons? Must an instruction manual be dry as the Sahara? Nay. Not anymore. We introduce a new line of VCRs that make recording a show easy as watching one. We introduce the Simple Touch™ remote control with only six buttons, for the stuff you really need 99% of the time.

Our new line of VCRs makes recording a show as easy as watching one.

The 35" RCA Home Theatre™ has Pic-in-Pic capability, a VHP picture tube, zoom and pan feature, Comb filter, and Sound Retrieval System.

The Simple Plus™ remote controls basic VCR functions.

The Simple Touch™ remote, just six buttons.

We introduce SRS (•)* [Sound Retrieval System], which surrounds you with stereo sound without stringing up extra wires or speakers. We bring you easy-to-read instruction manuals that you might actually read. There's even a toll-free number [1-800-336-1900] to help you find your nearest RCA dealer. Can it get any easier? Well, if so, we're working on it.

RCA
Changing Entertainment. Again.™

© 1991 Thomson Consumer Electronics. *SRS and (•) are registered trademarks of the Hughes Aircraft Company, a division of GM Hughes Electronics.

(*Southern Living* 27 (April 1992):37.)

"What a setting.
Water on the right, sand
on the left…"

"Sounds like our
golf game this morning."

Feel The Hyatt Touch.^{SM}

Hilton Head, South Carolina

Stroll on miles of white sandy beaches or drive the fairways on any of three championship, eighteen hole golf courses.

For reservations or more information about Hyatt Hotels and Resorts worldwide, call your travel planner or **1-800-233-1234.**

Hyatt Hotels and Resorts worldwide encompasses hotels managed by two separate companies – Hyatt Hotels Corp. and Hyatt International Corp.

(Southern Living. *February 1991. Copyright Hyatt Corp. 1990.*)

EXERCISE 5   Read each set of sentences carefully. The first sentence contains factual information. Use it to determine whether each sentence that follows is a fact (F) or an inference (I).

1. More than 60 percent of all Americans declare that they exercise at least three times a week.

   _____ Americans are exercising more.

   _____ Americans are concerned with fitness.

   _____ The increase in exercise has encouraged sales of sports equipment.

2. State universities usually cost less than private schools. For instance, Evergreen State charges only $2,500 a year for tuition. In contrast, Hall University, a private school, charges $10,000 for tuition.

   _____ State schools are less expensive than private ones.

   _____ Private universities offer more than state schools.

   _____ Students receive more individual attention at private schools.

3. Three new movies portray women as heroes. In each film, women abandon traditional roles and become corporate executives, artists, or criminals.

   _____ Only when women abandon traditional roles can they achieve success.

   _____ Women have not been considered heroes before.

   _____ These movies reflect a new trend in society with women as highly motivated individuals.

4. Only one-third of young adults aged 18–21 vote in national elections.

   _____ Young adults are apathetic about politics.

   _____ Young adults are more concerned with their own activities.

   _____ Politicians have not been able to attract young voters.

5. National tests for graduate, medical, and law schools now include at least two essays.

   _____ The professions value good writing.

_____ Applicants for these schools should be able to write well.

_____ Writing tells a great deal about an applicant.

EXERCISE 6

Read the following paragraphs carefully. At the end of each paragraph, you will be asked to make inferences about the passage.

1. The social consequences of the [Industrial Revolution] were enormous. Within decades hundreds of thousands of workers moved into the industrial centers, overwhelming the capacity of the cities to absorb them. Shanty towns grew up on the outskirts where the new workers lived in crowded, unsanitary conditions. The machines not only demanded regimentation of work but also reduced the need for skill or physical force. Especially in the cloth industry most operations involved in mechanized production could be performed by children, who were cheaper to hire than adults. By the middle 1820s a small boy working two looms could produce fifteen times more than an adult laborer working by hand.

   (Witt, Mary Ann Frese, et al. The Humanities. Vol. II. 3rd ed. Lexington, MA: Heath, 1989. p. 264.)

   a. What can you infer about the living conditions of many urban workers during the Industrial Revolution?

   _____

   _____

   _____

   _____

   b. What inferences can you draw about child labor?

   _____

   _____

   _____

   _____

2. [Prior to the 1992 referendum on apartheid,] South Africa was the only country in Africa where people of European ancestry still controlled the government. Large groups of settlers from both the Netherlands and Great Britain came to South Africa from the 1600s to the early 1900s. The people whose ancestors came from the Netherlands are known as Afrikaners. Ever since South Africa has been independent of Great Britain, Afrikaners have held political power.

Black South Africans outnumber whites by about five to one. However, the black population had few political rights. The South African government pursued a policy of apartheid, which means apartness. Under apartheid, the white minority held the economic and political power of the nation. This affected every part of life in South Africa. Blacks could live only in certain areas. They had separate—often very poorly maintained—schools, hospitals, parks, playgrounds, and beaches. There were also special laws that limited their actions and achievements.

(*Gritzner, Charles.* World Geography. *Lexington, MA: Heath, 1989. p. 445.*)

a. What can you infer about the balance of power in South Africa?

_____

_____

_____

_____

b. What can you infer about the quality of life for blacks in South Africa?

_____

_____

_____

_____

CONCLUSIONS

A conclusion is a logical decision based on factual evidence. In Chapter 4, you developed conclusions by identifying unstated main ideas in paragraphs. By examining the facts—the supports—within a paragraph, you reached a logical conclusion about the topic and the author's opinion on that topic. From this conclusion, you created a topic sentence.

As a conscious reader, you must draw conclusions from information given and be prepared to test the validity, or the correctness, of an author's stated conclusion. Analyze the following factual statement and the conclusions offered:

Fact: Within the past 15 years, after the introduction of fluoride into public water systems, American children have had fewer cavities than the generation before.

Conclusions: American children are more concerned now with dental hygiene.

Fluoride has had an impact on reducing the number of cavities children have.

American children have avoided cavity-causing foods in the past 15 years.

Which of these conclusions is valid? Which ones are not? If you analyze the information carefully, then you will see that only the second is a valid conclusion based on the information given. Sentence one is an inference. It may well be that children are more familiar with good dental care now and practice it. However, the factual information given does not point to this as a conclusion. Sentence three is also based on assumptions. Again, we now know far more about nutrition, so children may have been taught to avoid cavity-causing foods, such as candies and desserts. However, this sentence is not a conclusion. Remember that a conclusion is valid when it is based only on the information given. It is from this information alone that you must draw your conclusion.

EXERCISE 7

Read the following factual evidence. Then, read the three follow-up statements. In the space provided, indicate whether each statement offers a conclusion (C), an inference (I), or only a related fact (F).

1. In the 1970s, few high-school students worked after school. Today, over 60 percent of high-school students work 10–20 hours a week at part-time jobs. Within this time period, the economy has changed drastically. For instance, gasoline used to cost 50 cents a gallon; today, it costs over a dollar a gallon. This same inflation is seen in every aspect of consumers' lives.

   _____ Consumer goods cost more today than in the 1970s.

   _____ Because students' tastes and needs have changed in the past 20 years, they need money to buy more goods.

   _____ The changing economy has had an impact on the amount of money teenagers have. Many teenagers work to earn money.

2. The past ten years have seen an increase in medical technology. Today, doctors may use ultrasound, magnetic resonance imaging, and CAT scans to help in diagnosing illnesses.

   _____ Medical costs have risen with this new technology.

   _____ Doctors have more sophisticated means of diagnosing patients' problems.

   _____ More patients are saved with this new technology.

3.   The past year has seen a rise in the number of television programs dedicated to recreations of crime. Many of these programs ask for the viewer's assistance in solving cases.

_____ Americans are interested in crime stories.

_____ Private citizens have aided law officers in capturing 30 percent of the criminals shown on these programs.

_____ The average American citizen can now assist law officers in catching criminals.

JUDGMENTS

Judgments are evaluations based on the merits of given information. For instance, a mechanic makes a judgment based on the condition of a car. If a car loses fluid for cooling the engine, the mechanic must determine whether the hoses, water pump, or radiator is the cause of the loss of fluid. Based on his knowledge of cars and his experience with this situation, a mechanic will arrive at a judgment about the cause of the car's problem. The mechanic will then judge the best course of action. Each judgment is based upon the merits of the situation.

Of course, you use this same process in other situations. When you decide to rent an apartment, live in a dormitory, or stay at home during your college career, you judge the advantages and disadvantages of each location. When you buy a car, you examine a number of features on each potential purchase—price, gas mileage, style, reliability, and safety record. You then judge the cars on these features.

Conscious readers use judgments in two ways. First, they recognize the judgments made by authors and then determine whether those judgements are valid. Second, they arrive at their own judgments about issues and viewpoints presented in what they read.

EXERCISE 8   Read each paragraph carefully, and answer the questions that accompany the paragraphs.

1.   It is tempting to romanticize the tranquillity and isolation of the lighthouse keeper's life, but sometimes it was true hardship duty. Many keepers and their families fought a constant battle with loneliness, boredom, and bad weather. At the same time, most took fierce pride in their independence and considered it a sign of weakness to ask for help from the "mainland." They grew their own vegetables (soil conditions permitting); caught fish, lobsters, crabs; captured rain water in cisterns, and sometimes kept a cow for milk. They were responsible for maintenance and repair work, and they saw to the cleaning and polishing of their lanterns and brasswork with a zeal that was nothing less than astonishing. On light stations that were exposed to the full brunt of storms, the work was sometimes downright harrowing. During one ferocious blow in 1882, the keeper of the Tillamook Rock Light looked on in horror as waves pummeled the top of his tower, which loomed fully 133 feet above sea level. Some keepers were washed right off their islands or died when their lighthouses were destroyed by wind and waves; others perished trying to rescue seamen in distress.

(Hanson, Dennis. "For Lighthouses, a Brighter Future." Smithsonian 18 (August 1987):103.)

a. What is the author's opinion about the life of lighthouse keepers? How is this supported in the paragraph?

_____

_____

_____

_____

b. In your judgment, what other jobs are dangerous or difficult to perform? How would you support your judgment?

_____

_____

_____

_____

2.   Donora is twenty-eight miles south of Pittsburg and covers the tip of a lumpy point formed by the most convulsive of the Monongahela's many horseshoe bends. Though accessible by road, rail, and river, it is an extraordinarily secluded place. The river and the bluffs that lift abruptly from the water's edge to a height of four hundred and fifty feet enclose it on the north and east and south, and just above it to the west is a range of rolling but even higher hills. On its outskirts are acres of sidings and rusting gondolas, abandoned mines, smoldering slag piles, and gulches filled with rubbish. Its limits are marked by sooty signs that read, "Donora, Next to Yours the Best Town in the U.S.A." It is a harsh gritty town, founded in 1901 and old for its age, with a gaudy main street and a thousand identical gaunt gray houses. Some of its streets are paved with concrete and some are cobbled, but many are of dirt and crushed coal. At least half of them are as steep as roofs, and several have steps instead of sidewalks. It is treeless and all but grassless, and much of it is slowly sliding downhill. After a rain, it is a smear of mud. Its vacant lots and many of its yards are mortally gullied, and one of its three cemeteries is an eroded ruin of gravelly clay and toppled tombstones. Its population is 12,300.

(Roueche, Berton. "The Fog." The New Yorker (Sept. 30, 1950).)

a. This paragraph is full of objective details. What judgments can you make based on these details?

_____

_____

_____

_____

b. By mentioning the signs that read, "Donora, Next to Yours the Best Town in the U.S.A." what judgment does the author offer about the town? What supports this judgment?

_____

_____

_____

_____

c. The passage contains several subjective opinions: "a harsh gritty town," "old for its age," and "mortally gullied" yards, for example. How do these phrases affect your judgment of the town?

_____

_____

_____

_____

d. After reading this passage, what judgment can you make about the effectiveness of concrete detail on the description of a town?

_____

_____

_____

_____

SUMMARY

When you read critically, you enter a conversation with the author of a piece and recognize the opinions, inferences, conclusions, and judgments that the author presents or suggests. This ability to engage in a conversation with the author makes you a conscious reader. With your ability to analyze the elements of a paragraph—its topic, its topic sentence and controlling idea, its details, and its pattern or structure—and your ability to read critically, you are able to determine the validity of a passage.

Read the following selection carefully. Then, respond to the questions that follow.

Fishing

MA LIN

Last Saturday, for the first time, I went fishing. For a whole summer I'd longed to do that, but Uncle Qiao never took me with him. This time Mamma arranged it for me.

It was a lovely morning. We drove down the country road. It seemed that I hadn't breathed any fresh air for a long time. The Qinling mountains were to the south. The fields were painted full of vegetables.

The sun rose slowly, little by some little. In Xi'an, I couldn't see the sun rise at all because of the buildings. But here it was so different. So wild, so broad. I watched the sun rise from the very beginning and looked at it as it jumped from the right side to the left side of the car, then to the right again.

I didn't know why I felt so strange: How can the sun rise like that just out of the void? If there had been some clouds, maybe I wouldn't have had such thoughts.

After about two hours, the car drove on an uneven road which led us to a lovely place. The scene there was as beautiful as pictures. (I don't know why when people want to describe some real thing which is really wonderful they say it is almost real or compare it to something that is really unreal. Very interesting!)

I liked that place. It was a village at the foot of the mountains. Very peaceful and very nice. A narrow stream (maybe a river) flowed through many clean stones zigzag. There were some trees here and there full of persimmons, especially at the tops of the trees. The fruits were orange and some leaves were turning red. A black dog watched the car and wagged its tail.

We stopped near a pond. Uncle Qiao began to prepare the fishing tackle and chose a proper place. I was sent to buy some apples and persimmons. Following a peasant, I went to several cottages.

I hadn't often been to a small village like this, and I'd never been in a farmer's family. Most of them were kind and friendly. Their rooms were all big and empty and dark and dirty. Some of them were cooking lunch. The smell of burning wood pervaded the house and the yard. Those people's clothes were dingy, their expressions humble, and they smiled timidly (I don't know why, but it's true). From Uncle's friend I learned that many of them were saving money to buy a color TV or even a tractor.

After comparing the prices of the fruit, we chose to buy at a middle-aged man's. His family seemed quite special. The rooms were bright and new, yet still very empty. His wife helped me pick the apples. Several times she looked at me and smiled. Then she put the apples into the basket beside me. She touched my bare arm with her rough hand, as though not on purpose. I glanced at her face and saw her timid eyes. I smiled and kept on working.

After we finished, she gazed at my sweater for a while, then lifted her hand which was still full of dirt, fondled it, and said: "How nice, your life." If at another occasion or if another person was involved I might feel very uncomfortable or unpleasant to be touched like this. But I smiled at her the whole time and felt bitter in my heart.

"It's so hard," she said.

I said nothing.

The sun got warmer and warmer. I went back to see how many fish Uncle Qiao had got. But he told me the best time for fishing was 3 o'clock in the afternoon. I sat down on the dry grass beside him. There was a pile of dry stems behind me. There must have been a mouse or something in it. Every time I passed the pile, I could hear the sound of hurry moving.

I sat there and was comfortable. The pond was not big. We could hear people talking on the other side. The fishing line was quiet on the smooth water. I gazed at the other side from time to time, and chewed a biscuit.

A young man sat near us, and I thought he was about the same age as me. Maybe a few years younger. He looked at us, then called out: "Hi, college student!" (Many people call us in this way.)

"Do you think you can get a fish?" he asked.

"I'm not sure. But it doesn't matter. I just like sitting," I said.

"Nice?" he said. "There come ghosts from that pond." He was serious.

"What are you talking about? How do you know that?"

"Three people died here," he said. "When my teacher first told me about it, I didn't believe. But now I know it's true."

"Can people really die in a pond this small?" I asked.

"Sure!"

"It doesn't seem very logical," I said.

"Well," said the boy, "how do you explain this: There was a paralytic old man who couldn't move at all. But one night, when the wind was big, he heard someone call him. He got up and came here, and jumped into the water without any hesitation. When we found him his head was still stuck in the mud."

"Is that really true?" I noticed a group of children started to gather around and all of them nodded seriously.

"You don't believe me," the boy said. He seemed a little offended. "These ghosts often have a banquet here."

"I'll bet it's delicious," I smiled.

"I'm not lying," the boy yelled. "I didn't believe it at first either. But now, well . . . you're a college student. I'm waiting for your explanation."

"I don't know. I'm not clear about what happened here," I said.

"What else could it be?" the boy yelled once more. I knew the debate was useless. I digressed. "I like your village," I said. "It's very pretty."

"I hate my village. It's ugly," he answered.

"Why?" I was surprised.

"You don't live here. If you had to every day face the same thing, the remote mountains, the poor water, do the same thing every day, then old, then die, all the same! I'm not like you. You change your surroundings and breathe the fresh air for a while. But live here—it's another thing."

We left there. I don't know whether I could ever go back to that place and those people again. I don't know how to describe my feeling. The apples we bought were quite sweet but the persimmons were bitter. It took me a whole week to eat them up.

I got no fish that day. But I didn't get nothing.

(Lin, Ma. "Fishing." Baltimore Sun (21 May 1991):7A.)

1. Ma Lin is a college student who has little experience of life in Chinese villages. What facts in this piece indicate that her life is very different from that of the village farmers?

   _____

   _____

   _____

   _____

2. What is her opinion of the village? What supports this opinion?

   _____

   _____

   _____

   _____

3. Why does she feel uncomfortable when the farmer's wife touches her sweater? What inferences can you draw about this event?

   _____

   _____

   _____

   _____

4. Ma Lin's conversation with the young man suggests some of the differences between city and country dwellers. What can you infer about the differences in the lives of Ma Lin and the young man? What can you conclude about the beliefs of the farmers?

_____

_____

_____

_____

5. Ma Lin states, "I didn't know whether I could ever go back to that place and those people again. I don't know how to describe my feeling. The apples we bought were quite sweet but the persimmons were bitter. It took me a whole week to eat them up." Although she uses facts here—the sweet apples and bitter persimmons—she seems to be suggesting something far more. What in her story was sweet, and what was bitter? How does this statement represent her judgment upon the day in the village?

_____

_____

_____

_____

APPLICATION II

Read the following selection carefully. Then, respond to the questions that follow it.

Founding Mothers

LINDA GRANT DE PAUW

When our history books tell us of the birth of the United States, they emphasize the activities of the "founding fathers." These founders, they tell us, were the handful of wealthy, educated, white males who wrote the Declaration of Independence in 1776 and the Constitution of the United States in 1787. The American way of life, however, did not spring from these bits of parchment, although we are rightly proud of these documents. They express the principles of justice, humanity, and equality that have served as our national ideals for almost two hundred years. They still inspire us today as we continue to try to extend the "inalienable rights of man" to people of all races, to children, and to women. The men who wrote the Declaration of Independence and the Constitution did not, however, invent the ideals these documents embody nor did they make them operative. The real founders of the United States were not the small number of "founding fathers" but the two and a half million people who lived in the eastern part of North America and who made up our founding generation. It is obvious that without these ordinary people the nation we know today would not have been born. Only occasionally do our school books give us a glimpse of some of these ordinary people. We read about the common soldiers freezing at Valley Forge, of the black man Crispus Attucks who fell during the Boston Massacre, and of Indian warriors who fought on both sides during the war for American Independence. Such men should certainly be remembered along with the statesmen and generals. Even more hidden than the ordinary men of the Revolutionary generation are the women who lived through those historic years.

Almost half of the Revolutionary generation was female. Fine ladies, servant girls, black slave women, middle-class matrons, and American Indian women all contributed to the development of American life. They may be invisible in the history books but they were present everywhere that men were. They were on farms and plantations, in the cities and in the forests. They ran businesses, served with the armies, and participated in political decision-making. The sex stereotypes and legal restrictions in the nineteenth century were relatively weak in the eighteenth. Consequently, women participated in the social, economic, political, and military activities of the day in ways that would be thought highly improper if not impossible for women a generation later.

(De Pauw, Linda Grant, "Founding Mothers," in Roads Go Ever On. *Eds. Donna Alvermann et al. Lexington, MA: Heath, 1989. p. 379.)*

1. According to the author, why are the "founding fathers" given so much attention in our history books? Is this attention justified?

    _____

    _____

    _____

    _____

2. In addition to the "founding fathers," who else helped create the new nation? What facts support this?

   _____

   _____

   _____

   _____

3. What can you infer from the fact that women have been excluded from the history books? What conclusions can you draw from this exclusion?

   _____

   _____

   _____

   _____

4. The author states that women in the eighteenth century had more freedom than women in the nineteenth. What can you infer from this statement about the role of women in the United States?

   _____

   _____

   _____

   _____

5. What is the author's judgment about our history books? Do you agree or disagree with this judgment based on your knowledge of history textbooks? Have these history books changed over the past twenty years in any way? Are they changing now? Check your library or bookstore for current history books. Examine these books and list the changes, if any, that you note.

   _____

   _____

   _____

   _____

Chapter 10

READING FASTER

Objectives	1. To determine a purpose for reading.
	2. To adjust reading rate to purpose.
	3. To become a flexible reader.
	4. To scan effectively.
	5. To increase reading rates.
Key Concept	Conscious readers know why they read. Reading purpose is important because it affects reading rate and type of reading.

What do you actually do as you "read"? Think about why you read. Most people just sit down and begin to read. However, simply "beginning to read" is not the best course of action. If you approach all reading tasks the same way, then you read ineffectively and inefficiently. Conscious readers can have a variety of reasons for their activity, and their reasons influence their reading methods.

READING PURPOSE

How can your purpose for reading affect your reading method? Consider these different reading situations:

1. On a weekday night, before you begin to study for the next week's computer science test, you decide to read the newspaper for a few minutes.

2. After reading the newspaper, you begin to read your computer science textbook because you know next week's test will cover three chapters.

3. Your English instructor has assigned a research paper. Your chosen topic is Thomas Edison's inventions. From the library, you have taken out a biography of Edison, a book on nineteenth-century American inventions, and three journal articles. In addition, you have photocopied an encyclopedia

entry on Edison. You now have several pieces to read for your report.

4. Finally, the end of the semester has arrived. You have earned a rest. Therefore, you decide to spend a few days at the beach, relax, and read a good novel.

In each instance, you are performing the same task, reading. However, each task differs. You do not need to understand the novel as well as you need to understand the textbook. You do not read the newspaper in the same way you read the Edison encyclopedia piece. In each case, you have a different purpose and a different goal. By recognizing your purpose and goal each time you read, you can adjust your reading rate and comprehension.

Different Situations = Different Reading

All reading is not the same. All reading should not be done at the same speed. All reading does not require the same degree of concentration. All reading does not carry the same expectation for remembering the information later. Look again at the reading situations above.

Reading for Information

1. Reading the newspaper. You probably read the daily newspaper because you want to be informed. You want to know what is happening in your community, in the country, and in the world. In addition, you probably want to be able to understand and take part in your friends' conversations in the cafeteria tomorrow.

Those reasons will affect your rate of comprehension. Although you want to remember what you have read, you do not need or want to remember every story. If you are interested in a topic, then you will probably read the entire article. On the other hand, if you have no interest in certain topics, or if you already know what happened, you will probably skip those articles. Finally, if you are somewhat interested in a story, you may read the headline and just the first few paragraphs. In other words, you will read the paper selectively. You are not reading every word in the paper, but you are "reading the paper." In fact, if someone were watching you read the newspaper, it would seem to the observer that you had finished the paper quickly. He or she might conclude that you are a fast reader.

However, although you have "read" the paper, it is possible that, during a later conversation about an article, you may discover that you do not have a clue about what the other person is saying. You did not "comprehend" that specific article at all. As you can see, your reading purpose influenced your comprehension. You do not remember everything because you did not choose to remember it all. You read selectively.

Furthermore, although you want to be able to discuss the news the next day, do you want to talk about Tuesday's news on the following Monday? In other words, how long do you want to keep that information in your memory? In this case, the answer is probably only for a short time. You want to be able to discuss today's news tomorrow, not next month or next year. Consequently, the ideas you read in the paper will be stored in your short-term memory. They will be available to you to recall and use for only a brief time.

As you can see, your reading purpose affects your *rate* (how fast you read), *comprehension* (how much you understand), and *retention* (how much you remember). The type of reading described here is called *reading for information*. Many people use this kind of reading daily.

Reading for Information	
Reading purpose:	to be informed
Reading type:	selective
Reading rate:	moderate to fast (300–400 words per minute)
Reading comprehension:	general (70–80 percent)
Reading retention:	short-term memory

Reading for Academic Knowledge

2. *Reading the textbook.* Why do you read a textbook? First, you read because you expect to have a career. You assume that the information in the course and text will be useful to you and your career. Second, you read because the instructor has assigned specific chapters and will discuss them in class. Third, you read because you will be tested on the assigned chapters, and you want to do well on examinations.

Obviously, your reasons for reading the textbook differ from your reasons for reading the newspaper. Your approach to the text will be different too. A casual observer would see that you spend a great deal of time on the chapter, read everything slowly and carefully, and skip nothing. Furthermore, you use SQ3R because you want to learn from the text and remember as much as possible. Finally, you want and need to retain the information for a long time, perhaps a lifetime, so the information needs to be stored in your long-term memory.

Once again, your reason for reading has influenced the reading process. This type of reading is called *reading for academic knowledge*. Anyone in a new learning situation should read material this way.

Reading for Academic Knowledge	
Reading purpose:	to learn and use
Reading type:	study
Reading rate:	slow (150–250 words perminute)
Reading comprehension:	specific (90–100 percent)
Reading retention:	long-term memory

Reading for Rejection

3. Reading supplementary material. At some point during your academic career, you will be required to do extra reading. The additional material may be specifically assigned articles and books. It may be suggested by a research paper assignment. In either case, you will have to consider some questions before you begin:

> What do you already know about this topic?
>
> How much background knowledge of the topic do you have?
>
> How interested are you in the topic?
>
> How useful is the extra reading material to you?
>
> Can the additional reading fill in any gaps in your own knowledge of the topic?

Does the supplementary material present any new ideas or information? Some of these questions cannot be answered until you have familiarized yourself with the material. Familiarizing, however, does *not* mean a detailed, analytical reading. It means skimming, or quickly reading, to answer the questions. (For an explanation of skimming, see Chapter 7.)

Someone watching you skim an article would assume that you are a very fast reader. In reality, though, to gain familiarity, you trade comprehension and retention for speed. You try to cover the material quickly so that you can make an accurate assessment of its usefulness. Therefore, you do not understand it thoroughly, and you do not remember much of it. You read just enough to decide whether the article is useful to you or not. Once you have made your decision, you will handle the material in one of two ways:

1. *Useful*—If the material can be helpful to you, then you will read it more thoroughly later. You will either read it for information or for academic knowledge.

2. *Not useful*—If you decide that the material does not suit your purposes, then you will put it aside and quickly forget about it.

Skimming to judge the usefulness of an article is called *reading for rejection*. It is a first step in the reading process. When reading for rejection, you have two possible goals:

1. You will recognize that the material is helpful to you. In this case, you will read it more carefully later.

2. On the other hand, you may decide that it is not useful. Consequently, you will reject any further reading of it.

Reading for rejection can benefit you now as a student and later as a professional. As a student, it can help you focus your energy and time on the new and unfamiliar. You can avoid reviewing what you already know. As a professional, reading for rejection can make you aware of new developments and ideas in your chosen field. However, you do not have to waste time reading every article in a professional journal.

Reading for Rejection

Reading purpose:	to familiarize
Reading type:	skimming
Reading rate:	fast (500–800 words per minute)
Reading comprehension:	low (50 percent)
Reading retention:	short-term memory

Reading for Entertainment

4. Reading the novel. Your goal as you perform this task should be clear; you are *reading for entertainment*. You want to relax and enjoy the book. There will be no tests and no research papers based on this material. You will not need to remember every detail. As a matter of fact, you may store in your long-term memory only the title and your enjoyment of the book. After a while, you may be able to recommend the novel to friends as interesting or scary or well-written. But you probably could not summarize all the details of the plot for them. Because reading for entertainment is "light" reading, your rate is generally moderate and your memory is generally short.

Reading for Entertainment

Reading purpose:	to enjoy
Reading type:	general
Reading rate:	average (250–400 words per minute)
Reading comprehension:	varies
Reading retention:	short-term memory

READING FLEXIBILITY

As you can now see, all reading is not the same, and all reading tasks should not be approached in the same manner. If you still maintain that "all reading is reading," you will do yourself a disservice. You will plod slowly and carefully through all reading material, take a great deal of time, and expend much effort. Perhaps your time and effort will be rewarded with perfect comprehension and retention of every detail. However, is it really necessary to remember the specifics of a governor's current budget ten years from now?

A Vicious Cycle

More likely, as you read so carefully and slowly, you will get bored. As you plod through irrelevant details, you will lose your concentration. If you then force yourself to reread the article, reading it may seem to be an endless task. Consequently, you will read less of the article. The next time you begin reading, you will remember how difficult and time-consuming it was for you the last time. As a result, you will begin the new task with a defeatist attitude. This is how a cycle of reading failure starts. Eventually, you will classify reading as an "impossible" process, and you will avoid it, no matter what the cost.

Short-circuiting the Cycle

You can escape this cycle of failure. Simply recognize that *reading is a flexible process*, a variable task. Some material can be read quickly (or skimmed) with minimal comprehension. Other material must be analyzed slowly, carefully, and completely. Most material is generally read at a moderate pace with a satisfactory level of comprehension. Your first priority is to consider you purpose *before* you begin reading.

After establishing your reason for reading, you can vary your speed and limit your comprehension accordingly. This will make reading a manageable process. Then, as you read more, you will become more comfortable reading. Finally, as you recognize that your proficiency is increasing, you will be successful each time you read.

Below is a chart that distinguishes the different types of reading:

Purpose	Type	Retention	Rate	Words per Minute (WPM)
Entertainment	General	Short-term memory	Average	250–400
Information	Scan	Short-term memory	Fast	500–800
	Preview	Short-term memory	Fast	500–800
	Skim	Short-term memory	Fast	500–800
	Selective	Short-term memory	Average	250–400
Academic Knowledge	Study	Long-term memory	Slow	150–250
Rejection	Skim	Short-term memory	Fast	500–800

READING FACTORS

Two other factors influence your reading speed: the level of difficulty of the material and your background knowledge of and interest in the subject.

Level of Difficulty

Some materials read more easily than others. The material is deliberately written that way. Authors consider their intended audiences before they write. For instance, many people think *Reader's Digest* is easier to read than *Business Week*. More people read *National Geographic* than *Natural History*. Probably they consider the former easier to understand and faster to read than the latter. Consider the *Los Angeles Times* and *USA Today*. Both papers carry articles about current events. However, because the papers' intended audiences differ, so do the papers' reading levels. The first is more difficult to read than the second.

Now, consider the impact this level of difficulty has on textbooks. A college freshman might be able to read an introductory textbook without much difficulty. However, a graduate textbook on the same topic would be challenging to the same student. Furthermore, if that freshman were to read an article on that subject in a scholarly journal, the student might find the piece nearly impossible to read and understand.

In each case, the authors address different audiences. The introductory text is written with the beginner in mind. Details are kept to a minimum as the book provides an overview of the field. The more advanced textbook should cover each topic more thoroughly for readers who are already familiar with the basic principles. Finally, the journal article would probably examine one small aspect of the topic in great detail for an expert audience.

Authors change the level of details, abstractions, and language to meet different audiences' needs. Moreover, paragraph length varies as do the number of pictures, charts, or graphs. All of these factors change the level of difficulty.

If material is easy to read, you will be able to read it quickly with adequate comprehension. On the other hand, if the material is too difficult, you will read it slowly, with inadequate-to-poor comprehension. Obviously, you should try to choose your own reading material. When possible, pick material that you are comfortable reading. It should be neither too easy nor too difficult.

Unfortunately, you can not always choose your readings. Sometimes, the instructor assigns specific books and articles. If you have difficulty with an assigned work, then ask the instructor whether you can substitute another work for the required one. If you cannot make the substitution, then be sure to apply the reading techniques discussed in this book as you read. Also, try to organize a discussion group with other students. Their comments might help you better understand the material.

Background Knowledge and Interest

Your reading rate also depends on your knowledge of the topic. Presumably, knowing about a subject means that you are interested in it. Your knowledge will have been acquired over a period of time. As you begin to read material on an interesting topic, you will find yourself recalling previously learned information. You will also be able to retain new information easily because it needs only to be integrated with your current store of information. As a result, you will be able to read new material quickly and understand it easily.

However, if you know nothing about the topic and have no interest in it, you will probably consider reading about it to be a slow, boring task. You also may not remember much of an article's contents. The vocabulary may be unfamiliar to you. Possibly, an author may use jargon. These words are familiar to someone who knows the subject but are incomprehensible to an outsider: for example, a "hat trick" in hockey or "deconstruction" in literary analysis. Another problem might be that you are unfamiliar with the context of the article. For instance, if you are not aware of the controversy regarding gun-control legislation, you could not appreciate a discussion of the Brady bill. Likewise, if you and your family are healthy, you will not readily comprehend a discussion concerning the relative merits of a CAT scan versus an MRI as diagnostic tools.

Unfamiliarity with the subject and lack of interest affect your speed. You may find that reading an article on an unknown and boring topic is difficult. Both your speed and comprehension will decrease. If understanding the subject is vital to you, then be sure to use the SQ3R process as you read. (See Chapter 8 for a discussion of this technique.)

Your reading rate is not something that just happens. It is influenced by several variables: your purpose, the level of difficulty of the material, and your interest in the subject and background knowledge of it. Before you begin reading, you should be aware of these factors. Keep them in mind, so you can control your rate and successfully process the material.

Depending on these factors, you may read quickly or slowly, or you may even skim. These factors also influence your comprehension. In some instances, you may understand and remember everything. In others, you may understand most of the material, but remember it only briefly. Some readings you may not understand at all.

Unfortunately, some of the factors that affect your speed are beyond your control. You cannot change the level of difficulty of assignments. Nor can you quickly develop years of background knowledge. You can only deal with the material as it is assigned and use the most helpful reading techniques.

Consider Your Purpose

However, you can analyze your reading purpose. A few minutes before you begin, think about your reasons for reading the material. Those few minutes of analysis can make reading an easier, more enjoyable task for you. If, after analyzing your purpose, you recognize that you only need to preview the article, then you can spend less time with it. Also, you will not have to feel guilty about below-average comprehension. On the other hand, your analysis may indicate that you should study the chapter. In that case, you will delay working with the material until you have sufficient time to apply SQ3R as you read to learn. Finally, your analysis may demonstrate that you do not know how to best approach the material. Consequently, you can skim it to decide its usefulness. After skimming, you should either read it analytically or reject it.

In all of the previous examples, you were a flexible reader because you varied your speed and comprehension to suit your different purposes. In addition, your flexibility made you a more efficient and effective reader. You were able to take the ideas and information you needed from the material. In the process, you did not waste time. Efficiency, effectiveness, and flexibility characterize a mature, conscious reader.

Determine Your Goals

By taking the time to analyze your reasons for dealing with the material, you respond to the assignment maturely. Mature readers do not rush to complete the work. Instead, they take a few minutes to plan the most effective strategy. Consequently, your analysis should make your reading easier. Before you begin to read, ask yourself these questions:

1. Why am I reading this material?

2. What am I trying to achieve?

3. What is my goal?

4. Am I interested in the topic?

5. How much do I already know about this subject?

6. How much should I remember?

7. How long must I remember this information?

8. How long should it take me to process this material?

9. What method should I use to process it?

Consider your answers. Which reading technique do they indicate will be the most effective for you?

1. When I read this material, my purpose is _____.

2. When I read this material, my goal is _____.

3. When I read this material, I should retain the information for

   _____.

4. When I read this material, my rate should be _____.

SCANNING

You now recognize that all reading is not the same and that reading analytically is not always the most effective strategy. Sometimes, skimming or previewing may be the better choice. In some cases, scanning may be the preferred technique.

You are already familiar with scanning. In fact, you employ this technique daily. You may need a business's phone number, a word's definition, or a train's departure time. With the phone book, dictionary, or train schedule in hand, you scan to locate the particular item of information quickly. Using this technique makes you an efficient and effective reader, for you can quickly locate the item you need.

Scanning is fast, accurate, and specific; these are its advantages. For instance, you scan (read quickly) a column of names in the phone book until you find the company you want to call. Then, you slow down and read the phone number slowly and carefully. The phone number will probably be stored in your short-term memory. Eventually, you will forget it. Similarly, you scan the bold-faced entry words on a dictionary page until you see the specific word you need. Then, you slow your reading rate and read the definition carefully. In both situations, you scan a large amount of information quickly in order to focus on one specific item. Then you read that item carefully.

To scan effectively, you must be aware of two things:

1. the specific information you are seeking, and

2. the arrangement of the resource you are using.

Usually, resource material, such as a dictionary or index, is arranged alphabetically. Sometimes, however, the material will be arranged differently. For example, a bus schedule may be arranged according to destination and time. Class schedules are divided into day and evening sessions and then into academic disciplines.

To scan, let your eyes quickly contact each major item on the page until you find the specific item you need. Then, slow your reading rate and look for the information you need.

Scanning	
Reading purpose:	to find a particular item of information quickly
Reading type:	scanning
Reading rate:	fast
Reading use:	short-term memory

EXERCISE 1

The chart on the following page lists best-selling fiction and nonfiction books. Scan it to answer the following questions.

1. Is *Gone with the Wind* listed? _____

2. What nonfiction book is in fifth place? _____

3. Who wrote *Gerald's Game*? _____

4. Which best sellers this week were not on the list at all last

    week? _____

5. What is *Young Men & Fire* about? _____

    _____

October 4, 1992

THE NEW YORK TIMES BOOK REVIEW
Best Sellers

This Week	Fiction	Last Week	Weeks On List
1	**WHERE IS JOE MERCHANT?** by Jimmy Buffett. (Harcourt Brace Jovanovich, $19.95.) A couple on a wild chase through the Caribbean on the trail of a deceased rock star who has been sighted there.	2	6
2	**THE PELICAN BRIEF,** by John Grisham. (Doubleday, $22.50.) A woman law student probes the murder of two Supreme Court justices.	1	30
3	**WAITING TO EXHALE,** by Terry McMillan. (Viking, $22.) The friendships and romances of four black women in Phoenix.	4	19
4	**GERALD'S GAME,** by Stephen King. (Viking, $23.50.) Twenty-eight hours of horror suffered by a woman handcuffed to a bedpost.	3	12
5	**THE SECRET HISTORY,** by Donna Tartt. (Knopf, $23.) Close friends at a small college must deal with the consequences of a crime they committed.	6	3
6	**THE BRIDGES OF MADISON COUNTY,** by Robert James Waller. (Warner, $14.95.) A photographer and a lonely farmer's wife in Iowa.	8	8
7	**ALL THAT REMAINS,** by Patricia D. Cornwell. (Scribners, $20.) Searching for the truth behind the strange deaths of five young couples in Virginia.	5	6
8	**THE VOLCANO LOVER,** by Susan Sontag. (Farrar, Straus & Giroux, $22.) The story of Lord Nelson, his lover Emma Hamilton and her spouse.	7	6
9	**TANGLED VINES,** by Janet Dailey. (Little, Brown, $21.95.) Visiting her native Napa Valley, a television star encounters shades of her unhappy childhood and romance with the heir to a winery.	10	4
10	**THE LEGACY,** by R. A. Salvatore. (TSR, $15.95.) A fantasy tale about a spider queen's war to stop a band of elves in their quest for peace and security.	9	2
11	**THE CAT WHO WASN'T THERE,** by Lilian Jackson Braun. (Putnam, $18.95.) Jim Qwilleran has to contend with a series of crimes that occur during a bus tour of Scotland.	14	2
12	**BEFORE AND AFTER,** by Rosellen Brown. (Farrar, Straus & Giroux, $21.) A tragic event in a New England town pits members of a family against one another.		2
13	**SWEET LIAR,** by Jude Deveraux. (Pocket, $22.) In New York, a Kentucky woman copes with a mystery dating back to the Roaring Twenties.	11	6
14	**LIVE FROM GOLGOTHA,** by Gore Vidal. (Random House, $22.) The Gospel according to St. Timothy, recorded in A.D. 96 amid intrusions by 20th-century religious and media personalities.		1
15 *	**COLONY,** by Anne Rivers Siddons. (HarperCollins, $20.) A 90-year-old woman recalls what she saw as the doyenne of a Maine summer retreat.	13	12

This Week	Nonfiction	Last Week	Weeks On List
1	**THE WAY THINGS OUGHT TO BE,** by Rush H. Limbaugh 3d. (Pocket, $22.) Anecdotes and opinions offered by the radio talk show host.	1	3
2	**EVERY LIVING THING,** by James Herriot. (St. Martin's, $22.95.) Continuing the memoirs of the Yorkshire veterinarian.	2	5
3	**THE SILENT PASSAGE,** by Gail Sheehy. (Random House, $16.) The psychological and social significance of menopause for today's women.	3	19
4	**TRUMAN,** by David McCullough. (Simon & Schuster, $30.) A biography of the 33d President.	4	16
5	**EARTH IN THE BALANCE,** by Al Gore. (Houghton Mifflin, $22.95.) The Vice-Presidential candidate discusses factors affecting the environment and what must be done to save it.	5	17
6	**THE TE OF PIGLET,** by Benjamin Hoff. (Dutton, $16.) Aspects of Taoist philosophy explained through the actions of A. A. Milne's character Piglet.	10	2
7	**DIANA: HER TRUE STORY,** by Andrew Morton. (Simon & Schuster, $22.) A biography of the Princess of Wales.	9	14
8	**WOMEN WHO RUN WITH THE WOLVES,** by Clarissa Pinkola Estés. (Ballantine, $20.) A Jungian analyst reinterprets myths and folk tales to enable women to understand their psyches.	7	8
9 *	**THE LAST TSAR,** by Edvard Radzinsky. (Doubleday, $25.) The life of Nicholas II and his family, and their assassination in 1918; based in part on newly available material.	8	9
10	**YOUNG MEN & FIRE,** by Norman Maclean. (University of Chicago, $19.95.) An account of a disastrous fire in a Montana forest in 1949.	6	5
11	**UP IN THE OLD HOTEL,** by Joseph Mitchell. (Pantheon, $27.50.) Three dozen pieces about Manhattan life, published in The New Yorker during the past half-century.		2
12	**CARE OF THE SOUL,** by Thomas Moore. (HarperCollins, $20.) A psychotherapist's discussion of spirituality and everyday life.	13	3
13	**HEAD TO HEAD,** by Lester Thurow. (Morrow, $25.) The upcoming economic battle among Japan, Europe and the United States.	12	21
14	**WHO WILL TELL THE PEOPLE,** by William Greider. (Simon & Schuster, $25.) A journalist's account of how powerful monied interests and elite groups dominate the Federal Government.		19
15 *	**KISSINGER,** by Walter Isaacson. (Simon & Schuster, $30.) A biography of the former national security adviser and Secretary of State.	15	2

EXERCISE 2   Scan the map below to answer these questions.

1. Does Afghanistan have any oil fields? _____

2. Is Saudi Arabia a land-locked country, or does it have a sea-coast? _____

3. Name two countries that border the Arabian Sea. _____

_____

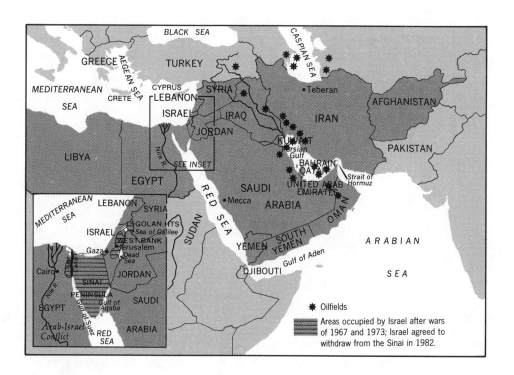

(Kennedy, David M. *The Brief American Pageant. 3rd ed. Lexington, MA: Heath, 1989.*
p. 524.)

EXERCISE 3   Scan the television listings on the following page to find the answers to these questions.

1. Is *The Cosby Show* listed? _____

2. What program will be shown on Channel 11 at 7:30 P.M.?

   _____

3. When will the news be broadcast on Channel 56?

   _____

4. How long is the movie *Big*? _____

5. Who stars in *Running Scared* on Channel 38? _____

   _____

WEDNESDAY PRIMETIME

	6:00	6:30	7:00	7:30	8:00	8:30	9:00	9:30	10:00	10:30	11:00	11:30
2	MacNeil/Lehrer 58740		Wednesday Group	Are You Served?	Live from Lincoln Center: "New York City Opera: Cavalleria Rusticana/Pagliacci" 145108						Are You Served?	Nova 81363
4	News 50108		NBC News 1295	Entertainment	Unsolved Mysteries 6837		Seinfeld 7450	Mad About You	Law & Order: "Conspiracy" 9160		News 9716108	The Tonight Show
5	News 66130		ABC News 6769	Chronicle 3547	The Wonder Years	Doogie Howser	Home Improve.	Laurie Hill 86547	Civil Wars 18160		News 3158498	◄11:35 Nightline
6	News 4653	CBS News 5905	A Current Affair	You Bet Your Life	The Hat Squad 33479		The 26th Annual Country Music Association Awards 36566				News 15585	Dangerous Curves
7	News 8479	CBS News 2059	Wheel of Fortune	Jeopardy! 1943	The Hat Squad 20905		The 26th Annual Country Music Association Awards 23092				News 3143566	◄11:35 Jeopardy!
9	News 4295	ABC News 5547	Entertainment 7653	Hard Copy 4059	The Wonder Years	Doogie Howser	Home Improve.	Laurie Hill 49127	Civil Wars 74740		News 40295	Nightline 66382
10	News 2837	NBC News 3189	Hard Copy 5295	Entertainment 5301	Unsolved Mysteries 99059		Seinfeld 36092	Mad About You	Law & Order: "Conspiracy" 72382		News 8485363	The Tonight Show
11	MacNeil/Lehrer 22450		Business Report	Carmen Sandiego	Copland's Appalachian Spring		The Shakers: Hands to Work ...		Roger & Me ★★★ (1989, Documentary) 54498			
12	News 7905	ABC News 1585	Wheel of Fortune	Jeopardy! 7769	The Wonder Years	Doogie Howser	Home Improve.	Laurie Hill 32837	Civil Wars 67450		News 8410059	◄11:35 Nightline
25	Cosby 61699	The Wonder Years	Married ... 76127	Married ... 83905	Beverly Hills, 90210 (R) 57653		Melrose Place 44189		Roseanne 90943	Roseanne 76363	Studs 46059	Infatuation 45566
27	Amo y Senor	Noticiero 89189	Marielena 66301		Mundo de Fieras 42721		Cine de Telemundo 52108				Noticiero 31127	Paid Programming
38	M*A*S*H 3721	M*A*S*H 7301	Cheers 3479	Murphy Brown	Running Scared ★★ (1986, Comedy-Drama) Gregory Hines, Billy Crystal. 190498				Hogan's Heroes		Cheers 95769	Honeymooners
44	◄5:30 Sesame St.	Nightly Business	MacNeil/Lehrer 58635		Fire on the Rim 80905		Korea: Unknown War 58699		P.O.V.: "Maria's Story" 20896		Nightly Business	Wednesday Group
50	The Wonder Years	Infatuation 924479	Star Trek: The Next Generation		Death Wish 4: The Crackdown ★ (1987) Charles Bronson, Kay Lenz. 391127				All in the Family	All in the Family	Whoopi Goldberg	Arsenio Hall
56	Full House 577585	Who's the Boss?	Star Trek: The Next Generation		Used Cars ★★★ (1980, Comedy) Kurt Russell, Jack Warden. 732585				News 711092		Arsenio Hall: Raven-Symone. 346837	
68	Frontiers 1458837		Feature Story	Feature Story	One Norway Street: Issues. 4475479		Childhood: A Journey 4488943		Rodina: "Russian Homeland" 4481030		50 Years Ago	Feature Story

	6:00	6:30	7:00	7:30	8:00	8:30	9:00	9:30	10:00	10:30	11:00	11:30
A&E	Rockford Files: "The Big Ripoff" 781030		New Wilderness	In Search Of ...	Our Century 521585		American Justice	Spies 760547	First Flights	TravelQuest	An Evening at the Improv 945301	
BRAVO	Off the Air				Duchess of Duke Street 736301		La Traviata ★★★ (1982, Musical) Teresa Stratas, Placido Domingo. 706160				Loneliness of Long Distance Runner	
CNN	The World Today 327856		Moneyline 565027	Crossfire 707943	Primenews 165943		Larry King Live 152479		World News 155566		Sports Tonight	Moneyline 846566
DISNY	Young Musicians Symphony Orchestra		Totally Minnie 729011		$1,000,000 Duck ★★ (1971, Fantasy) Dean Jones. 7336030		My Fair Lady (9:35) ★★★ (1964, Musical) Audrey Hepburn, Rex Harrison. (12:30)► 10995437					
ESPN	Inside the PGA	Up Close 722127	Sports-Center	Baseball 223653						Baseball Tonight	SportsCenter 387363	
FAMILY	Rin Tin Tin	New Zorro 321547	Life Goes On 599011		The Young Riders 515059		Father Dowling Mysteries 595295		The 700 Club (R) 598382		Scarecrow & Mrs. King 123127	
HBO	◄(4:45) My Blue ...	A Fine Mess ★ (1986) Ted Danson, Howie Mandel. 662419			Truth or Dare ★★★ (1991, Documentary) 967363				Tales from Crypt	Dream On 415585	One-Night Stand	Road House
LIFE	Supermarket	Shop/Drop 327721	China Beach 502585		L.A. Law: "Gorilla My Dreams" 588905		A Cry for Help: The Tracey Thurman Story ★★ (1989) Nancy McKeon. 581092				Mahatma Gandhi: The Great Soul	
MAX	Cahill, US Marshal (6:15) ★★ (1973) John Wayne, George Kennedy. 97842160				Diner ★★★ (1982, Comedy-Drama) Steve Guttenberg, Mickey Rourke. 591479				The Haunting of Morella ★ (1990) David McCallum. 354160			Ultimate Desires
MC	◄(4:30) Delta/2	Johnny Be Good ★ (1988) Anthony Michael Hall. 416295			Big ★★★ (1988, Fantasy) Tom Hanks, Elizabeth Perkins. 378301				Freddy's Dead: The Final Nightmare ★ (1991) 140740			Deadly ...
NESN	Sportfishing 23585	Fishing the West	Red Sox Digest	Baseball: Boston Red Sox at Toronto Blue Jays. 832943					Baseball Action		High Five 33547	Baseball 550837
NICK	What Would	Wild Kids 362769	Looney Tunes	Bullwinkle 351653	Get Smart 639943	Superman 18450	Mary Tyler Moore	Dick Van Dyke	Dragnet 511491	Alfred Hitchcock	Lucy Show 874189	Green Acres
SHOW	The Search for Signs of Intelligent Life in the Universe ★★★ (1991) 166672				Child's Play 2 ★ (1990) Alex Vincent, Jenny Agutter. 268522		Mr. Saturday N't		Kinjite: Forbidden Subjects ★★ (1989) Charles Bronson, Perry Lopez. 9887160			
SPORT	Rockingham	Thoroughbred	Forever Baseball	1992-93 Whalers	NBA Basketball: Celtics Encore: Milwaukee Bucks at Boston Celtics. (R) 372127				Sportswriters on TV (R) 351634		Eddie Andelman's Tuesday/Football	
TBS	Three's Company	Andy Griffith	Beverly Hillbillies	Sanford & Son	Runaway ★★ (1984, Science Fiction) Tom Selleck, Cynthia Rhodes. 163585				Nighthawks ★★★ (1981, Suspense) Sylvester Stallone, Billy Dee Williams. 411634			
TDC	Mother Nature	Wildlife Chronicles	Man Who Loved Birds		Mac & Mutley	Incredible Animals	Wings: "JU-87 Stuka" 516653		Beyond 2000 519740		Mac & Mutley	Incredible Animals
TNT	Pink Panther	Captain Planet	Jetsons 200301	Bugs Bunny	Nevada Smith ★★★ (1966, Western) Steve McQueen, Karl Malden. 361108						The Carpetbaggers ★★ (2)► 57088301	
USA	MacGyver: "Deathlock" 312924		Quantum Leap 141363		Murder, She Wrote 150011		The Haunting of Sarah Hardy ★★ (1989) Sela Ward, Michael Woods. 160498				MacGyver: "The Odd Triple" 583585	
WPIX	Full House 63127	The Wonder Years	A Different World	Murphy Brown	Creepshow 2 ★ (1987, Horror) Lois Chiles, George Kennedy. 11837				News 23672		Cheers 73189	Honeymooners
WWOR	Cosby 115769	Who's the Boss?	Gimme a Break	Temperatures	Ironside 369653		Quincy, M.E. 356189		News 359276		Love Boat 979189	

The Boston Sunday Globe (*September 27, 1992*).

READING FASTER

Many students ask why they should read faster. They say they are comfortable reading at their present rate and insist that their speed suits their comprehension. They believe that their understanding will suffer if they read faster.

However, you *should* work to increase your reading rate because you will be reading for the rest of your life. Every day, every waking hour, you read. Sometimes, you read only street signs and directions. Sometimes, you read a two-paragraph memo or a letter from a friend. At other times, you read important reports or articles. In our literate society, you read—you must read—on a daily basis.

Reading Obligations

News reports and government studies regularly refer to America's "information explosion." Computer technology has made storing information easier and has also helped to develop that information and publish it. All that information exists to be read and used.

Professionals have an obligation to be well-read. Twenty years ago, an accountant had to read only one monthly periodical and stay familiar with a few yearly changes in tax laws. An accountant who did that, then, had fulfilled all professional obligations. Today, however, there are ten accounting journals to be familiar with, and current tax laws plus their regulations can run to thousands of pages. Certainly, the accountant, as a professional, must be aware of changes in the field. However, how can anyone read all that material?

All professionals face the same dilemma. They must be aware of current events in their fields. Usually, though, they lack the time to complete all the necessary reading. As a student, you too are a professional, and you are in the same situation.

Students have an obligation to read, yet they lack the time to do a thorough job. Besides textbooks, they must read supplementary material. Although they may think that they have enough time to do it all, an honest appraisal of their life-styles would reveal that time is not on their side. Most students cannot devote all their waking hours to the reading and studying required by four to six courses. Many students hold part-time jobs. Others may also have household or family responsibilities. Understandably, they may want a social life too. Lacking the time to accomplish everything, students have to set priorities. Their teachers hope that course work will be at the top of the list.

As you can see, you must be well-read now and also continue reading for the rest of your life. As a professional, you must read and understand large quantities of material.

Too Much to Read/Too Little Time

Fortunately, you *can* solve the dilemma of having too much reading. Course work does not have to, and should not, absorb all of your time. Analyze your situation. Consider the solutions:

1. *First, be a flexible reader.* You have already discovered that not all the material must be read analytically. In other words, consider your purpose, and decide which type of reading approach the material requires.

2. *Second, increase your reading rate.* Reading faster does not mean understanding less. It means dealing with more material in the same amount of time, or, if that does not suit your schedule, it means reading the same amount of material in half the time. In either case, you win.

Increasing Your Reading Rate

What can you do to increase your speed? By considering how the eye functions as you read, you will recognize ways to increase your rate.

Fixations. The eye is blind when it is in motion; it can "see" only when it stops. The stops are called fixations. Frequently, slow readers stop, or fixate, for too long. Long fixations are a bad habit that usually develop when children first learn to read. If they did not know a word, they were taught to "sound it out," or use the context or its structure to help them determine the word's meaning. Those techniques required them to fixate on the word for a moment. Even though you are no longer a beginning reader, you may still act upon some of those first reading instructions.

Now, as a mature reader, you should *decrease the length of your fixations.* You do not have to stop for a long time as you read. Your eyes do not have to acknowledge each letter in every word. You can let your eyes glide across the line of print. By doing so, you will begin to read faster.

Eye Span. When your eyes stop, they look at a specific number of words. If you are a slow reader, then you probably look at just one word at a time. That is, your eyes fixate on each word separately as you read. This inefficient, word-by-word technique wastes time. You do not need to focus on each word, nor do you need to give each word equal emphasis. Some words in a line (verbs, for example) are more useful to you because they carry the meaning of the sentence. Other words (adjectives and prepositions, for instance) are frequently fillers. They may make the sentence flow more smoothly or add more details, but they do not convey the essential meaning of the sentence.

Therefore, you should *increase your eye span*. Read phrase by phrase rather than word by word. When reading phrases, concentrate on the important words in the sentence. Articles, prepositions, and adjectives can be read, but not emphasized. Such phrase-reading will help your comprehension, too. It is sometimes difficult to construct meaning from a sentence if you are examining each element (word) individually, in isolation. Phrase-reading groups the words for your eye and helps you to place ideas in their logical relationship to each other. This grouping will help your understanding.

Look at this example:

> It / is / sometimes / difficult / to / construct / meaning / from / a / sentence / if / you / are / examining / each / element / (word) / individually, / in / isolation. /

If you are a word-by-word reader, then your eyes will stop twenty times as you read the sentence above. Furthermore, you will give each word equal emphasis. It will be difficult to recognize whole ideas that are essential to the sentence's meaning. Read the sentence again, grouping words into meaningful phrases.

> It is sometimes *difficult* / to construct *meaning* / from a *sentence* / if you are *examining* / each *element* (word) / *individually*, in isolation. /

A phrase-by-phrase reader would fixate only six times while reading the same sentence. Obviously, that saves much time. In addition, noting the important word in a phrase is a relatively simple task. A phrase-by-phrase reader, then, can construct meaning more easily and quickly.

Regressions. Regressions are another bad habit that some students develop. Students who are uncomfortable reading may lack confidence in their ability to extract information. When that happens, they fail to recognize how their mind functions. They do not recognize that, if their eyes have seen something (for instance, the printed word as they read), then that something has made an impression on their mind. In other words, if they read something, then it is available to them. However, lacking confidence, the students regress—or go back and reread the material—to confirm the impression it has made. Clearly, regressions waste time.

To read faster, *stop rereading material*. If you read the material once, you can assume that your mind has received its message. If you read without regressing, then you will see that, in general, your comprehension does not suffer.

Of course, you must keep the material's level of difficulty in mind. If the subject is unfamiliar to you—for instance, if the material is directed to an expert in the field—then you may indeed have to read it several times in order to understand it. Difficult material often requires reading an entire piece several times. However, merely regressing—going back over a paragraph or a sentence—does not help. Such piecemeal reading is not useful because you cannot organize ideas as you understand them. Therefore, although you may need to read difficult and unfamiliar material more than once, you still should not regress as you read it.

Practice. Efficient and effective reading is a skill that you develop by using proven techniques. Like other techniques—making a jump shot, baking bread, driving a standard transmission—reading techniques must be practiced. They do not develop automatically. They must be learned and, once learned, practiced so that they can be applied skillfully and effortlessly. You want to master the techniques so that you can use them unconsciously. In that way, you can concentrate on understanding the material's message and, when necessary, learning that message.

Therefore, *practice reading faster.* Apply these techniques to a variety of materials: newspapers, magazines, novels, textbooks, nonfiction works. Make an effort every day to read a little faster. The more you practice, the more skilled you will be.

Work on revising these four elements of your reading style in order to read faster:

1. Decrease the length of your fixations.

2. Increase your eye span.

3. Stop regression.

4. Most important—practice, practice, practice!

SUMMARY

The reading process is a composite of skills based on techniques. A conscious reader knows which skills are most effective in different situations and applies the appropriate reading techniques. As a conscious reader, you should recognize your purpose for reading, because this purpose guides your choice of reading type and rate. To read efficiently and effectively, you must read as quickly as possible with adequate comprehension. To do that, you must practice.

APPLICATION I

Read the questions and then scan the chart below to find the answers.

1. What were the three most populous cities in the Soviet Union? _____

2. What percentage of the country's land is forested?

   _____

3. Which republic has the largest population? _____

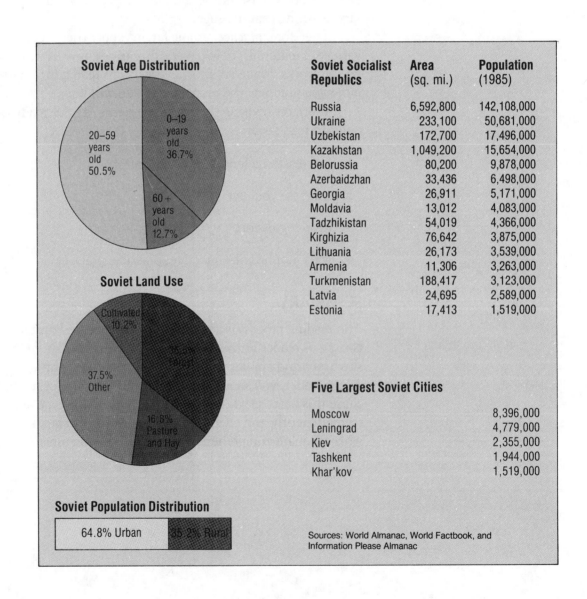

Soviet Socialist Republics	Area (sq. mi.)	Population (1985)
Russia	6,592,800	142,108,000
Ukraine	233,100	50,681,000
Uzbekistan	172,700	17,496,000
Kazakhstan	1,049,200	15,654,000
Belorussia	80,200	9,878,000
Azerbaidzhan	33,436	6,498,000
Georgia	26,911	5,171,000
Moldavia	13,012	4,083,000
Tadzhikistan	54,019	4,366,000
Kirghizia	76,642	3,875,000
Lithuania	26,173	3,539,000
Armenia	11,306	3,263,000
Turkmenistan	188,417	3,123,000
Latvia	24,695	2,589,000
Estonia	17,413	1,519,000

Soviet Age Distribution

0–19 years old 36.7%
20–59 years old 50.5%
60 + years old 12.7%

Soviet Land Use

Cultivated 10.2%
35.5% Forest
37.5% Other
16.8% Pasture and Hay

Five Largest Soviet Cities

Moscow	8,396,000
Leningrad	4,779,000
Kiev	2,355,000
Tashkent	1,944,000
Khar'kov	1,519,000

Soviet Population Distribution

64.8% Urban   35.2% Rural

Sources: World Almanac, World Factbook, and Information Please Almanac

(Gritzner, Charles F. World Geography. Lexington, MA: Heath, 1989. p. 341.)

Scan the excerpt from the textbook index on the next page to answer the following questions.

1. Does the book discuss Venus? _____

   If so, on what page(s)? _____

2. Does the book discuss smog? _____

   If so, on what page(s)? _____

3. Does the book discuss time? _____

   If so, on what page(s)? _____

   If so, do you think it offers a detailed discussion of the topic?

   Explain. _____

4. Does the book discuss volcanoes? _____

   How many subdivisions of volcanoes are listed? _____

5. Might this book be a useful source for a five-page research

   paper on "temperature"? Explain your answer. _____

   _____

   _____

   _____

   _____

   _____

(*Tilley, Bill W. Earth Science. Lexington*, MA: *Heath, 1987. p. 531.*)

PART THREE

Reading Applications

SELECTION 1
Secrets of the Sleep Merchants
WILLIAM LINDSAY GRESHAM

1   Before a hushed audience of perspiring farmers and their wives, a gaunt, sallow man with lank hair falling to his shoulders motioned for quiet. Behind him, on a stage lit with candles backed by tin reflectors, a boy of twelve lay with his feet on one chair, his shoulders on another. On his mid-section reposed a king-sized rock.

2   The hyponotist announced in his melodious voice, "And now, ladies and gentlemen, a demonstration of the uncanny powers of mind over matter. You see here a young man in a perfect cataleptic trance in which his body assumes the rigidity of an iron bar. I shall take this sledge hammer and apply sufficient force to this paving stone to smash it, without waking the lad or causing him the slightest injury."

3   He swung the sledge. The rock split and fell to the floor with resounding thumps. The boy remained stretched between chairs, as immobile as a statue.

4   The stone-breaking routine is as old as the hills, but it is still in use. The rigidity of catalepsy is imitated by taking a very short person, such as a wiry girl or young boy, and placing his shoulders on one chair, his feet on another. This position can be held for some time. The "paving stone" is a hunk of soft sandstone. The blow which breaks it is distributed through the bulk of the stone and is not felt by the subject underneath.

5   Let there be no doubt that there is such a thing as hypnotism. It had been known for thousands of years to the learned men of the Far East when, nearly 200 years ago, it began to be studied by Western medical men. The first of them to recognize its possibilities was Anton Mesmer, who, in Paris in the 1780's, was acclaimed a miraculous healer. His power, he said, came from "magnetism" applied to physical ills through magnets, magnetized water, and bottles of iron filings. He did "cure" a lot of people, although they may have felt a little rusty afterward. What had effected the cures was hypnotic suggestion, helped by his prestige and the elaborate magnetic contraptions.

6   Just what is hypnotism? So far as we know, it is a state of mind resembling sleep, artificially induced by outside suggestions: those of a hypnotist. It is not true sleep. A hypnotized subject can be left standing rigid

in the center of a stage. No one could do this in normal sleep.

7   There are many methods of inducing a hypnotic trance, but all have one thing in common. The subject's attention is caught and held on some object: the tip of a pencil held above the level of the eyes, a finger or even a glaring glass eye held in the fist of the operator. Whatever it is, the subject is told to gaze at it steadily. Soon his eye muscles tire and his eyes begin to droop or flicker. At this point the hypnotist tells him that his eyelids are growing heavy, a feeling of drowsiness is overcoming him, he is sinking deeper and deeper into a dreamless sleep.

8   About one out of five persons actually goes right to "sleep" at this point. But while the subject seems to be asleep he is attentive to commands by the hypnotist. Stage hypnotists, however, do not always rely on real hypnotism. Many times they use stooges for dramatic effects.

9   A friend I call Professor, a retired hypnotist, is a gold mine of data on pseudohypnosis. "It's very seldom you see an operator who does a full show of nothing but fake stuff," he explains. "The reason is that it's easier to use real hypnosis, after you get the hang of it, than to train stooges to act hypnotized. A good hypnotist's subject will give a better performance than any stooge. And you don't have to pay him; he's already paid you for a ticket.

10   "When you get enough experience you can pick out your 'one-in-fives' easy enough. Only one person in five, on an average, will go into deep hypnosis the first crack out of the box. So you get a good-sized crowd on stage and tell 'em to clasp their hands. Then you give them a lot of suggestions that their hands are stuck fast, they can't open them no matter how hard they try, and so on. If you watch you'll be able to pick out those who really can't open their hands until you tell them they can. They're your prospects. A couple of other tests will screen out the very best ones. You can usually get at least three from a crowd of twenty-five. Then you go to town.

11   "Right from the first you start conditioning the audience in a belief in your powers. There's nothing like a couple of set-up demonstrations to get them to believing that you really do what you say you will."

12   The professor would seat his volunteers in a large semicircle on stage and give a brief orientation talk on

the powers of suggestion. Then he would take a silver sugar bowl from a side table.

13 "I shall hold this lump of sugar in the air above your heads, and one at a time I shall command you to taste the sugar without touching it. Please raise your hand when the sweet taste registers on your tongue."

14 Under one armpit he had hidden a bulb filled with saccharin powder. A rubber tube as thin as a knitting needle was taped to his arm, leading from the bulb to the edge of his shirt cuff. At the opportune moment a squeeze of the arm sent a little puff of saccharin into the air about the subject's face. Licking his lips, the gullible fellow naturally tasted the saccharin and was convinced of the suggestive powers of the hypnotist.

15 "In working the sticks, barnstorming," the professor told me in a reminiscent mood, "you'd invariably come up against some tough customers. Every now and then one would force his way on stage and roar out a challenge to hypnotize him.

16 "For such hard cases I had a beautiful system. After asking if his heart were sound, I would lead the loud-mouth to a sort of throne, an armchair on a little platform. On each side is an incense burner, going full blast. You seat the skeptic in the chair and have him loosen his collar and tie. With mystic passes you set out by telling him that he is getting drowsy, his eyelids feel heavier and heavier.

17 "Now this is a combination of hypnosis and devious trickery. For in one hip pocket you have a flat flask of chloroform. In your side pocket is a rubber bulb connected with the flask by a tube. Another tube leads from the flask up your sleeve and down to the cuff. As one hand makes the passes, the other goes to the side pocket and starts squeezing the bulb, which sends a spray of anesthetic into his face. The incense hides the acrid odor of the chloroform.

18 "You don't put a man all the way out with the chloroform, of course. It just knocks the cutting edge off his conscious mind so that the suggestion can begin to work, and he's under."

19 Although hypnotism was rediscovered by the West only a century ago, there is little about it that is really new. Even its most recent development, the use of sedatives to assist in creating a hypnotic trance, goes all the way back to earliest times. Modern investigators have found that the administration of a drug derived from *Cannabis indica*, sometimes called "In-

dian Princess" or more commonly, marijuana, a plant found all over the world, enables them to hypnotize the insane and other subjects not accessible to suggestion alone.

20   Yet witch doctors since the dawn of ages have known the Indian Princess. The witch doctor places his patient on a mat, kindles a fire and, throwing herbs on it, fans the smoke into the patient's face. If the herbs contain a few leaves of *Cannabis indica*, the suggestions given during the treatment take effect with sledgehammer power.

21   And finally, science has given hypnotism a gimmick which is today one of the most closely guarded secrets of the art. To the electronics expert it's a simple device: an oscillator tube hooked up to an amplifier. Set up in the wings of the stage, it is tuned up until its squeal is just out of range of the human ear. Then the volume is turned on full force. There is something about this silent screech, according to hypnotists, that makes ordinary people unusually susceptible to hypnosis and makes good hypnotic subjects fall over like tenpins.

22   But as one operator recently told me, "You want to watch out with that oscillator that you don't get yourself groggy with it. I nearly fluffed a show until I regained my composure enough to tell my assistant backstage to turn the darned thing off: it was knocking me out."

Gresham, William Lindsay. "Secrets of the Sleep Merchants." Adapted from True, The Man's Magazine. *Copyright, 1955, Fawcett Publications, Inc.*

QUESTIONS

1. Define *hypnotism*.

   _____

   _____

2. What one element is absolutely essential to inducing a hypnotic trance?

   _____

   _____

   _____

3. Are all demonstrations of hypnosis real? Are any of them based on tricks?

_____

_____

_____

4. "Mesmerized" is a synonym for "hypnotized." What do you think is the derivation of the word "mesmerized"?

_____

_____

_____

5. What is "Indian Princess"?

_____

_____

_____

6. Explain how an oscillator tube helps some hypnotists.

_____

_____

_____

7. Define "working the stick" and "barnstorming."

_____

_____

_____

8. Some showmen occasionally use tricks to help them demonstrate their hypnotic powers. Name two tricks that might be used.

_____

_____

_____

Think about hypnosis. Do you think it works, or is it just "smoke and mirrors"? Has anyone you've known ever relied on hypnosis to quit smoking or lose weight? Was hypnotic therapy a success? Do you think hynotists should be encouraged (or even allowed) to influence people's unconscious minds, or is that giving one person too much control over another?

Many people think hypnotism is like advertising; both seek to pursuade people by using the power of suggestion. However, some people think that using "suggestions" is an unfair and unethical way to change people's minds because they might not even recognize they are being manipulated and influenced. Perhaps, it might be fairer to be straightforward when a person presents logical arguments. In a paragraph, discuss persuasion versus argumentation. Is one method more valid than the other? Is one more appropriate in certain situations? Should one be used most of the time, with the other being reserved for only occasional use?

SELECTION 2
The Library Card
RICHARD WRIGHT

1   One morning I arrived early at work and went into the bank lobby where the Negro porter was mopping. I stood at a counter and picked up the Memphis *Commercial Appeal* and began my free reading of the press. I came finally to the editorial page and saw an article dealing with one H. L. Mencken. I knew by hearsay that he was the editor of the *American Mercury*, but aside from that I knew nothing about him. The article was a furious denunciation of Mencken, concluding with one, hot, short sentence: Mencken is a fool.

2   I wondered what on earth this Mencken had done to call down upon him the scorn of the South. The only people I had ever heard denounced in the South were Negroes, and this man was not a Negro. Then what ideas did Mencken hold that made a newspaper like the *Commercial Appeal* castigate him publicly? Undoubtedly he must be advocating ideas that the South did not like. Were there, then, people other than Negroes who criticized the South? I knew that during the Civil War the South had hated northern whites, but I had not encountered such hate during my life. Knowing no more of Mencken than I did at that moment, I felt a vague sympathy for him. Had not the South, which had assigned me the role of a non-man, cast at him its hardest words?

3   Now, how could I find out about this Mencken? There was a huge library near the riverfront, but I knew that Negroes were not allowed to patronize its shelves any more than they were the parks and playgrounds of the city. I had gone into the library several times to get books for the white men on the job. Which of them would now help me to get books? And how could I read them without causing concern to the white men with whom I worked? I had so far been successful in hiding my thoughts and feelings from them, but I knew that I would create hostility if I went about this business of reading in a clumsy way.

4   I weighed the personalities of the men on the job. There was Don, a Jew; but I distrusted him. His position was not much better than mine and I knew that he was uneasy and insecure; he had always treated me in an offhand, bantering way that barely concealed his

contempt. I was afraid to ask him to help me to get books; his frantic desire to demonstrate a racial solidarity with the whites against Negroes might make him betray me.

5 Then how about the boss? No, he was a Baptist and I had the suspicion that he would not be quite able to comprehend why a black boy would want to read Mencken. There were other white men on the job whose attitudes showed clearly that they were Kluxers or sympathizers, and they were out of the question.

6 There remained only one man whose attitude did not fit into an anti-Negro category, for I had heard the white men refer to him as a "Pope lover." He was an Irish Catholic and was hated by the white Southerners. I knew that he read books, because I had got him volumes from the library several times. Since he, too, was an object of hatred, I felt that he might refuse me but would hardly betray me. I hesitated, weighing and balancing the imponderable realities.

7 One morning I paused before the Catholic fellow's desk.

8 "I want to ask you a favor," I whispered to him.

9 "What is it?"

10 "I want to read. I can't get books from the library. I wonder if you'd let me use your card?"

11 He looked at me suspiciously.

12 "My card is full most of the time," he said.

13 "I see," I said and waited, posing my question silently.

14 "You're not trying to get me into trouble, are you, boy?" he asked, staring at me.

15 "Oh, no, sir."

16 "What book do you want?"

17 "A book by H. L. Mencken."

18 "Which one?"

19 "I don't know. He has written more than one?"

20 "He has written several."

21 "I didn't know that."

22 "What makes you want to read Mencken?"

23 "Oh, I just saw his name in the newspaper," I said.

24 "It's good of you to want to read," he said. "But you ought to read the right things."

25 I said nothing. Would he want to supervise my reading?

26 "Let me think," he said. "I'll figure out something."

27 I turned from him and he called me back. He stared at me quizzically.

28   "Richard, don't mention this to the other white men," he said.

29   "I understand," I said. "I won't say a word."

30   A few days later he called me to him.

31   "I've got a card in my wife's name," he said. "Here's mine."

32   "Thank you, sir."

33   "Do you think you can manage it?"

34   "I'll manage fine," I said.

35   "If they suspect you, you'll get in trouble," he said.

36   "I'll write the same kind of notes to the library that you wrote when you sent me for books," I told him. "I'll sign your name."

37   He laughed.

38   "Go ahead. Let me see what you get," he said.

39   That afternoon I addressed myself to forging a note. Now, what were the names of books written by H. L. Mencken? I did not know any of them. I finally wrote what I thought would be a foolproof note: *Dear Madam: Will you please let this nigger boy*—I used the word "nigger" to make the librarian feel that I could not possibly be the author of the note—*have some books by H. L. Mencken?* I forged the white man's name.

40   I entered the library as I had always done when on errands for whites, but I felt that I would somehow slip up and betray myself. I doffed my hat, stood a respectful distance from the desk, looked as unbookish as possible, and waited for the white patrons to be taken care of. When the desk was clear of people, I still waited. The white librarian looked at me.

41   "What do you want, boy?"

42   As though I did not possess the power of speech, I stepped forward and simply handed her the forged note, not parting my lips.

43   "What books by Mencken does he want?" she asked.

44   "I don't know, ma'am," I said, avoiding her eyes.

45   "Who gave you this card?"

46   "Mr Falk," I said.

47   "Where is he?"

48   "He's at work, at the M—— Optical Company," I said. "I've been in here for him before."

49   "I remember," the women said. "But he never wrote notes like this."

50   Oh, God, she's suspicious. Perhaps she would not let me have the books? If she had turned her back at that moment, I Would have ducked out the door and never gone back. Then I thought of a bold idea.

51   "You can call him up, ma'am," I said, my heart pounding.

52   "You're not using these books, are you?" she asked pointedly.

53   "Oh, no, ma'am. I can't read."

54   "I don't know what he wants by Mencken," she said under her breath.

55   I knew now that I had won; she was thinking of other things and the race question had gone out of her mind. She went to the shelves. Once or twice she looked over her shoulder at me, as though she was still doubtful. Finally she came forward with two books in her hand.

56   "I'm sending him two books," she said. "But tell Mr. Falk to come in next time, or send me the names of the books he wants. I don't know what he wants to read."

57   I said nothing. She stamped the card and handed me the books. Not daring to glance at them, I went out of the library, fearing that the woman would call me back for further questioning. A block away from the library I opened one of the books and read a title: *A Book of Prefaces*. I was nearing my nineteenth birthday and I did not know how to pronounce the word "preface." I thumbed the pages and saw strange words and strange names. I shook my head, disappointed. I looked at the other book; it was called *Prejudices*. I knew what that word meant; I had heard it all my life. And right off I was on guard against Mencken's books. Why would a man want to call a book *Prejudices?* The word was so stained with all my memories of racial hate that I could not conceive of anybody using it for a title. Perhaps I had made mistake about Mencken? A man who had prejudices must be wrong.

58   When I showed the books to Mr. Falk, he looked at me and frowned.

59   "That librarian might telephone you," I warned him.

60   "That's all right," he said. "But when you're through reading those books, I want you to tell me what you get out of them."

61   That night in my rented room, while letting the hot water run over my can of pork and beans in the sink, I opened *A Book of Prefaces* and began to read. I was jarred and shocked by the style, the clear, clean, sweeping sentences. Why did he write like that? And how did one write like that? I pictured the man as a raging demon, slashing with his pen, consumed with

hate, denouncing everything American, extolling everything European or German, laughing at the weaknesses of people, mocking God, authority. What was this? I stood up, trying to realize what reality lay behind the meaning of the words . . . Yes, this man was fighting, fighting with words. He was using words as a weapon, using them as one would use a club. Could words be weapons? Well, yes, for here they were. Then, maybe, perhaps, I could use them as a weapon? No. It frightened me. I read on and what amazed me was not what he said, but how on earth anybody had the courage to say it.

62   Occasionally I glanced up to reassure myself that I was alone in the room. Who were these men about whom Mencken was talking so passionately. Who was Anatole France? Joseph Conrad? Sinclair Lewis, Sherwood Anderson, Dostoevski, George Moore, Gustave Flaubert, Maupassant, Tolstoy, Frank Harris, Mark Twain, Thomas Hardy, Arnold Bennett, Stephen Crane, Zola, Norris, Gorky, Bergson, Ibsen, Balzac, Bernard Shaw, Dumas, Poe, Thomas Mann, O. Henry, Dreiser, H. G. Wells, Gogol, T. S. Eliot, Gide, Baudelaire, Edgar Lee Masters, Stendhal, Turgenev, Huneker, Nietzsche, and scores of others? Were these men real? Did they exist or had they existed? And how did one pronounce their names?

63   I ran across many words whose meanings I did not know, and I either looked them up in a dictionary or, before I had a chance to do that, encountered the word in a context that made its meaning clear. But what strange world was this? I concluded the book with the conviction that I had somehow overlooked something terribly important in life. I had once tried to write, had once reveled in feeling, had let my crude imagination roam, but the impulse to dream had been slowly beaten out of me by experience. Now it surged up again and I hungered for books, new ways of looking and seeing. It was not a matter of believing or disbelieving what I read, but of feeling something new, of being affected by something that made the look of the world different.

64   As dawn broke I ate my pork and beans, feeling dopey, sleepy. I went to work, but the mood of the book would not die; it lingered, coloring everything I saw, heard, did. I now felt that I knew what the white men were feeling. Merely because I had read a book that had spoken of how they lived and thought, I

identified myself with that book. I felt vaguely guilty. Would I, filled with bookish notions, act in a manner that would make the whites dislike me?

65   I forged more notes and my trips to the library became frequent. Reading grew into a passion. My first serious novel was Sinclair Lewis's *Main Street.* It made me see my boss, Mr. Gerald, and identify him as an American type. I would smile when I saw him lugging his golf bags into the office. I had always felt a vast distance separating me from the boss, and now I felt closer to him, though still distant. I felt now that I knew him, that I could feel the very limits of his narrow life. And this had happened because I had read a novel about a mythical man called George F. Babbitt.

66   The plots and stories in the novels did not interest me so much as the point of view revealed. I gave myself over to each novel without reserve, without trying to criticize it; it was enough for me to see and feel something different. And for me, everything was something different. Reading was like a drug, a dope. The novels created moods in which I lived for days. But I could not conquer my sense of guilt, my feeling that the white men around me knew that I was changing, that I had begun to regard them differently.

"The Library Card" from Black Boy *by Richard Wright. Copyright 1937, 1942, 1944, 1945 by Richard Wright. Reprinted by permission of Harper & Row, Publishers, Inc.*

QUESTIONS

1. What initially interested Wright in reading? How did this incident relate to Wright's own life?

   _____

   _____

   _____

2. What effect did reading H. L. Mencken's *A Book of Prefaces* have on Wright? How did Wright apply this new knowledge to his own life?

   _____

   _____

   _____

3. Because Wright had read very little, he had some problems with Mencken's book. Name those problems and Wright's solutions.

_____

_____

_____

4. Wright says, "Reading grew into a passion." What specifically did Wright learn from his readings?

_____

_____

_____

5. What is Wright's unstated thesis about reading?

_____

_____

_____

6. What were Wright's living conditions? Did these have any effect on his desire to read?

_____

_____

_____

7. What obstacles did Wright face in obtaining a library card? What can you infer from them about Memphis in the 1920s? How did Wright overcome these obstacles?

_____

_____

_____

8. Define the following words: *castigate* (2), *solidarity* (4), *imponderable* (6), and *prejudice* (55).

_____

_____

_____

How important was an education to Wright? What does Wright say that reading allowed him to do? Why do you believe that education is crucial? Are your reasons similar to Wright's? If not, how do they differ? Is reading as important to you as it was to Wright?

For Wright, the experience of reading one book changed his views about how words are used. "[Mencken] was using words as a weapon, using them as one would use a club" (61). Wright later became a writer himself and described the experience of blacks. Think of one book you have read that had a impact on you. In a paper, describe the book and your reaction to it. (You may substitute a play or movie for a book.)

SELECTION 3

Snow Job: Scientists Help Olympic Bobsledders Go for the Gold

ERIC WEINER

1   *WHOOSH! SNOW FLIES. A TINY SLED HURTLES BY. INSIDE CROUCH TWO MEN IN HELMETS. IT'S THE U.S. TWO-MAN BOBSLED TEAM. THEY'RE GOING 80 MILES PER HOUR! ZOOM! THE SLED BANKS THROUGH ANOTHER STEEP, ICY CURVE.*

2   These bobsled athletes are preparing for this month's Olympic Winter Games in France. (The Games begin on February 8.) And this time, the U.S. sledders believe they have a shot at a medal. If they're right, it will be the first U.S. medal in bobsledding since 1959. But the athletes will have to share that honor. As the bobsledders themselves will tell you, they can't do it alone. To make fast time, they need the help of a team of scientists.

3   "Bobsledding has really become a sport of science and technology," notes Brian Richardson, one of the top bobsledders on the U.S. team. "If teams don't have good scientists behind them, they just can't compete." Before the athletes ever race each other down a hill, scientists all over the world spend years racing each other to develop faster and faster sleds. The scientists also try to develop better training methods for sledders and new ways to get the athletes into tip-top shape.

4   "In the last Olympics we lost the two-man bobsled race by six seconds!" Brian says sadly. "That may not sound like much, but you have to remember: Bobsled races can be decided by less than one second. The only way to lose by six whole seconds is to lose the technology race first. This year I think it will be a different story."

What a Drag!

5   A bobsled sits in the middle of a long concrete tunnel. The helmeted driver stares straight ahead. There is a muffled roar. A 250 mile-per-hour wind begins to blow. Only a dummy would stay in the sled. Luckily, it *is* a dummy, a wooden figure.

6   This is the wind tunnel at the Flight Research Institute in Seattle, WA. Normally a place for testing airplane models, the site is now being used by a team of 10 engineers to help them design better bobsleds. The sleds are attached to a series of levers. The wind

shoves the sled back. Electronic measuring devices then record the amount of wind resistance—or drag— created by sled and driver.

7   "No one's allowed in the tunnel during a test," explains the lead scientist, Jerry Baer. "They would break up the air flow. We use dummies because they stay in one position. That way, we know they'll be causing exactly the same amount of wind resistance each time."

8   If you've ever sledded down a hill, you know you go faster lying down than you do sitting up. That's because, when you're sitting up, you create more surface area for the wind to hit. And this creates more wind resistance.

9   Baer and his crew want to find a shape that cuts through the air cleanly. "Every time we reduce the drag on the sled, we say, 'That's it. We'll never be able to get it any faster than that! But then we do!" The ultimate, Baer says, would be a sled that went 90 miles per hour. "But there are certain Olympic rules about the bobsled's size and shape that hold us back."

Shake, Rattle and Roll

10   The need to reduce wind resistance is only one of the problems facing bobsled scientists. Trying to get a smoother ride is another, says Baer. "Some team members rode the sled down a hill. They said it was like driving on concrete with square tires. These things shake, rattle and roll like crazy!"

11   The engineers were sore all over. But they had learned an important lesson. They realized that all that shaking meant a loss of energy for the speeding sleds. So the search began for a sled design that shook less.

12   Tiny devices—called accelerometers—were attached to the bobsleds. The instruments measured the speed of different parts of the sled. This helped scientists to measure the sled's vibrations. Meanwhile, other scientists searched for new materials to coat the sled's runner blades. They hoped to cut down the friction of the blade against the snow. Each improvement shaved valuable hundredths of a second off the sled's time.

Do It Yourselfer

13   When bobsledder Brian Richardson heard about Baer's research, he knew he had to take part. "I decided that if I was going to have a shot at a medal, I'd have to get my sled into that wind tunnel," Brian

14 Brian's homemade red sled went through test after test. After each trial, Brian and the other scientists made adjustments. They added strong tape to the fiberglass coat and styrofoam in other spots, trying to find the best sled shape. "Once I got out there with a saw and hacked away at it!" says Brian.

Before paragraph 14:

recalls. Brian has an advantage over many other bobsledders. He's also an engineer, and he designs and builds his own equipment. In fact, he wants to go for the gold in one of his own sleds.

15 After days of work, he and the engineers had managed to reduce the sled's drag by 15 percent. Next, Brian covered the sled with wax, making a mold. Then he used the mold to pour a new fiberglass shell. The result, he hopes, will carry him to a gold medal.

Jumping Into Shape

16 As in every sport, bobsled athletes need more than great equipment. They need to be in peak physical condition. Scientists are helping here too. They recommend "plyometrics."

17 It's a new method of exercise that helps develop the muscles' power. In plyometrics, the athlete uses very rapid movements—such as bounding and twisting. "It basically means I do hours of jumping up and down," laughs Brian. "But the exercises do help me when it comes time to push the sled. I get off to a faster start."

18 With scientists working on the athlete's equipment and training, is bobsledding still a sport?

19 "I believe everyone should be made to use the same equipment," says Jerry Baer. "That way you'd just be testing the athlete, not the scientists. But the athlete is still the most important person. In a bobsled race, it's 50 percent athlete, 25 percent technology and 25 percent luck!"

20 Brian agrees that bobsledding will never be pure science. He remembers his first bobsled experience, at a special school for sled driving in Lake Placid, NY. "I learned that it isn't really something anyone can teach you," he says. "They basically put you in a sled and kick you down the hill!"

21 Bobsledding is a dangerous sport. Taking icy curves at high speeds leads to accidents. Sledders are sometimes badly hurt—even killed. So an engineer at the University of California is currently working on a bobsled simulator. Thanks to a computer screen, the simulator will help athletes learn to steer a fast course without risking their lives.

22   That's the idea, anyway. But Brian Richardson believes there will never be any substitute for the real thing—going down the hill: "You're concentrating so hard, all you can see is the pitch of ice right ahead of you. For that one minute, the rest of the world just disappears."

Weiner, Eric. "*Snow Job: Scientists Help Olympic Bobsledders Go for the Gold.*" Contact (Jan./Feb. 1992): 24–27.

QUESTIONS

1. When did a U.S. bobsledding team last win an Olympic medal?

   _____

   _____

   _____

2. How does technology help bobsledders?

   _____

   _____

   _____

3. How do scientists help bobsledders?

   _____

   _____

   _____

4. Define the following words: *drag* (9), *accelerometers* (12), and *plyometrics* (16).

   _____

   _____

   _____

5. Why do bobsledders use a wind tunnel?

   _____

   _____

   _____

6. Name two problems bobsledders face.

_____

_____

_____

7. Is bobsledding solely a scientific endeavor? Explain your answer.

_____

_____

_____

FOR DISCUSSION

Originally, the Olympic Games were athletic contests between amateurs. Nowadays, however, science, technology, and corporate sponsorship, not athletic prowess, frequently provide the winning edge. In your opinion, is this trend beneficial or harmful to the sports world?

WRITING ASSIGNMENT

Today, there is no need to travel by fast sled; other means of transportation have replaced it. So, bobsledders risk their lives just for entertainment purposes, merely for competitive goals. Should they be encouraged to participate in such a dangerous sport? Should they even be allowed to take such risks?

SELECTION 4

Seven Secrets of Peak Performance

MORTON HUNT

1 Two of my classmates in college hoped to have careers in publishing. Each was talented, personable, ambitious. Yet Roger now heads a multimillion-dollar book company while Jack has a dull, modestly paying job editing business directories.

2 Why has one man flown so much higher than the other? Not because of luck, connections or dedication to work—but simply because Roger is a peak performer and Jack is not.

3 Charles Garfield, associate professor at the University of California's medical school in San Francisco and head of his own research institute, the Peak Performance Center, in Berkeley, has studied 1500 outstanding achievers in nearly every walk of life. He finds they all have certain traits in common—traits that are not innate but which *can be learned by anyone.*

4 This doesn't mean that everyone can become a company president or win an Olympic medal. It *does* mean that all of us can learn to make much more of the gifts we have. Here, based on Garfield's research, are seven steps that can lead to peak performance:

5 *1. Lead a well-rounded life.* High achievers, we often hear, are inevitably "Type A" personalities—hard-driving, obsessed people who bring work home and labor over it until bedtime. Not so, according to Garfield. "Such people tend to peak early," he says, "then go into a decline or level off. They become addicted to work itself, with much less concern for results."

6 High performers, in contrast, are willing to work hard—but within strict limits; for them, work is not everything. When Garfield interviewed top executives in ten major industries, he found that they knew how to relax, could leave their work at the office, prized close friends and family life, and spent a healthy amount of time with their children and intimates.

7 *2. Select a career you care about.* Although he really wanted to edit children's books, my former classmate Jack chose business-directory publishing as a likelier path to a large salary. For 30 years he has dragged himself out of bed five days a week to work at something he doesn't care about—and which has never produced the hoped-for pay. If Jack had done what he

really wanted to do, he might—or might not—have made more money. But he almost certainly would have been a happier and more successful human being.

8   Garfield's data show that high performers choose work they truly prefer, and spend over two-thirds of their working hours doing it and only one-third on disliked chores. They want *internal* satisfaction, not just *external* rewards such as raises, promotions and power. In the end, of course, they often have both. Because they enjoy what they are doing, their work is better and their rewards higher.

9   *3. Rehearse each challenging task mentally.* Before any difficult or important situation—a board meeting, a public appearance, a key tennis match—most peak performers run through their desired actions in their minds over and over. Famed golfer Jack Nicklaus, for example, never takes a golf shot without first mentally visualizing the precise trajectory of his swing, the flight of the ball, the spot where it lands.

10   Nearly all of us daydream about important coming events. But idle daydreaming isn't the same as a deliberate mental workout that hones the skills actually used in the activity. A pianist in China, imprisoned for seven years during the Cultural Revolution, played as well as ever soon after he was released. His explanation: "I practiced every day in my mind."

11   *4. Seek results, not perfection.* Many ambitious and hard-working people are so obsessed with perfection that they turn out little work. A professor I know has spent ten years preparing a study about a playwright. Haunted by the fear that she has missed something, she has yet to send the manuscript to a publisher. Meanwhile, the playwright—who was at the height of his fame when the project began—has faded from public view. The professor's study, even if finally published, will interest few.

12   When University of Pennsylvania psychiatrist David D. Burns, author of *Feeling Good: The New Mood Therapy*, tested a major insurance company's top 69 salesmen, he found that those who had perfectionist tendencies earned from $8,000 to $10,000 less a year than those who did not. This does not surprise Garfield. High performers, he has found, are almost always free of the compulsion to be perfect. "They don't think of their mistakes as failures," he says. "Instead, they learn from them so they can do better the next time."

13   *5. Be willing to risk.* Most people stay in what Garfield

calls the "comfort zone"—settling for security, even if it means mediocrity and boredom, rather than taking chances. I know an opera soprano who has a splendid voice and is a fine actress but who has sung only the smallest roles. "I don't want the responsibility of a major role," she says, "the whole evening depending on me, the audience listening to my every note."

14 This woman—and there are many people like her—isn't necessarily cowardly. She simply has made no effort to think through what might happen if she did fail. High performers, by contrast, are able to take risks because they carefully consider exactly how they would adjust—how they would salvage the situation—if, in fact, they did fail. "When I want to take a leap of some sort," one business executive told Garfield, "I construct a catastrophe report for myself. I imagine the worst that could happen if I tried my new plan, and then ask myself what I would do. Could I live with it? Frequently I can. If not, I don't take the chance."

15 Constructing a "worst-case scenario," as Garfield calls it, allows you to make a rational choice. If you remain immobilized by fear, you have no choice at all.

16 *6. Don't underestimate your potential.* Most of us think we know our own limits. But much of what we "know" isn't knowledge at all but belief—erroneous, self-limiting belief. "And self-limiting beliefs," says Garfield, "are the biggest obstacle to high-level performance."

17 For many years everyone "knew" that running a mile in less than four minutes was "impossible." Articles published in journals of physiology "proved" that the human body couldn't do it. Then, in 1954, Roger Bannister broke the four-minute barrier. Within two years ten other athletes had followed suit.

18 This is not to say there are *no* limits on how fast a human being can run—or on how much weight a person can lift or how well one can do any particular task. The point is: we rarely *really* know what these limits are. Thus too many of us too often set our individual limits far below what we could actually achieve.

19 High performers, on the other hand, are better able to ignore artificial barriers. They concentrate instead on themselves—on their feelings, on their functioning, on the momentum of their effort—and are therefore freer to achieve at peak levels.

20 *7. Compete with yourself, not with others.* High per-

formers focus more intently on bettering their own previous efforts than on beating competitors. In fact, worrying about a competitor's abilities—and possible superiority—can often be self-defeating.

21   Because most high performers are interested in doing the best possible job by their own standards, they tend to be "team players" rather than loners. They recognize that groups can solve certain complicated problems better than individuals and are therefore eager to let other people do part of the work. Loners, often over-concerned about rivals, can't delegate important work or decision-making. Their performance is limited because they must do everything themselves.

22   Such are the skills of high performers. If you want to make more of your talents—to live up to your full potential—then learn to use them. As Garfield explains, "I'm *not* saying 'Try harder' or 'Why don't you do better?' I *am* saying that you have the power to change your habits of mind and acquire certain skills. And if you choose to do so, you can improve your performance, your productivity and the quality of your whole life."

Hunt, Morton. "Seven Secrets of Peak Performance." Reader's Digest 121 (Sept. 1982): 85–88.

QUESTIONS

1. What is the author's thesis? Where is it located?

_____

_____

_____

2. What are the seven secrets of peak performance?

_____

_____

_____

3. What facts or studies does Hunt offer to support each of his seven points?

_____

_____

_____

4. Why is it important to select a career that truly interests you?

_____

_____

_____

5. What is the advantage of rehearsing each challenging task mentally? What types of examples does the author include to support this tactic?

_____

_____

_____

6. Why is it important not to underestimate your potential?

_____

_____

_____

7. Why is this advice about performance secrets valuable? Why does Garfield state, "I'm *not* saying 'Try harder' or 'Why don't you do better?' I *am* saying that you have the power to change your habits of mind and acquire certain skills." What judgment does Garfield make about this approach?

_____

_____

_____

8. Define the following words: *personable* (1), *"Type A" personalities* (5), *compulsion* (12), *mediocrity* (13), and *immobilized* (15).

_____

_____

_____

Consider carefully some people you regard as successful. What characteristics do they share? What makes these people successful?

When have you been successful or a peak performer? Select a task that you performed well. You may want to consider athletics, friendships, hobbies, and interests as well as academic achievements. What made your performance successful? In a paragraph, describe the task and its situation, your success, and your feeling about your accomplishment.

SELECTION 5
Hooray for the Hot Dog
BARBARA SMALLEY

1   Movie stars prefer them on gold-banded plates. Some people think they're gourmet food. Babe Ruth once downed a dozen between the games of a double header. Frankly, Americans love hot dogs. Some 14 billion— enough to reach the moon and back three times—are manufactured each year in the United States alone. According to the National Hot Dog and Sausage Council, hot dogs are served in 95 percent of American homes. Studies suggest that adults eat more franks than children do and that women eat more of them than men do. Some 50 million are eaten in the United States every day year-round. That's about 80 hot dogs a year for every person.

2   Hot dogs also have tickled the taste buds of some unusual people. Franklin D. Roosevelt once served them with beer to England's King George VI. Queen Elizabeth II served them at a royal dinner for the American Bar Association in 1957. Apollo astronauts took them to the moon. Skylab crew members ate them in outer space.

3   Hot dogs are a favorite snack food at fairs, circuses, amusement parks, and picnics. They are especially popular at sporting events. According to concession-aires, 60 percent of the fans in attendance end up eating hot dogs. During the baseball season, the num-ber of franks sold at ball parks averages about 80 percent of attendance figures.

4   The term *hot dog* was coined in 1901 at the home of the baseball Giants. One cold April day, concession-aire Harry Stevens wasn't making any profits selling ice cream and soda. He came up with the idea of selling hot "dachshund" sausages instead. He sent his sales force into the stands to bark that now-familiar chant: "They're red hot! Get your red hots here!" Sports cartoonist Ted Dorgan drew a cartoon of barking sausages. He wasn't sure how to spell dachshund, so he called them hot dogs. Dorgan's cartoon was an instant success and the name stuck. Today, according to the U.S. Department of Agriculture, hot dogs also are officially known as wieners, frankfurters, and franks.

5   The basic hot dog is made of meat. They may be labeled "all meat" or simply "frankfurters," "hot dogs,"

or "wieners." Those labeled "all meat" are made of beef or a mixture of beef and pork. They are not made of just any kind of meat. They are made of muscle meat only. They do not contain meat by-products, fillers, or binders, unless these ingredients are featured on the label: for example, beef franks with soy flour. As with all hot dogs made of meat, they can contain no more 30 percent fat.

6   Franks which are not labeled "all meat," but simply "frankfurters," are made of a combination of meats, usually beef and pork. They may also include fillers, such as soy flour and milk powder.

7   Recently, chicken and turkey hot dogs have become very popular. These are made without any fillers or binders. The fat content is not regulated by law, but it is usually lower than that of meat franks.

8   No matter what the hot dog is made of, the process is the same. The meat is cured, seasoned, finely ground, stuffed into casings, and linked. Franks then are lightly smoked and given a hot-water bath. After this, they are ready to eat when purchased. Differences in flavor are the results of spices and seasonings used in carefully guarded recipes. Hot dogs typically range from bite-size to foot-long. The longest hot dog on record—a 165-footer—was made for the First Baptist Church of New Philadelphia, Ohio.

9   There is some argument about the origin of the hot dog. Frankfurt-am-Main, Germany, is usually credited with originating the frankfurter. But, the people of Wien (or Vienna), Austria, point to the word *wiener* to prove their claim as the birthplace of the hot dog. Some historians believe that the hot dog was first made in the late 1600s by a butcher in Coburg, Germany. They say he later traveled to Frankfurt to promote his new product.

10   The origin of the hot dog bun is also in doubt. Some reports credit a German immigrant. He sold sausages with milk rolls and sauerkraut from a pushcart in New York City during the 1860s. Others favor Charles Feltman, a German butcher who opened the first Coney Island stand in 1871. In his first year of business, Feltman sold 3,684 sausages with milk rolls. The hot dog bun as we know it today, however, was introduced in 1904 at the Louisiana Purchase Exposition in St. Louis. Bavarian concessionaire Anton Feuchtwanger loaned white gloves to his customers to hold

his piping-hot sausages. But souvenir hunters began to make off with the gloves. So Feuchtwanger asked his brother-in-law, a baker, to come up with a roll that would hug the meat.

11   But, no matter who discovered the hot dog or its bun, the pair has since come to mean big business. Oscar Mayer Foods Corporation of Madison, Wisconsin, is the leading seller of hot dogs. It produces 38,000 franks per hour. The company uses an electronically controlled process it calls the "hot dog highway."

12   Close behind Oscar Mayer is Hygrade Food Products Corp. and its Ball Park franks. This brand is No. 1 in Detroit and outsells any other by a mile. But, that's not the reason Ball Park franks hit the national news and TV networks in 1983. That was the time when Hygrade received some horrifying news. A woman said she had found a razor blade in one of its franks!

13   When the report came in, Hygrade sent one of its top men, Charles Ledgerwood, to talk to her. Ledgerwood examined the hot dog and blade. The blade was not part of a machine blade. The woman's husband remarked that it was the same kind of razor blade that he used to shave. Ledgerwood did not think the remark was important at the time.

14   He went back to Hygrade and the company decided to give out a statement to the press. The company took the blame. It said that a crazed worker in its plant must have placed the blade in the frank. Hygrade and Ball Park franks hit the headlines and TV with a bang. The next day, several other people reported finding razor blades in Ball Parks.

15   Hygrade stopped production at its Livonia plant and called back 350,000 Ball Parks. But, these new reports also provided clues that hoaxers had been at work. The company worked around the clock, inspecting every one of the called-back hot dogs. Nothing was found. Then, two days later, the woman Ledgerwood had talked to admitted lying.

16   Happily, the newspapers and TV played up this good news just as heavily as they had the bad. The town of Livonia went all out in support of its company by staging a Livonia Loves Hygrade Week. Its goal was for each Livonia man, woman, and child to eat one Ball Park frank. On windup day, thousands of Livonians lined up in bitter cold to buy and eat a Ball Park. When the count was in, 104,000 Livonians had eaten over

150,000 Ball Parks! That showed that Ball Park's strength was back. Shortly, its loyal fans pushed sales way ahead of where they had been before the hoax.

17   But, Detroit and Livonia are not the only places where people are loyal to the hot dog. More than 100,000 franks are eaten on a single summer weekend at New York City's Coney Island. More than 2 million hot dogs a year are sold at Chicago's O'Hare International Airport. This is more than are sold at any other single location in the world. On special occasions, hot dog sales soar. In 1976, for example, onlookers watching Operation Sail in New York Harbor gobbled 10 million hot dogs. That same year, 1.5 million wieners were eaten in Montreal at the Olympics.

18   What makes franks so doggone popular? They are cheap, convenient, and come ready to eat. A wiener in a bun offers a good amount of protein. They are low enough in calories to be included on the official Weight Watchers program. They can be boiled, broiled, barbecued, and stuffed. They can be cooked almost any way and with almost any other food. Most important, hot dogs are fun to eat.

19   The best way to dress a dog has become a matter of geographic preference. The Chicago hot dog is served on a poppy seed bun. Added to that is mustard, relish, onion, tomato, and a dash of celery salt. The Kansas City dog is served with sauerkraut and melted Swiss cheese on a seeded roll. The official New York City dog is topped with cheese and bacon, But, sidewalk sellers smother theirs in stewed onions. And at Coney Island, frankfurters come buried in a special spicy sauce. Californians prefer to dip their hot dogs in cornmeal batter and deep-fry them. Bostonians like theirs piled high with either onions or sauerkraut.

20   No matter the topping, Americans have long been saying "hot diggety" to the dog. In 1957, the U.S. Chamber of Commerce officially named July as National Hot Dog Month. Recently, the National Hot Dog and Sausage Council said that Americans ate 18 million more wieners than they did the year before. One wit said: "The noblest dog of all is the hot dog. It feeds the hand that bites it."

Smalley, Barbara. "Hooray for the Hotdog." Guided Reading Study Guide FF. Huntington Station, NY: Instructional Communications Technology, Inc., pp.14–17.

1. Define *gourmet* (1) and *concessionaires* (3).

   _____

   _____

   _____

2. Name at least three synonyms for *hot dog*.

   _____

   _____

   _____

3. Who is credited with naming the hot dog? Tell the story.

   _____

   _____

   _____

4. What kind of hot dog has the lowest fat content?

   _____

   _____

   _____

5. When, where, and why was the hot dog roll invented?

   _____

   _____

   _____

6. Which place holds the record for most hot dogs sold in one location?

   _____

   _____

   _____

7. Which month is National Hot Dog Month?

   _____

This article praises hot dogs as low-calorie, tasty, and convenient. However, many people point to hot dogs as the prime example of all that is wrong with Americans' diets. What do you think of Americans' eating habits? How might you improve your own eating habits?

WRITING ASSIGNMENT

Some people maintain that if Americans would eat properly and wisely, they would live longer, healthier lives. Others feel that the quest for extended life is unrealistic. They believe the human body has a built-in self-destruct mechanism. What do you think? Can the key to long life be found? Or should resources be concentrated on improving the quality of life, even if that life cannot be extended to one hundred years?

SELECTION 6
Job Hunting? Watch What You Say!
LEIGH KNOTTS

1   All over the country the Class of 91 is graduating, and soon many of us will be looking for jobs, confident our hard-earned degree will impress job interviewers. But there's at least one more thing my fellow graduates need to know before they head off to the first interview:

2   They should be careful of what they say and how they say it. It will make a difference, especially for women. And I can prove it. During my senior year at Hood College, I researched speech patterns and how they affect a job search. What I found out is scary for women hoping to land that big job.

3   Women realize they aren't starting on equal ground with men in the work place. We've seen the research on pay equity and on women in top management. But few of us know that we have to watch how we say things even more than what we say when we go for an interview.

4   Numerous researchers have shown that women, more often than men, use certain phrases or clauses in their speech. We'll call it "women's language." I wanted to see if personnel managers reacted differently to job candidates using "women's language" than to those who did not.

5   I picked four features of women's language to use in my research—tag questions, hedges, hesitation and intensifiers.

6   A "tag question" is a statement followed by a questioning phrase. For example (all examples are taken from a script I used in my research), "A reliable person is important in the work place, isn't she?" "Isn't she" is a tag question. It isn't needed and allows the speaker to avoid forcing an opinion on the listener.

7   A "hedge" is a phrase that blunts a statement or makes the statement more tentative. "I guess one adjective to describe me is reliable." "I guess" is a hedge. Other hedges include "sort of" and "kind of." Hedges help the speaker soften the impact of a statement that might provoke negative reactions.

8   A "hesitation" denotes tentativeness on the part of the speaker. "In the past, I have worked independently on several projects and, um, have completed them on time." Words like "um," "uh" and "well" are hesita-

tions. A hesitation allows the speaker to avoid appearing dominant or assertive in the conversation.

9 An "intensifier" is an intonational emphasis, the equivalent of underlining the written language. "I come to work on time and I really do not take days off unnecessarily." "Really," "so" and "such" are intensifiers.

10 To gauge the effects of women's language in an interview, I recorded my honors adviser, a psychology professor, using and then not using women's language while reading a script presenting her qualifications as a job candidate. The tapes were reviewed by 27 personnel officers, all women. Half heard one version of the tape, the others heard the alternative version.

11 The personnel officers judged the "applicant" on potential success, acceptance and likability. The woman who spoke without using women's language was rated significantly higher all around, including more likely to be hired for a management position in a large corporation, more likely to be effective in handling the job and more likely to be promoted. She also was rated as having more power and as more likely to receive support from superiors. There were several other categories, but the bottom line was the same—women's language is not the language that business people want applicants to speak. Even women don't want to hear it. They want a woman to talk like a man.

12 My test results are consistent with past research showing that people using women's language are judged as lacking knowledge, authority and power, and as unassertive. The research also shows that women using women's language are seen as not having what it takes to be good managers—traits such as aggression, directness, knowledge and leadership ability.

13 The frightening implication of my study is that previous research has understated the effect of the use of women's language on the evaluation of an individual, in particular, job applicants. Much of the previous research was based on the critiques of college students looking at job applicants. I went straight to personnel officers, people responsible for hiring.

14 Further, it is shocking to discover that men are not the only ones who limit the access of females to power based on their aversion to women's language. This might be because the business world is a man's world, and these personnel officers have adopted the standards of men in order to be accepted themselves.

15   What should we do? What can we do? Do we give up a language that is unique to women? Women's language does serve a purpose, according to sociologists. All of the features are effective in creating a sense of community and stimulating cooperation. That's the way women tend to operate. Men use language for power and to dominate. That's the way men tend to operate.

16   We can give up women's language and talk like men so we can "fit in" with the power structure. Or we can continue to use women's language and take the chance that the personnel officer looks beyond *how* we say it to see *who* is saying it.

17   My advice is to be practical. In the ideal business world women could be themselves without fear of rejection. But first, personnel officers and others have to be educated as to the usefulness of women's language. Women need to watch how they speak in an interview. But once they land that job, they should try their best to educate personnel officers and managers about bias.

Knotts, Leigh. "Job Hunting? Watch What You Say!" Baltimore Evening Sun (17 May 1991):A9.

QUESTIONS

1. What is the author's thesis? Where is it located?

   _____

   _____

   _____

2. What terms does the author define as she describes her study on women's speech patterns? What do these terms mean?

   _____

   _____

   _____

3. How did Knotts conduct her investigation of women's speech patterns? What were the steps involved?

   _____

   _____

   _____

4. What were the results of the author's study? What evidence does the author provide to support these results?

_____

_____

_____

5. What are the implications of this study? What can you infer about women job applicants who use women's language? What are their chances of being hired for management positions?

_____

_____

_____

6. What inferences can you make from the fact that all the personnel officers in the study were women? What does this suggest about the officers' reaction to other women?

_____

_____

_____

7. What solutions does the author offer for this problem? Which is the most reasonable one? Why?

_____

_____

_____

8. What is the connection between women's language and its reception in the business world?

_____

_____

_____

Why do women tend to use this type of language? Does this language of hesitations, tag questions, hedges, and intensifiers reflect the way women think? Or does it reflect the way women believe they are supposed to respond? How would you describe men's language? How might society influence our language? Should people be judged by their language? Consider, for instance, that certain regions of the country have certain dialects. The same is true for many ethnic groups. How can we avoid judging people by their use of language?

Conduct your own evaluation of the way people use language. In conversations with friends, listen carefully for keys to their use of language. Do friends use slang terms, for instance? If so, why? What is your reaction? Report your findings in a paragraph.

SELECTION 7
Magma, P. I.
BRIANNA POLITZER

1   A hot wind blew through a village in Indonesia. Today was the day that Barry Voight and his team of scientists would climb Merapi, the 9,500 foot mountain of fire. Its violent eruptions have killed thousands of people throughout the centuries. But today, the scientists were not afraid. They had carefully studied the volcano before the climb. They knew that the angry giant was napping. The chance of their being killed by a wave of fiery melted rock, called molten lava, was small. In fact, it was less than the risk of being hit by a car while crossing the street.

2   Even so Merapi *is* an active volcano. "I don't want to be up there when Merapi is ready to go off," Voight [said]. After all, Voight knows firsthand what it's like to have a close call. He had to make a run for a helicopter when Mount St. Helens blew its top!

3   Although the climb would be short—only five hours or so—it wouldn't be easy. The slopes were crumbly and steep. And the group carried heavy packs filled with equipment, batteries, water and camping supplies. They also carried gas masks to protect themselves from poisonous gases. (The gases come from cracks and openings near the volcano's peak, or summit.) Without the masks, one belch of gas would scorch the scientists' lungs.

4   The climbers wandered through farms on the volcano's lower slopes. Bursting from fields were sweet potatoes, soybeans and tobacco. The group followed the trail up into a belt of humid jungle, then out onto misty ridges and grassy slopes. Then they were above the vegetation line. Above this point, the colder temperatures and rocky soil prevent even the most hardy grasses from growing. When the group arrived on the volcano's level summit, they pitched their tents.

Blast from the Past

5   "If you were looking for the most active and dangerous volcano in the world today, Merapi might be it," says Voight. And that's exactly why he's there. Voight is a volcanologist—an expert in the science of volcanoes. His main job is to predict the exact moment when a volcano will erupt.

6   The equipment that Voight and his team place on

Merapi will give them important information. It will help them learn what is going on inside the volcano. These clues might help them figure out when the mountain of fire will erupt again, throwing up geysers of hot lava and ash.

7   Why is it important to know when Merapi might blow? If many of the people living around the volcano's base don't leave in time, they could be killed. Hurricanes of 1,400 degree F. volcanic ash would burn the villagers and farmers. Or flows of mud caused by heavy rain mixed with the ash would bury them alive.

8   Merapi has erupted about 70 times in the past 1,000 years. In 1930, an eruption killed 1,300 people who lived around the volcano's base. In 1984, there was another huge eruption. But that time, the people got away, and nobody was hurt.

9   Why do people keep moving back? One reason, Voight says, is that the rich lava soil around the volcano is perfect for farming.

10   "A volcano is like a window into the inside of the Earth," Voight says. "It is a place where the molten material inside the Earth, called magma, can get out." Magma that the volcano spits out is called lava, he explains.

11   Voight says that there's a reason why most volcanoes are shaped like large, upside-down ice-cream cones. When the volcano erupts, piles of lava, rock and other material are thrown out of the volcano. Each eruption adds another layer to the pile, causing the mountain to grow and grow.

12   Volcanoes erupt when magma from deep within the Earth rises. This causes the older rock clogging the hole in the volcano to be pushed upwards or sideways. The pressure becomes too much for the rock to withstand. BOOM! The volcano erupts in an explosion of fiery lava, pieces of rock, steam and gas. Voight says the eruption is like opening a bottle of soda that has been shaken up. The minute you pop off the cap—whoosh!—the soda blasts out in a foamy spray of liquid.

13   Before a volcano erupts the ground swells and rumbles as the magma squeezes into the chamber in the volcano's core. Temperatures on the volcano's surface grow hotter. Gas and steam may rise more furiously. These are some of the signs that Barry Voight watches for at Merapi.

Measuring Up

14   "The ground is stretching around the volcano because more and more magma is being pumped into it," Voight explains. "We measure the amount of stretching. Before it goes, the ground may start making creaks and groans because earthquakes are happening. We measure those, too."

15   Voight measures the movement in the surface of the rock with three different types of instruments. The first kind, called a tiltmeter, measures changes in the angle, or slope of the ground. The changing ground is a sign that the rock is beginning to swell or bulge. The second, a seismograph (say *SIZE-mo-graff*), measures earthquakes.

16   The third instrument is a mirror placed high on the mountain. It can be spotted from the valley five miles away. Scientists shoot lasers, or beams of light, toward the mirror. The light bounces back and hits a device that figures the distance between itself and the mirror. If the distance has changed the next time they measure, they know the reflector has moved—and that the rock is swelling.

17   The scientists placed all three types of measuring devices on Merapi. They attached solar-powered radio transmitters to the devices to beam the information to computers in a city about 20 miles away. There, scientists put together the information to help determine the rock's breaking point.

18   Voight says, "We want to predict the point in time when the magma will break through the rock and come out of the hole."

19   Voight has come up with a math formula to predict this breaking point. He is convinced that if engineers can use math to figure out when bridges will break under strain, then it can also be used to predict when a volcano will explode.

20   Who knows when Merapi will blow next? Will it be next week, next month, next year? Could it happen while a scientist is standing on top of the huge crater, installing instruments? "I'm not afraid on Merapi," says Voight. "Not unless the instruments show us something unusual." Meanwhile, he says, he plans to keep on doing what he's doing—"wiring up" dangerous volcanoes and studying what makes them tick.

Politzer, Brianna. "Magma, P.I." Contact, (Jan./Feb. 1992): 24–27.

1. Why did the climbers carry gas masks?

_____

_____

_____

2. What is the *vegetation line* (4)?

_____

_____

_____

3. What is Merapi? Find out where it is located.

_____

_____

_____

4. Define *magma* and *lava*.

_____

_____

_____

5. Explain how volcanoes erupt.

_____

_____

_____

6. What are the signs that indicate a volcano may soon erupt?

_____

_____

_____

7. What three instruments do scientists use to measure the movement of the earth near a volcano? How does each work?

_____

_____

_____

FOR DISCUSSION

Voight says people keep moving back to the slopes of volcanoes, even though they know it is a dangerous place to live. Similarly, people build on barrier beaches and rebuild on flood plains. What does this disregard for the power of nature indicate about humans and our needs?

WRITING ASSIGNMENT

Some people might argue that studying volcanoes should not be an immediate concern to scientists. They would say that more pressing problems facing humanity, such as hunger, disease, and pollution, should be addressed before scientists spend their time and resources on volcanoes, the deep ocean, or the moon. What do you think? Is there any compelling reason why such topics as literature, hieroglyphics, or the planets should be studied? Or should only those areas of immediate, practical significance be studied?

SELECTION 8
The Buried Treasure of Oak Island
RALPH H. MAJOR, JR.

1   On a windswept, mile-and-a-half-long island only fifty-four miles from Halifax, Nova Scotia, lies one of the world's most famous buried treasures. Over the past two centuries, more than a million dollars has been spent in attempts to penetrate the 160-foot pit where submerged wooden chests, believed to be full of precious metal and coins, await someone with the engineering genius to wrest them from the ground.

2   Of all the so-called "treasures" in North America, the secret cache on Oak Island is perhaps the most fabled, the most sought after, the best verified, and yet the one most fraught with mystery. Buried, according to legend, by Captain Kidd's lieutenants around 1720, this prize has defied recovery ever since three youngsters from the mainland stumbled upon the grass-overgrown pit. Since then, no less than twenty diligent attempts have been made to retrieve what experts have called "the world's most perfectly buried treasure."

3   Oak Island is a heavily wooded islet off Nova Scotia's rugged coast. First to discover what must stand as one of the most phenomenal engineering achievements of its time were Jack Smith, Tony Vaughan, and Daniel McInnes, three youths from nearby Lunenburg on Nova Scotia.

4   This trio landed from their canoe one day in 1795 and soon noticed, about 400 feet from shore, a majestic oak from which a long lower limb projected over a depressed square of earth. The limb showed signs of block-and-tackle pressure; the depressed ground indicated a one-time excavation.

5   Next day, the three returned to Oak Island equipped with shovels, axes, and picks. They began to dig. Ten feet down they hit something hard. It turned out to be a platform of six-inch-thick oak planks. Why was it there? To protect an exotic store of riches? The boys were enthralled. Ten feet further they hit another oaken barrier. Thirty feet down a similar platform halted their progress.

6   The youths returned week after week to probe deeper into the pit until exhaustion forced them to curtail their digging for a time. Back in Nova Scotia, they began asking guarded questions about the isle.

7   Oak Island, they learned, was under some cryptic curse. Back in 1720, so the story went, mainlanders had seen strange lights flickering there. Several boatmen ventured close enough to observe pirate-garbed men working amid roaring bonfires. Two fishermen furtively rowed in to inspect the activity. They were never seen again, and no one ever discovered what actually had befallen the men.

8   Through the years, the three young Nova Scotians doggedly continued to nourish their dream. They were joined by a Dr. Lynds who raised capital to buy equipment and hire labor, and the work on Oak Island continued in earnest. At forty feet, another platform interrupted the digging. Still another was uncovered at fifty feet. On they dug, encountering platforms of oak or hardened putty every ten feet.

9   At ninety feet, the shovels struck a perplexing new mystery, a flat stone tablet, three feet by sixteen inches, covered with curious engraved characters. Although scientists at the time were unable to decipher the hieroglyphics, the Rev. A. T. Kempton of Cambridge, Mass., in 1928 translated them to read: "FORTY FEET BELOW, TWO MILLION POUNDS ARE BURIED."

10   Inspired by the discovery of the strangely engraved stone, the diggers worked furiously. Down and down they delved with inspired perseverance. Then, one hundred feet below the surface, they found what they believed would prove to be the last barrier above a crypt. Exuberant, Dr. Lynds ordered work stopped until next morning.

11   When the sun rose, a despondent cry came from the workers' lips. For, overnight, water had risen in the shaft to within thirty-five feet of the top! Cursing and perspiring, the workmen bailed and pumped for weeks, until bad weather necessitated suspension of the operations.

12   The next summer, Dr. Lynds and his friends were back on the job. Now they dug a new shaft beside the flooded treasure pit, hoping to divert into it water which sealed off the underground chamber. At ninety-eight feet they began to cut horizontally toward the flooded pit. But when a shovel sliced through the last few feet of earth, tons of water poured into the auxiliary shaft, drowning three workmen. The water quickly rose to the same level as in the treasure pit. Disillu-

sioned and broke, the Lynds company gave up the search.

13   Later, Dr. Lynds and Tony Vaughan set off for Oak Island with a newly recruited crew and drilling equipment developed for coal mining. Just above the water level they built a platform from which a special type of drill was lowered into the shaft. When the drill was raised, a shout of joy rose from the crowd about the pit. Three massive gold links were entwined about the end of the bit.

14   From the chain links and pieces of wood brought to the surface, the company's engineer deduced that the treasure consisted of several oaken chests and casks, each brimming with metal in various forms. But seventy-five feet of water still separated them from the hoard and finally discouraged their attempt. Another attempt was made in 1863, when a powerful engine and pump were brought to the island. They succeeded in keeping water in the shaft well below the previous level. But when an engineer warned that the shaft was about to cave in, this attempt was also abandoned with chagrin.

15   In 1865 and 1874, still other companies poured more than $70,000 into the watery pits. Then, in 1893, perhaps the most ambitious scheme of all was launched. It was the Oak Island Treasure Company, Inc., organized by Judge Frederick L. Blair of Amherst, Nova Scotia.

16   Blair's outift reopened and widened the treasure shaft and began a new one. Drills soon reached the unprecedented depth of 108 feet. Samples removed from the bits helped engineers plot the area of a subterranean room, seven feet square surrounded by a twenty-inch framework of wood and cement. Borings produced more evidence of human activity—one, a tiny ball of parchment on which, when flattened out, the letters *ui, vi,* or *wi* were found to have been written in black ink.

17   For four more years, work continued. New shafts went down, some as deep as 160 feet. But in 1897, the syndicate gave up. Still obsessed with dreams of riches, however, Blair bought out his other backers and kept plugging away. In 1903, even he belatedly admitted defeat.

18   In the 1930's, Gilbert D. Hedden, a retired steel manufacturer from Newark, New Jersey, bought parts

of the island and engaged a mining and drilling firm to sink a new shaft, 155 feet deep. However, success eluded them and this project was abandoned in 1939.

19   In 1949 Mel Chapparal and Whitney Blake bought the island and secured the right to search for the treasure from the Blair estate. They made several excavations but met with no success. Although Chapparal still owns the island and the rights to search for treasure on it, he has allowed several people to search for the treasure.

20   In 1955 a Texas oilman, George J. Greene, brought a four-inch core drill to the island and began drilling holes around the excavations made by Chapparal. He found the same layers of oak timbers that the three boys had found. However, in the fourth hole he drilled, he found an eight-inch layer of oak covering a forty-five foot cavern. In an attempt to discover the entrance to the cavern, he pumped 100,000 gallons of water into it. It leaked out as expected, but unfortunately he could not find where the water had gone. He was finally forced to give up his attempts when urgent business called him away.

21   Since the Oak Island treasure pit was discovered 170 years ago, some twenty separate expeditions have been organized to exhume the hoard from its inaccessible water-guarded tomb. More than $1,500,000, by conservative assessment, has been poured into the thirty-eight shafts which today honeycomb the island.

22   Who was responsible for this engineering enigma? He is still anonymous. For years it was popularly believed that successors to the pirate, Captain Kidd, executed in 1701, had buried the treasure. A later theory held that the cache was part of loot captured by Spanish marauders in the fifteenth and sixteenth centuries and diverted from shipments earmarked for Spain.

23   Whatever the theories about the origin, the fact remains that the burial of the Oak Island treasure involved a stupendous feat of engineering. It is almost inconceivable, but true, that more than 200 years ago unschooled and untrained men were able to conceive and laboriously construct a subsurface hiding place that has defied the best brains and talents of the modern engineering world.

Major, Ralph H., Jr. *"The Buried Treasure of Oak Island."* Controlled Reading Study Guide II. *Stanford E. Taylor et al. New York: McGraw, 1963, pp. 48–49.*

1. What is the buried treasure of Oak Island?

   _____

   _____

   _____

2. Why is it still buried and not yet recovered?

   _____

   _____

   _____

3. Where is Oak Island?

   _____

   _____

   _____

4. How many attempts have been made to recover "the world's most perfectly buried treasure"?

   _____

   _____

   _____

5. Besides the possibility of finding buried treasure, what else about Oak Island is intriguing?

   _____

   _____

   _____

6. Describe the structures devised to protect the treasure.

   _____

   _____

   _____

7. Define the following words: *phenomenal* (3), *excavation* (4), *exotic* (5), *doggedly* (8), *chagrin* (14), and *exhume* (21).

_____

_____

_____

FOR DISCUSSION

Is it possible that treasure really is buried on Oak Island? Is it probable? What other explanation could there be for the elaborate shaft constructed on the island?

WRITING ASSIGNMENT

Many people are willing to gamble a little. They will purchase a lottery ticket or join a sport-betting pool. But few people are willing to take a chance with a lot of money, as the treasure hunters in this article did. Why do you think this is true? What makes most people hesitate? Is it the sum of money? Is it the level of risk?

How much of a risk-taker are you? Do you believe in luck? Write about chance, luck, and risk-taking. Think about your family, friends, and associates. Categorize them according to their tolerance for risk-taking.

SELECTION 9
Does America Still Exist?

RICHARD RODRIGUEZ

1   For the children of immigrant parents the knowledge comes easier. America exists everywhere in the city—on billboards, frankly in the smell of French fries and popcorn. It exists in the pace: traffic lights, the assertions of neon, the mysterious bong-bong-bong through the atriums of department stores. America exists as the voice of the crowd, a menacing sound—the high nasal accent of American English.

2   When I was a boy in Sacramento (California, the fifties), people would ask me, "Where you from?" I was born in this country, but I knew the question meant to decipher my darkness, my looks.

3   My mother once instructed me to say, "I am an American of American descent." By the time I was nine or ten, I wanted to say, but dared not reply, "I am an American."

4   Immigrants come to America and, against hostility or mere loneliness, they recreate a homeland in the parlor, tacking up postcards or calendars of some impossible blue—lake or sea or sky. Children of immigrant parents are supposed to perch on a hyphen between two countries. Relatives assume the achievement as much as anyone. Relatives are, in any case, surprised when the child begins losing old ways. One day at the family picnic the boy wanders away from their spiced food and faceless stories to watch other boys play baseball in the distance.

5   There is sorrow in the American memory, guilty sorrow for having left something behind—Portugal, China, Norway. The American story is the story of immigrant children and of their children—children no longer able to speak to grandparents. The memory of exile becomes inarticulate as it passes from generation to generation, along with wedding rings and pocket watches—like some mute stone in a wad of old lace. Europe. Asia. Eden.

6   But, it needs to be said, if this is a country where one stops being Vietnamese or Italian, this is a country where one begins to be an American. America exists as a culture and a grin, a faith and a shrug. It is clasped in a handshake, called by a first name.

7   As much as the country is joined in a common culture, however, Americans are reluctant to celebrate

the process of assimilation. We pledge allegiance to diversity. America was born Protestant and bred Puritan, and the notion of community we share is derived from a seventeenth-century faith. Presidents and the pages of ninth-grade civics readers yet proclaim the orthodoxy: We are gathered together—but as individuals, with separate pasts, distinct destinies. Our society is as paradoxical as a Puritan congregation: We stand together, alone.

8   Americans have traditionally defined themselves by what they refused to include. As often, however, Americans have struggled, turned in good conscience at last to assert the great Protestant virtue of tolerance. Despite outbreaks of nativist frenzy, America has remained an immigrant country, open and true to itself.

9   Against pious emblems of rural America—soda fountain, Elks hall, Protestant church, and now shopping mall—stands the cold-hearted city, crowded with races and ambitions, curious laughter, much that is odd. Nevertheless, it is the city that has most truly represented America. In the city, however, the millions of singular lives have had no richer notion of wholeness to describe them than the idea of pluralism.

10   *"Where you from?" the American asks the immigrant child. "Mexico," the boy learns to say.*

11   Mexico, the country of my blood ancestors, offers formal contrast to the American achievement. If the United States was formed by Protestant individualism, Mexico was shaped by a medieval Catholic dream of one world. The Spanish journeyed to Mexico to plunder, and they may have gone, in God's name, with an arrogance peculiar to those who intend to convert. But through the conversion, the Indian converted the Spaniard. A new race was born, the *mestizo*, wedding European to Indian. José Vasconcelos, the Mexican philosopher, has celebrated this New World creation, proclaiming it the "cosmic race."

12   Centuries later, in a San Francisco restaurant, a Mexican-American lawyer of my acquaintance says, in English, over *salade niçoise*, that he does not intend to assimilate into gringo society. His claim is echoed by a chorus of others (Italian-Americans, Greeks, Asians) in this era of ethnic pride. The melting pot has been retired, clanking, into the museum of quaint disgrace, alongside Aunt Jemima and the Katzenjammer Kids. But resistance to assimilation is characteristi-

cally American. It only makes clear how inevitable the process of assimilation actually is.

13 For generations, this has been the pattern. Immigrant parents have sent their children to school (simply, they thought) to acquire the "skills" to survive in the city. The child returned home with a voice his parents barely recognized or understood, couldn't trust, and didn't like.

14 In Eastern cities—Philadelphia, New York, Boston, Baltimore—class after class gathered immigrant children to women (usually women) who stood in front of rooms full of children, changing children. So also for me in the 1950s. Irish-Catholic nuns. California. The old story. The hyphen tipped to the right, away from Mexico and toward a confusing but true American identity.

15 I speak now in the chromium American accent of my grammar school classmates—Billy Reckers, Mike Bradley, Carol Schmidt, Kathy O'Grady. . . . I believe I became like my classmates, became German, Polish, and (like my teachers) Irish. And because assimilation is always reciprocal, my classmates got something of me. (I mean sad eyes; belief in the Indian Virgin; a taste for sugar skulls on the Feast of the Dead.) In the blending, we became what our parents could never have been, and we carried America one revolution further.

16 "Does America still exist?" Americans have been asking the question for so long that to ask it again only proves our continuous link. But perhaps the question deserves to be asked with urgency—now. Since the black civil rights movement of the 1960s, our tenuous notion of a shared public life has deteriorated notably.

17 The struggle of black men and women did not eradicate racism, but it became the great moment in the life of America's conscience. Water hoses, bulldogs, blood—the images, rendered black, white, rectangular, passed into living rooms.

18 It is hard to look at a photograph of a crowd taken, say, in 1890 or in 1930 and not notice the absence of blacks. (It becomes an impertinence to wonder if America *still* exists.)

19 In the sixties, other groups of Americans learned to champion their rights by analogy to the black civil rights movement. But the heroic vision faded. Dr. Martin Luther King Jr. had spoken with Pauline elo-

quence of a nation that would unite Christian and Jew, old and young, rich and poor. Within a decade, the struggles of the 1960s were reduced to a bureaucratic competition for little more than pieces of a representational pie. The quest for a portion of power became an end in itself. The metaphor for the American city of the 1970s was a committee: one black, one woman, one person under thirty. . . .

20   If the small town had sinned against America by too neatly defining who could be an American, the city's sin was a romantic secession. One noticed the romanticism in the antiwar movement—certain demonstrators who demonstrated a lack of tact or desire to persuade and seemed content to play secular protestants. One noticed the romanticism in the competition among members of "minority groups" to claim the status of Primary Victim. To Americans unconfident of their common identity, minority standing became a way of asserting individuality. Middle-class Americans—men and women clearly not the primary victims of social oppression—brandished their suffering with exuberance.

21   The dream of a single society probably died with *The Ed Sullivan Show*. The reality of America persists. Teenagers pass through big-city high schools banded in racial groups, their collars turned up to a uniform shrug. But then they graduate to jobs at the phone company or in banks, where they end up working alongside people unlike themselves. Typists and tellers walk out together at lunchtime.

22   It is easier for us as Americans to believe the obvious fact of our separateness—easier to imagine the black and white Americas prophesied by the Kerner report (broken glass, street fires)—than to recognize the reality of a city street at lunchtime. Americans are wedded by proximity to a common culture. The panhandler at one corner is related to the pamphleteer at the next who is related to the banker who is kin to the Chinese old man wearing an MIT sweatshirt. In any true national history, Thomas Jefferson begets Martin Luther King Jr. who begets the Gray Panthers. It is because we lack a vision of ourselves entire—the city street is crowded and we are each preoccupied with finding our own way home—that we lack an appropriate hymn.

23   Under my window now passes a little white girl softly rehearsing to herself a Motown obbligato.

Rodriguez, Richard. "Does America Still Exist?" in 75 Readings: An Anthology (McGraw); first appeared in Harper's, March 1984.

QUESTIONS

1. The author answers his title question by asserting that America does exist. Where does it exist? What proof of its existence does he offer?

   _____

   _____

   _____

2. Rodriguez identifies certain characteristics of recent immigrants. What traits do recent immigrants display?

   _____

   _____

   _____

3. The author describes American society as "paradoxical." Explain the paradox.

   _____

   _____

   _____

4. When did the dream of a single society die? Why?

   _____

   _____

   _____

5. In the end, what is the author's vision of America?

   _____

   _____

   _____

6. Is that vision an accurate one?

   _____

   _____

   _____

7. Define the following words: *assimilation* (7, 12), *diversity* (7), *orthodoxy* (7), *paradoxical* (7), *nativist* (8), and *pluralism* (9).

   _____

   _____

   _____

FOR DISCUSSION

Currently, some people are questioning the view of America as a "melting pot." They feel that a more realistic, acceptable goal for diverse America is to strive for a "mosaic," or "salad," of cultures and ethnic groups. What do you think should be the country's goal? Should immigrants be encouraged to blend into American society, or should they actively maintain their own cultures?

WRITING ASSIGNMENT

Richard Rodriguez provides some details of the evolution of an immigrant family into an American family. Change is a process that happens to everyone. Sometimes, the change is beneficial; sometimes it is not. In a paragraph, discuss a change that you have witnessed or experienced. (You might want to focus on the evolution of a farm into a housing development or a shopping mall. You might think of a change in your grandparents, from spry senior citizens into frail, elderly invalids. You might consider a change in American culture: eating habits, life-styles, or literacy skills, for instance.)

SELECTION 10

Set Your Body's Time Clock To Work for You

BARBARA ROWES

1   As the first days of sunlight filter over the hills of California's Silicon Valley, Charles Winget opens his eyes. It is barely 5 A.M., but Winget is raring to go. Meanwhile, his wife pulls up the covers and buries her face under the pillow.

2   "For the past fifteen years," says Winget, "we've hardly ever gotten up together."

3   The Wingets' situation is not uncommon. Our bodies operate with the complexity of clocks, and like clocks, we all run at slightly different speeds. Winget is a morning person. His wife is not at her best until hours after nightfall.

4   Behavioral scientists long attributed such differences to personal eccentricities or early conditioning. This thinking was challenged in the late 1950s by a theory labeled chronobiology by physician-biologist Franz Halberg. In a Harvard University laboratory, Dr. Halberg found that certain blood cells varied predictably in number, depending on the time of day they were drawn from the body. The cell count was higher at a given time of day and lower 12 hours later. He also discovered that the same patterns could be detected in heart and metabolic rates and body temperature.

5   Halberg's explanation: instead of performing at a steady, unchanging rate, our systems function on an approximately 25-hour cycle. Sometimes we are accelerating, sometimes slowing down. We achieve peak efficiency for only a limited time each day. Halberg dubbed these bodily cadences "circadian rhythms."

6   Much of the leading work in chronobiology is sponsored today by the National Aeronautics and Space Administration. Charles Winget, a NASA research physiologist and authority on circadian rhythms, says that circadian principles have been applied to astronauts' work schedules on most of the space-shuttle flights.

7   The space-age research has many useful applications here on earth. Chronobiologists can tell you when to eat and still lose weight, what time of day you're best equipped to handle the toughest challenges, when to go to the dentist with your highest threshold of pain and when to exercise for maximum effect. Says Winget, "It's a biological law of human

efficiency: to achieve your best with the least effort, you have to coordinate the demands of your activities with your biological capacities."

8   Circadian patterns can be made to work *for* you. But you must first learn how to recognize them. Winget and his associates have developed the following approach to help you figure out your body's patterns:

9   Take your temperature one hour after getting up in the morning and then again at four-hour intervals throughout the day. Schedule your last reading as close to bedtime as possible. You should have five readings by the end of the day.

10   Now add your first, third and fifth readings and record this total. Then add your second and fourth readings and *subtract* this figure from the first total. That number will be an estimate of your body temperature in the middle of the night—consider it your sixth reading.

11   Now plot all six readings on graph paper. The variations may seem minuscule—only one-tenth of a degree in some cases—but are significant. You'll probably find that your temperatures will begin to rise between 3 A.M. and 6 A.M. reaching a peak sometime in the late morning or early afternoon. By evening the readings start to drop. They will steadily decline, reaching their nadir at around 2 A.M.

12   Of course, individual variations make all the difference. At what hour is *your* body temperature on the rise? When does it reach its highest point? Its lowest? Once you have familiarized yourself with your patterns, you can take advantage of chronobiology techniques to improve your health and productivity.

13   We do our best physical work when our rhythms are at their peak. In most people, this peak lasts about four hours. Schedule your most taxing activities when your temperature is highest.

14   For mental activities, the timetable is more complicated. Precision tasks, such as mathematical work, are best tackled when your temperature is on the rise. For most people, this is at 8 or 9 A.M. By contrast, reading and reflection are better pursued between 2 and 4 P.M., the time when body temperature usually begins to fall.

15   Breakfast should be your largest meal of the day for effective dieting. Calories burn faster one hour after we wake up than they do in the evening. During a six-year research project known as the Army Diet Study,

Dr. Halberg, chronobiologist Robert Sothern and research associate Erna Halberg monitored the food intake of two groups of men and women. Both ate only one, 2000-calorie meal a day, but one group ate their meal at breakfast and the other at dinner. "All who ate dinner either maintained or gained weight."

16   If foods are processed differently at different times of day, certainly caffeine, alcohol and medicines will be too. Aspirin compounds, for example, have the greatest potency in the morning, between 7 and 8. (So does alcohol.) They are least effective between 6 P.M. and midnight. Caffeine has the most impact around 3 in the afternoon. Charles Walker, dean of the College of Pharmacy at Florida A & M University, explains, "Stimulants are most effective when you are normally active, and sedatives work best when you're naturally sedate or asleep."

17   Knowing your rhythms can also help overcome sleep problems. Consult your body-temperature chart. Your bedtime should coincide with the point at which your temperature is lowest. This is between 11 P.M. and 2 A.M. for most people.

18   Dr. Michael Thorpy of the Sleep-Wake Disorders Center at Montefiore Medical Center in New York City offers other circadian sleep tips: go to bed at the same time every night and get up at the same time every morning, even on weekends. "Irregularity in sleep and waking times is the greatest cause of sleep problems," Dr. Thorpy says. The best way to recover from a bad night's sleep is simply to resume your normal cycle. Beware of sleeping pills. "Most sleeping pills won't work for periods longer than two weeks," warns Dr. Thorpy. And there is real danger of drug accumulation in the blood.

19   Visit a doctor or dentist as early in the day or as late in the evening as possible, since your highest pain threshold is between 8 P.M. and 8 A.M.

20   Winget and fellow NASA chronobiologist Charles DeRoshia also offer advice to diminish the debilitating effects of jet lag: a week or so before departure begin adjusting your daily activities so that they coincide with the time schedule of your destination. Eat a small, high-protein, low-carbohydrate meal just before your trip. Get plenty of sleep in the days before your trip. In flight, eat very little, drink lots of water and avoid alcohol and caffeinated drinks. When you

arrive, walk around, talk to people, try to adapt to your environment. Before retiring, have a light meal, high in carbohydrates. Take a warm bath.

21   Knowing your body's patterns is no guarantee of good health. But what chronobiology reveals is the importance of regularity in all aspects of your life and of learning to act in synchronization with your body's natural rhythms.

Rowes, Barbara. "Set Your Body's Time Clock to Work for You." Reader's Digest 125 (Dec. 1984): 146–148. Condensed from Family Circle, August 21, 1984.

QUESTIONS

1. What is the author's thesis? Where is it located?

   _____

   _____

   _____

2. What were the first explanations of differences in people's body clocks? What explanation has been accepted since the 1950s? Discuss this explanation and its consequences.

   _____

   _____

   _____

3. Why is NASA interested in circadian rhythms?

   _____

   _____

   _____

4. What are some advantages of knowing one's body clock?

   _____

   _____

   _____

5. What are the steps involved in determining one's peak periods of the day?

   _____

   _____

   _____

6. Why should breakfast be the largest meal of the day? What evidence supports this claim?

   _____

   _____

   _____

7. In addition to food, what other drugs or chemicals does the body process differently at various times of the day? What can you infer from this information?

   _____

   _____

   _____

8. Define the following words: *cadences* (5), *chronobiology* (6), *nadir* (11), *potency* (16), *sedate* (16), *coincide* (17), and *synchronization* (21).

   _____

   _____

   _____

FOR DISCUSSION

Do people truly have different body clocks? What has your experience told you about studying, taking classes, exercising, working, or having fun? What impact does the time of day have on you and your friends?

WRITING ASSIGNMENT

Since you cannot schedule every activity in your life around your own circadian rhythms, how do you adjust to others' time schedules for your activities? For instance, although you study best in the morning, you may have to take some classes or work then. How do you adapt? How do you study at a later time and still study effectively? Report your findings in a paragraph for your instructor.

APPENDIX

Orientation Lecture

There are several differences between the student who makes it in college and the student who doesn't. One major difference, and probably the most important difference, is how much the student understands about what goes on in a university learning situation. How much academic know-how does the student have? So, today, I want to look at this factor of academic know-how. I want to do what I can to provide some insight into how a student gets on at a university.

I'm going to begin by pointing out three things that the college instructor assumes about students. The first thing the college instructor assumes is that the student knows what he's [or she's] doing. The college instructor assumes that the student is capable of deciding what courses he [or she] wants to take, capable of deciding whether he [or she] wants to attend class, whether he [or she] wants to do assignments. Now the instructor is going to point out certain things which should be done—certain standards in the class. He [or she] assumes that the student is capable of deciding whether he's [or she's] going to do those things or not. If the student doesn't do them, he [or she] fails the course. But very few college instructors will bother the student about doing these various assignments, attending class, or anything else. That's the student's business whether he [or she] wants to stay in college or not. That's the first assumption. The student knows what he's [or she's] doing.

The second assumption that the college instructor makes is that he [or she], the instructor, is there to present material and the student is there to learn. He [or she] assumes that the student will meet him [or her] halfway. Most college instructors try to make their lectures, their courses, at least listenable, at least bearable, but they, the instructors, do not assume that they have to pound something into the student's mind. The instructor does not assume that he [or she] is concerned with the student's personal behavior in class. In fact, discipline problems, in this sense, do not exist at the college level.

Okay, the student is there to learn. The third assumption the college instructor makes is that the student has to show some evidence of learning, some consistent performance of assignments in order to pass the course, even with a "D." The student will have to produce.

Now if you stop and think for a minute, you'll realize that what the college instructor is really assuming is that this student himself [or herself] is mature enough to know what he's [or she's] about, mature enough to make his [or her] own decisions, mature enough to know why he's [or she's] in college. And the college instructor is there to provide a service. He's [or she's] there to provide information, he's [or she's] there to distinguish between those who are understanding it and those who are not understanding it and not comprehending it.

I'm going to be negative for a moment, and I'm going to look at the major causes of student failure. I'm going to get down to a very practical level here. I'm not dealing with educational theory, or motivational theory, or any other theory. I'm dealing with the instructor who looks out at a group of freshman students, observes what's going on, and notices why some students fail. And this is going to be a kind of negative view of things.

I've singled out five of these basic, simple reasons why students seem to fail out of college in this first semester, this first year.

The first reason I've noticed is that a student will wait to be warned by someone that he's [or she's] in trouble. He'll [or she'll] wait for the instructor to say, "You've been cutting a lot of classes. That's pretty bad." Or he'll [or she'll] wait for an instructor to say, "You haven't been turning in your assignments. I think we ought to look into that." As a matter of fact, in most college courses no one will ever warn the student. The wise student knows that he's [or she's] going to have to perform, do well in class, and he [or she] doesn't wait for somebody to tell him [or her] that he's [or she's] not doing well.

The second of these reasons why students seem to fail is that the student will put off working during the semester. In many courses there's not a great deal of day-to-day or even week-to-week work. The instructor will assign readings. He [or she] will assume that the student is doing the reading and is coming to class and comprehending the material. The student, on the other hand, puts things off, until suddenly around midterm time he's [or she's] faced with an impossible amount of reading, papers to write, exams and problems that he [or she] has to work out. Sometimes it hits in the middle of the semester, sometimes it doesn't really hit until the end of the semester. Then it's too late. The student realizes that he [or she] can't get all of it done. Therefore, facing this impossible task, he [or she] will give up.

A third reason for student failure is that a student will miss an occasional assignment and figure it will make no real difference. Let me explain something to you about grading policy in college. Very seldom will an instructor give an assignment and put a grade on it without counting that grade in your final work. And in most instructors' grading systems undone assignments do not count merely as an "F"; they count as a zero. You cannot miss an occasional assignment because you don't feel like doing it. Do every assignment, even though some of them may be done relatively poorly. Be sure you do them, and do them on time.

The fourth of these mechanical causes for failure is the student doesn't really understand assignments. He [or she] doesn't take notes on assignments, and doesn't read the assignment in the syllabus. I am not talking about the student who doesn't understand the reading material and the reading assignment. I'm talking about the student who doesn't understand what the instructor is talking about when the instructor makes an assignment. An instructor will often have assignments specified in a syllabus or course schedule, and he [or she] may mention them in class. If you don't understand what he [or she] is driving at, you have to ask him [or her]. An instructor may make an assignment for a major paper and it may not be due for two months. The student will not take any notes on the assignment. He'll [or she'll] think, "Yeah, I'll remember that." A month later, when he [or she] starts working on his [or her] paper, he [or she] doesn't know what the assignment is all about. So he [or she] does the wrong thing. In most university courses, if you write a brilliant paper on the wrong subject, it's worth zero. The instructor does not want the assignment done on something that you thought he [or she] might like better than what he [or she] assigned.

The fifth and last of these mechanical causes of failure, and I suppose the most obvious, is the student who starts cutting classes. Now as I said, very few instructors will call your attention to whether you're cutting classes or not. They don't have time. They are there to teach, not to see if people come to class. Some instructors will tell you that they don't take roll; they are not interested in whether you are there or not. Now beware of this. In most of these situations where the instructor tells you that he [or she] doesn't care if you come to class, he [or she] is leaving it up to you whether you want to come or not. But he [or she] is still going to be very much aware of who is there and who isn't. Later, in a close decision on a grade, your attendance will help him [or her] decide which grade to give you.

The last section of material that I'm going to deal with is to make three very simple positive suggestions which mark the good student. I'm talking now about the student who is working pretty near his [or her] capacity, that is, his [or her] capacity in terms of the energy and intelligence that he [or she] has. The student, in other words, is a professional: he [or she] knows what he's [or she's] about, and he [or she] operates efficiently in an academic situation.

I'm going to make a few simple suggestions that are basic for academic success. The first of these suggestions is to take complete lecture notes. Take lots of notes on lectures and class discussions. In many courses most of the material you'll be expected to know is given to you in these lectures. There are lots of specific techniques for taking lecture notes. The basic point that I'm making here is you can't know that material when you prepare for an examination unless you've got it in your notes to begin with. I see freshmen, sometimes half the students or more in a freshman class, who will sit and wait for me to say, "Now this is absolutely important." Sometimes even when I tell them, "I'm going to test you on this," they still don't take notes.

The professional student, on a condensed lecture, will take, on regular-sized notebook paper, three or four pages of notes per class period. It's hard work. But that's where you get much of your material.

The second suggestion I'm going to make is to keep up with reading assignments. And don't just read the material passively. Try to understand what is in these reading assignments. Read the assignments, or at least scan them before they are discussed or lectured on in class, because this is usually the most efficient way to get the most out of both the lectures and the readings. The good student, the conscientious student, the person who's going to make it, is the person who will at least scan a reading assignment before going into the class; then this student will read that reading assignment afterwards.

The third suggestion I'm going to make for the good student is to review occasionally your reading notes and your lecture notes. Go back over the material you have read and your lecture notes. That will fix it in your mind. It will cause you to think about it, become a little bit involved and interested in it, and it will make the continuity in a course much easier.

Okay, these are three basic positive suggestions— take complete lecture notes, keep up with the reading, review and think about the material. I'll conclude by saying that learning is the name of the game. Really learning material is what the college academic experience is all about. I think if you try it, try to apply some of these things I've said, you'll discover that your freshman year can be really successful.

From a lecture by James A. Wood in College Reading and Study Skills, *2nd ed. Nancy V. Wood. 1982. CBS College Publishing.*

ACKNOWLEDGMENTS

Ad for Hyatt Regency at Hilton Head, South Carolina, reprinted with permission of Hyatt Corporation.

Ad for the U.S Army, "If you'd like a career with a high-tech company, start with one of ours," reprinted with permission of the U.S. Army.

Ad for Canon, "Wildlife as Canon Sees It," reprinted with permission of Canon Inc.

"The Nazca Drawings" from *Ancient Monuments* by Daniel Cohen, Copyright © 1971 by Daniel Cohen. Used with permission of McGraw-Hill Book Company.

Ad for CUNA Mutual Insurance Group, reprinted with permission of CUNA Mutual Insurance Group.

"Don't Know Much About History?" by Jean Grasso Fitzpatrick, reprinted from the March 10, 1992 issue of *Family Circle* magazine. Copyright © 1992 The Family Circle, Inc.

Ad for General Motors, "One way or another, we will destroy this car," reprinted with permission of General Motors Corporation.

"Seven Secrets of Peak Performance," by Morton Hunt, reprinted with permission from the September 1982 *Reader's Digest*. Copyright © 1982 by the Reader's Digest Association, Inc."

Leigh Knotts, "Job Hunting? Watch What You Say!" from the *Baltimore Evening Sun*, May 17, 1991.

Ad for Lane Furniture, "When's the last time you were this comfortable?" Reprinted with permission of Lane Furniture.

Ma Lin, "Fishing," the *Baltimore Sun*, May 21, 1991.

Ralph H. Major, Jr. Adapted from "The Buried Treasure of Oak Island" by Ralph H. Major, Jr. *Coronet*, July 1954, copyright 1954 by Esquire, Inc. Courtesy of the Hearst Corporation.

"Contents" from Gove, Philip Babcock, ed. *Webster's Third New International Dictionary*, 1976, p. 3a. By permission, © 1976 published by Merriam-Webster Inc., publisher of the Merriam-Webster ® dictionaries.

"Biography" and "Broadcast" by permission from *Webster's New Collegiate Dictionary*, © 1961, pp. 86, 106, publisher of the Merriam-Webster ® dictionaries.

New York Times, list of Best Sellers from *The New York Times Book Review*, October 2, 1992. Copyright © 1992 by The New York Times Company. Reprinted by permission.